THE CRUCIAL HOURS

*When Time And Eternity Converged
To Determine The Destiny Of Mankind*

by

Wm. A. Lauterbach

NORTHWESTERN PUBLISHING HOUSE

Milwaukee, Wisconsin

Second edition, 2013

All rights reserved. This publication may not be copied, photocopied, reproduced, translated, or converted to any electronic or machine-readable form in whole or in part, except for brief quotations, without prior written approval from the publisher.

Library of Congress Card 76-51660
Northwestern Publishing House
1250 N. 113th St., Milwaukee, WI 53226-3284
www.nph.net
© 1977 by Northwestern Publishing House
Published 1977
Printed in the United States of America
ISBN 978-0-8100-0050-6
ISBN 978-0-8100-2625-4 (e-book)

CONTENTS

Foreword page v

CHAPTER ONE: JESUS' READINESS TO SUFFER AND DIE
A. Jesus Determines The Time And Manner Of His Death 3
B. The Rulers Conspire Against Jesus 5
C. Judas Iscariot Covenants To Betray Jesus 7
D. Preparation For The Passover 11
E. Strife At The Passover Meal 15
F. Jesus Washes The Disciples' Feet 19
G. Treason Present Among The Twelve 23

CHAPTER TWO: JESUS' AGONY OF SOUL IN GETHSEMANE
A. The Shadow Of The Betrayal 29
B. The Traitor Is Exposed 31
C. The Son Of Man Glorified 34
D. The Lord's Supper Instituted 35
E. Peter Is Warned 37
F. Jesus Warns Of Coming Danger 41
G. Peter's Second Warning 42
H. Jesus Enters Gethsemane 45
I. The Agony In The Garden 47
J. Jesus Prays For The Removal Of The Cup 48
K. The Disciples Sleep During The Master's Agony 49
L. "Rise, Let Us Be Going!" 52

CHAPTER THREE: JESUS BEFORE THE SANHEDRIN
A. Jesus Meets The Multitude 57
B. Jesus Betrayed With A Kiss 60
C. Peter Strikes With The Sword 62
D. Jesus Rebukes The Multitude 65
E. Jesus Is Bound 67
F. Jesus Before Annas And Caiaphas 69
G. Peter Enters The High Priest's Palace 71
H. Peter's First Denial 72
I. Peter's Second And Third Denials 74
J. Jesus Questioned By The High Priest 77
K. Jesus Placed Under Oath By The High Priest 80
L. Jesus Mocked By The Servants 84

CHAPTER FOUR: JESUS SENT FROM CAIAPHAS TO PILATE
A. The Morning Session Of The Sanhedrin 89
B. Jesus Delivered To Pilate 90
C. Judas' Remorse And End 92

D. The Potter's Field Bought With The Price Of Blood 94
E. Pilate Demands The Accusation 95
F. They Begin To Accuse Jesus 97
G. Jesus Answered Nothing 101
H. Jesus Before Herod 102

CHAPTER FIVE: JESUS CONDEMNED TO DEATH
A. Pilate Offers To Chastise Jesus And To Release Him 107
B. Jesus Or Barabbas 108
C. Pilate Is Warned By His Wife 109
D. "Release Unto Us Barabbas" 110
E. Jesus Is Scourged And Mocked 112
F. "Behold The Man!" 115
G. "No King But Caesar" 119
H. Pilate Washes His Hands 121
I. Barabbas Released — Jesus Delivered 123
J. The Via Dolorosa 123
K. The Lamenting Daughters Of Jerusalem 126

CHAPTER SIX: JESUS' DEATH ON THE CROSS
A. The Crucifixion 133
B. The Title On The Cross 138
C. The Parting Of The Garments 141
D. Jesus Mocked On The Cross 143
E. The Penitent Malefactor 148
F. The Mother Of Jesus At The Cross 152
G. Darkness Prevails — Jesus Forsaken 157
H. Jesus Dies On The Cross 160
I. The Veil Of The Temple Rent And The Tombs Opened 164
J. "Truly, This Was The Son Of God!" 166
K. Jesus' Side Pierced 170

CHAPTER SEVEN: JESUS' BURIAL
A. The Body Of Jesus Requested 175
B. The Body Taken Down From The Cross 177
C. Jesus Laid In The Tomb 179
D. The Women At The Tomb 181
E. The Guard At The Sepulcher 182

FOREWORD

Not Normandy, not Waterloo, not Gettysburg, nor any other decisive clash of armed forces which changed the course of human events, can claim to be history's most crucial hour — not when we are aware of what took place almost 2,000 years ago in a small vassal state of the mighty Roman Empire and without force of combat. When Jesus of Nazareth paid His last visit to Jerusalem, time and eternity converged to determine the destiny of mankind.

The world shrugged off the activity of these eventful hours as the mere suppression of an eccentric rabbi. However, a much higher assessment had already been made on the holy mount by the transfigured Lord Jesus and His heavenly visitors, the glorified Moses and Elijah. Their sublime conversion centered on the path that Jesus had to follow and the work that He had to fulfill at Jerusalem.

Never in all history were the stakes so high or the results so far-reaching.

If heaven now resounds with the voices of praise proclaiming, "Worthy is the Lamb that was slain!" can those on earth redeemed by His blood remain silent or lose interest in the events of Holy Week? Can a child of God ever be more properly or profitably engaged than in searching and examining the sacred record of the crucial hours when man's redemption was being secured, and in glorifying Christ for His supreme act of love?

The primary sources of the material presented in this volume are the sacred Scriptures of the Old and New Testaments. The annals of secular history, where available, serve as a secondary source to help us understand the events and customs of that day. Wherever there is a reference to a tradition or a legend, the reader will find that it has been identified as such. Where the records are silent, the author has not ventured to speak, since speculation easily gives birth to distortion and may lead to false conclusions.

For the sequence of events and the division of the material, the author has adopted the arrangement of "The Passion History" in *The Lutheran Lectionary* (quoted with the permission of the publishers, *viz.* Concordia Publishing House, St. Louis, Missouri). "The Passion History" quotations appear in **bold type** as the introduction to each division. The paragraphs that follow in *italics* give the Scripture passages from which the compilation was derived.

The goal of this book is to aid the reader in understanding and appreciating our Savior's redeeming love — that he may be led to a deeper knowledge and a bolder confession of His glorious name. The constant focal point is Christ and His sacrificial work. All other persons in the account are important only in relation to Him, and as their actions have bearing upon His redemptive acts.

Wm. A. Lauterbach

CHAPTER ONE
Jesus' Readiness To Suffer And Die

— A —
Jesus Determines The Time And Manner Of His Death

Now the Feast of Unleavened Bread drew nigh, which is called the Passover. And Jesus said unto His disciples, "Ye know that after two days is the feast of the Passover, and the Son of Man is betrayed to be crucified." (TLL, p. 260)

He said unto His disciples, "Ye know that after two days is the Feast of the Passover, and the Son of Man is betrayed to be crucified." (Matt. 26:1b,2)
After two days was the Feast of the Passover and of Unleavened Bread. (Mark 14:1a)
Now the Feast of Unleavened Bread drew nigh, which is called the Passover. (Luke 22:1)

Jesus Himself identified the day on which He declared the time and manner of His death as the twelfth of Nisan. That is clear from His remark to His disciples, "AFTER TWO DAYS IS THE FEAST OF THE PASSOVER." The Passover falls on the fourteenth of Nisan.

Since the fourteenth of Nisan in that year apparently fell on Thursday, this day was Tuesday — the great Tuesday, so full of labor, conflicts, and teaching, of which such a comprehensive report has been preserved for us (Matt. 21:23-26:5; Mark 11:20-14:2; Luke 20:1-22:2).

THE GREAT TUESDAY

This was one of the busiest days in the public life of Jesus. It began with the journey from Bethany to Jerusalem. Jesus stayed at Bethany on the nights preceding the feast. On the way to Jerusalem the withered fig tree became an object lesson by the Master on the tremendous power of faith, causing the disciples to be amazed. The Temple was the scene of Jesus' last public teaching, of His warning to the Pharisees and Sadducees, and of His final call to national repentance. Here too the Greeks, representatives of the Gentile people, expressed their desire to "see Jesus," even as the leaders of His own people were manifesting their increasing hostility toward Him.

His public teaching at the Temple concluded, Jesus proceeded to the Mount of Olives with His disciples. There He conversed with them on the destruction of Jerusalem and the Last Judgment, making fitting applications in parables. Near the close of this eventful day Jesus spoke the words which determined the time and manner of His death.

Announcement of His sacrificial suffering, including the manner of His death, had been made previously by Jesus:

1. At the first cleansing of the Temple (John 2:19-22)
2. To Nicodemus (John 3:14,15)
3. At Caesarea Philippi (Matt. 16:21-23)
4. At the close of the Galilean ministry (Matt. 17:22,23)
5. On the last journey to Jerusalem (Matt. 20:17-19)

Here He announces the exact time of His suffering. It was to coincide with the regularly established observance of the Feast of the Passover. This indicates more than a prediction and more than supernatural knowledge. This was an act of determining, or fixing, the time. Here He demonstrates His authority. Regardless of any plans of the Jewish leaders, it would be as He directs — Thursday night and Friday, and no other time.

AN ACT OF DETERMINING

The feast was really a twofold festival: A. The Passover (Heb., *pesach*), which lasted only one day, from sunset of the 13th until sunset of the 14th of Abib (or Nisan, as the month was later called) B. The Feast of Unleavened Bread, so called because of the removal of all leaven (yeast) from the homes. This feast lasted seven days, from sunset of the 14th until sunset of the 21st. From the beginning, the Feast of Unleavened Bread was connnected with the Passover (Exod. 12:15), and in a later Jewish era they were merged into one festival lasting eight days. They were alternately designated as the Passover and the Feast of Unleavened Bread.

THE FEAST

The Passover commemorated the dreadful night of judgment and deliverance, the birth-night of the nation, while the Feast of Unleavened Bread was to remind the Children of Israel of the Exodus itself (Exod. 12). The festival was instituted at the time of the Exodus, and annual repetition was commanded. Other laws governing the festival are found in Leviticus 23:5-14; Numbers 9:10-14; 28:16-25. This Passover was to be unlike any other. It was set apart from all that had gone before as the one in which the true Lamb of God, symbolized by the countless paschal lambs of fifteen centuries, was to be offered as the sacrifice for all time.

THE BIRTH-NIGHT
OF THE NATION

The title "Son of Man" is found 84 times in the New Testament. It was coined by Jesus Himself and was used exclusively by Him, except in John 12:34 and in Acts 7:56. It is derived from Daniel 7:13,14. The term draws attention to the human nature of Jesus, yet at the same time the things that are attributed to Him imply that He was also far more than an ordinary man. It points to His divine nature and reminds us that "the Word was made flesh and dwelt among us" (John 1:14). Jesus preferred the term "Son of Man" over "Messiah" because of the unfortunate political implications His contemporaries had learned to read into the latter term.

THE SON OF MAN

The present tense, "is betrayed" (delivered up), is to be understood in a prophetic sense, or as an expression of certainty of what was about to occur. It indicates that the betrayal process had already begun. His enemies were even now plotting His betrayal. It might also be stated that in the eyes of the omniscient Lord the betrayal by Judas had already taken place in the heart of this avaricious "disciple." On other occasions when Jesus' enemies tried to take Him He escaped from them. Now, when they desired not to take Him, He willed to be taken, and His will had to prevail.

BETRAYED

The manner of His death was not to be a matter of chance, but that too was determined beforehand. The Jewish mode of execution, in which the flesh was bruised and crushed, and the bones shattered by the impact of the stones hurled upon the victim, was not suited for the slaying of the Paschal Lamb. Care had to be taken not to break a single bone of His body (see pages 170,171). For that reason the Roman form of execution by crucifixion was much more suitable. It was furthermore necessary that He be "lifted up" before mankind as an object of faith (John 3:14,15), and that He bear "the curse" as our Substitute (Gal. 3:13).

TO BE CRUCIFIED

Jesus not only knew that His hour had come, but He also knew the bitter shame that awaited Him in that hour when He would be executed like a criminal. Yet He did not flinch or waver in His purpose to fulfill the mission given Him by the Father.

— B —

The Rulers Conspire Against Jesus

Then assembled together the chief priests, and the scribes, and the elders of the people, unto the palace of the high priest, who was called Caiaphas, and consulted that they might take Jesus by subtilty, and kill Him. But they said, "Not on the feast day, lest there be an uproar among the people." For they feared the people. (TLL, p. 260)

Then assembled together the chief priests, and the scribes, and the elders of the people, unto the palace of the high priest, who was called Caiaphas, and consulted that they might take Jesus by subtilty and kill Him. But they said, "Not on the feast day, lest there be an uproar among the people." (Matt. 26:3-5)
And the chief priests and the scribes sought how they might take Him by craft and put Him to death. But they said, "Not on the feast day, lest there be an uproar of the people." (Mark 14:1b,2)
And the chief priests and scribes sought how they might kill Him; for they feared the people. (Luke 22:2)

That same evening, at the very time when Jesus was predicting His crucifixion during the Passover festival, the council was plotting His death. The Evangelists name the constituent groups — the chief priests, the scribes, and the elders of the people — rather than saying "the council." This supreme religious tribunal of the Jewish nation consisted of seventy-one members: priests, scribes, and laymen who were the elders of the people. It was known as the Sanhedrin. The Talmud traces its origin to Moses and his appointment of seventy elders, who, together with him, were to act as magistrates and judges of the nation (Num. 11:16).

THE COUNCIL

This meeting of the council, or Sanhedrin, was an irregular one, as is shown both from the time of the meeting as well as the place. The Sanhedrin sat in regular ses-

AN IRREGULAR MEETING sions every day, except on the Sabbath and festival days, from the close of the morning sacrifice until the time of the evening sacrifice. Its regular meeting place was in the Hall of Polished Stones of the Temple. Because the hall would be closed for the lateness of the hour, this meeting was held in the palace of Caiaphas. No doubt the change of meeting place was welcomed by the leaders so that they could better avoid public attention and keep their plottings secret.

The high priest stood at the pinnacle of the priestly office in Israel. The priestly office, according to its divinely prescribed duties and functions, was an office of reconciliation and mediation. The **THE PRIESTLY OFFICE CORRUPTED** priests were to represent the people before God. In addition, the priests, and especially the high priest, were to lead God's people in God's ways. They were to be an example in holiness. As a symbol of holiness the high priest wore the crown of holiness upon his forehead. On the gold plate were inscribed the words "Holiness to the Lord" (Exod. 28:36). When the priests offered up daily sacrifices, these words also reminded the people of the sacrifice of the coming Savior, which would truly bring holiness for all.

How far the office had fallen from its high ideal! In the days of Christ this exalted office was occupied by Caiaphas, who was from the house of Annas, which supplied no fewer than eight high priests: father, five sons, one son-in-law (Caiaphas), and a grandson. This dynasty was notorious for corruption — for political pressure to gain its selfish ends, thereby causing the perversion of justice and the lowering of moral standards.

Joseph Caiaphas was the high priest, not by the grace of God, but by the favor of the Romans, who changed the occupancy of the office at will in search of someone pliant enough to submit to their will. He was appointed to the office **CAIAPHAS** by Valerius Gratus, predecessor of Pontius Pilate, and occupied it for eleven years, from 25 A.D. to 36 A.D. Caiaphas was the son-in-law of Annas, a former high priest still active in Jewish politics, and like him belonged to the sect of the Sadducees, who were rationalistic in their philosophy and materialistic in their outlook. They were generally wealthy, belonged to the ruling class, and had close political connections with the Romans. They denied the resurrection of the dead and the existence of angels and other spirits (Acts 23:8). Because Jesus warned against their false doctrine (Matt. 16:6,12), exposed their wickedness (Matt. 16:3,4) and their ignorance (Matt. 22:29; Mark 12:24), and by His teachings undermined their influence on the people, the Sadducees hated Him with burning intensity.

Caiaphas is credited with first demanding the judicial murder of Jesus as an act of political necessity by recalling the well-known Jewish saying that it is better one man should die than that the nation perish (cf. John 11:48-50). At the same time, as St. John points out, in his capacity as high priest Caiaphas unwittingly spoke a word of prophecy when he proposed the death of Jesus for the benefit of the people.

The Sanhedrin had charge of all matters pertaining to religion and religious institutions. Formerly it inflicted not only corporal punishment, but also capital pun-

THE SANHEDRIN RESTRICTED ishment. While it was the policy of the Roman government to interfere as little as necessary in the religious affairs of its subject people, they did take the power of inflicting capital punishment away from Israel forty years before the destruction of the Temple. Even though the Jewish leaders knew that their action was restricted, the determination to kill Jesus dominated the meeting. They "consulted that they might take Jesus by subtilty, and kill Him." The concern of these men was where and how it should be done. Subtilty must be employed so that the murder might appear to be in the best public interest.

The timing called for the murder to take place after the feast, when the pilgrims would have departed and returned home. At the time of the feasts, especially the Passover, a great influx of people crowded the **THEY FEARED THE PEOPLE** streets of Jerusalem. Among them were many religious enthusiasts whose presence had a potential to make the crowds very volatile. The very enthusiastic welcome which had been given to Jesus by the people, especially on Palm Sunday, had not gone unnoticed. The leaders were afraid that if they should take Jesus during the feast and kill Him, the people would create an uproar. This was a human judgment and would probably have been correct if they had been dealing with a Jewish nationalist insurgent. He would have taken advantage of the acclaim of the multitude to raise a tumult among the people. But because Jesus acted in an entirely different way their calculation proved to be incorrect. He was killed on Good Friday, the day of preparation for the great Passover Sabbath, and no uproar arose in His favor.

The hostility against the Old Testament prophet Jeremiah was a type of this scheming against Jesus. He had written, "But I was like a lamb . . . that is brought to the slaughter; and I knew not that they had devised devices [planned schemes] against me, saying, 'Let us destroy the tree with the fruit thereof, and let us cut him off from the land of the living that his name may be no more remembered'" (Jer. 11:19). The hope of the enemies in both cases was to nullify the work of Jeremiah and Jesus.

Tyranny as exercised here by the Sanhedrin is also described by the Psalmist: "They gather themselves together against the soul of the righteous and condemn the innocent blood" (Ps. 94:21).

— C —

Judas Iscariot Covenants To Betray Jesus

Then entered Satan into Judas, surnamed Iscariot, being of the number of the Twelve. And he went his way, and communed with the chief priests and captains, how he might betray Him unto them. And when they heard it, they were glad, and promised to give him money. And he said unto them, "What will ye give me, and I will deliver him unto you?" And they covenanted for thirty pieces of silver. And he promised and sought opportunity to betray Him unto them in the absence of the multitude. (TLL, pp. 260-261)

Then one of the Twelve, called Judas Iscariot, went unto the chief priests and said unto them, "What will ye give me, and I will deliver him unto you?" And they covenanted with him for thirty pieces of silver. And from that time he sought opportunity to betray Him. (Matt. 26:14-16)
And Judas Iscariot, one of the Twelve, went unto the chief priests to betray Him unto them. And when they heard it, they were glad and promised to give him money. And he sought how he might conveniently betray Him. (Mark 14:10,11)
Then entered Satan into Judas surnamed Iscariot, being of the number of the Twelve. And he went his way and communed with the chief priests and captains how he might betray Him unto them. And they were glad and covenanted to give him money. And he promised, and sought opportunity to betray Him unto them in the absence of the multitude. (Luke 22:3-6)

The "then" indicates the time when Judas bargained with the Jewish leaders for the betrayal of his Master. However, there is a difference of opinion as to which time that was. It appears to be quite generally accepted by expositors that it points to Tuesday evening, the time when Jesus was setting Thursday as the day for His suffering to begin. Others, such as Lange and Lenski, connect it with the anointing of Jesus at Bethany and the rebuke of Judas by Jesus. They therefore see the possibility that the deal between Judas and the high priests might have been made as early as Saturday evening.

THEN ENTERED SATAN INTO JUDAS

The conduct of Judas brings us face to face with a deep mystery. Was it only covetousness, grown so mighty, that prodded him on? Was it resentment against Jesus because Jesus had not fulfilled Judas' ambitious hopes for material power and advantages? Was he greatly disappointed because Jesus refrained from taking part in a public uprising and spoke of a cross instead of a crown? Of all the explanations for his conduct (and there are many offered) none satisfies as well as the statement of Scripture, "then entered Satan into Judas." Entry was made through the open door of his heart, out of which Jesus had been thrust. To gain this entry was a masterpiece of Satan. How does Luke know that Satan entered into Judas? The subsequent acts of Judas testify to it; but chiefly this knowledge was imparted by the Holy Spirit, under whose guidance Luke was writing.

This was not a case of demonic possession, where Satan entered by compulsion to rule in the members of the body; but rather, Judas willingly yielded control of the mind, heart, and will to the Prince of Darkness and became his obedient tool.

Two of the disciples were named Judas. To distinguish them one is called the brother (NASB, NIV; BECK:"son") of James (Luke 6:16), while the other is identified as Iscariot. This name he derived from his father, Simon Iscariot (John 6:71). Its apparent origin is *Ish Kerioth* (man of Kerioth), meaning that his home town was Kerioth in Judea (Joshua 15:25). Accordingly, Judas Iscariot was the only one of the Twelve who came from Judea. The other eleven were from Galilee. Attempts to connect his defection with his Judean origin are too farfetched to be given any weight.

JUDAS ISCARIOT

Judas Iscariot was infamous as the betrayer. When the Evangelists write of him they always add a modifier, "Which also betrayed Him" (John 12:4).

OF THE TWELVE "The Twelve" were the disciples whom Jesus had chosen from among His followers and later elevated to the apostleship. Judas was chosen at the same time as Peter and John. Outwardly he was connected with the cause of Christ, but inwardly he was not one with Him. An entire year before His final suffering and death, and following His discourse on the Bread of Life, Jesus had sorrowfully told His disciples: "Have not I chosen you twelve, and one of you is a devil?" (John 6:70.) It is not for us to question why Jesus had chosen Judas, knowing from the beginning "who they were that believed not and who should betray Him" (John 6:64). When our faith turns to sight we shall also understand this mystery. We need not be surprised to find that question any more difficult than another: why has He chosen you and me?

NO BETTER OPPORTUNITY The words "of the Twelve" ring in our ears with unmistakably plain and clear warning that the mere outward association or connection with the kingdom of God is no guarantee of salvation. No one ever had a better opportunity than Judas Iscariot. He was a member of the select group of Jesus' disciples, dwelling together with the Son of God. As such he had the benefit of hearing instruction directly from Jesus' lips. He beheld Jesus' divine works, and he was elevated to the apostleship, destined for one of the apostolic thrones in heaven. Yet he spurned his Lord and Savior and became a willing tool of Satan. What a solemn warning to us that, unless we are always on our guard and heed the voice of the Good Shepherd, we too could be lost in spite of our outward affiliation!

JUDAS WENT TO THE CAMP OF THE ENEMY The disciples were not under guard, so the betrayer was free to go as he chose. Luke tells us, "And he went his way and communed with the chief priests and captains." The captains were officers of the Levitical Temple police. To obtain an audience with the chief priests Judas was probably obliged to go first to these commanders. They were apparently also present when the deal was made. Of his own volition Judas offered his despicable services to them. The idea was his, and he took the first steps in that infamous deal. It was not a case of yielding to a tempting offer, or a persuasive argument about his patriotic duty. Judas conceived the plan and sought out the enemies of Jesus.

Betrayal was the wicked proposal which this false disciple had to offer. He would use his position of privilege and trust to perpetrate treachery. He would betray HIM — no ordinary man, his Lord and Master, his best and truest Friend, and, above all, the Son of God.

What was there to betray? Who He was, or where He kept Himself? That was not necessary. His whereabouts were no secret. He had not gone underground. He could challenge the Sanhedrin: "I sat daily with you teaching in the Temple" (Matt. 26:55). They were seeking an opportunity to apprehend Him "in the absence of the multitude." Judas knew his Master's habits and places of retreat. He agreed to "deliver Him" under the circumstances favorable to the Jewish leaders.

The pages of history tell us of many acts of treachery and atrocity; of faithlessness and violation of trust; of virtue, love, and truth betrayed for a paltry pittance, a sordid advantage, or for spite and vengeance. But this act of treachery surpasses all others. It was not done to a mere man, but it was an offense against the Son of God. It was rejection of the Messiah and treason against his own Savior and Redeemer. The members of the council were glad about the offer of betrayal as a thing desired, but unexpected. What they had previously dreaded to attempt now seemed safe and easy. They felt joy and showed it, revealing their baseness. They were especially pleased that their hated enemy was being betrayed by one of His own trusted followers, thereby reflecting discredit upon His cause. Had they been of nobler character, the members of the council would have been repelled by such a violation of trust.

UNSURPASSABLE TREACHERY

So pleased were the Jewish leaders at the turn of events that they immediately "promised to give him money." There is no indication of haggling about the price. Judas' demand for immediate payment seems to have been readily met. He would do nothing unless the money was paid first. "What will you give me?" means right here and now. He would not run the risk of collecting later. The bargain was promptly struck and the money weighed out (*Gr., estesan* — "covenanted," Matt. 26:15; cf. also Zech. 11:12). It would appear that "weighing out" money was an ancient form of speech retained after the practice had become obsolete, for coined money was in general use. Judas left with the money in the bag.

THEY PROMISED HIM MONEY

To us the price of betrayal seems an insignificant amount. However, to some men a small amount takes on a greater proportion than to others. Satan vainly offered Christ all the kingdoms of the world and their glory when he tempted Him in the wilderness. Judas succumbed when a mere thirty shekels were dangled before him. Changing the sum into modern coin leaves an entirely false impression of the amount. We must remember that the purchasing power of money was very much higher in those days. Thirty shekels represented at least four months' wages for a workingman. In the Law of Moses that amount was significantly the price required as a penalty for accidentally killing a slave (Exod. 21:32). Joseph was sold into slavery by his brothers for twenty pieces of silver (Gen. 37:28).

THIRTY PIECES OF SILVER

It has been suggested that Judas might have successfully held out for more, but it is just as true that he had maneuvered himself into a position where he could have been compelled to take less. The real reason for this amount was the directing hand of God, which fixed the sum in harmony with the five-hundred-year-old prophecy of Zechariah 11:12,13. Matthew, the only one of the Evangelists to report the amount, connects it with this prophecy when he tells that the money was invested in the potter's field (27:9). It is certainly irony when the prophet calls the thirty pieces "a goodly price" for the Shepherd of Israel.

THE HAND OF GOD

Modern kidnappers have appraised their victims much higher than the Lord of heaven and earth was valued by these conspirators. Ransom demands and payments sometimes amount to millions of dollars.

If Judas sold his Lord and Savior for so little, it is equally true that the official leaders of Israel bargained for, bought, and paid for, the blood of the Messiah at a price that reflects their scorn and disdain. The Lord was sold cheaply, but in the end it cost the participants in the unholy bargain dearly. Most likely they paid Judas from the Temple money which was intended for (among other things) the purchase of sacrifices.

Mary of Bethany had been far more generous in her appraisal of Jesus. No less an authority on the value of a shekel than Judas, the treasurer of the Twelve, she valued her sacrifice of love at a figure two-and-a-half times as much as the thirty shekels which changed hands between him and the chief priests.

— D —
Preparation For The Passover

Now on the first day of the Feast of Unleavened Bread, when the passover must be killed, the disciples came to Jesus, saying unto Him, "Where wilt Thou that we go and prepare for Thee, that Thou mayest eat the passover?" And He sent forth two of His disciples, Peter and John, and saith unto them, "Go and prepare us the passover, that we may eat." And they said unto Him, "Where wilt Thou that we prepare?" And He said unto them, "Go ye into the city, and behold, when ye are entered into the city, there shall meet you a man, bearing a pitcher of water; follow him into the house where he entereth in. And wherever he shall go in, say ye unto the goodman of the house, 'The Master saith unto thee: My time is at hand; I will keep the Passover at thy house with My disciples. Where is the guestchamber, where I shall eat the passover with My disciples?' And he shall show you a large upper room furnished and prepared; there make ready for us." And His disciples went forth and came into the city, and found as He had said unto them; and the disciples did as Jesus had appointed them, and they made ready the passover. (TLL, p. 261)

Now the first day of the Feast of Unleavened Bread the disciples came to Jesus, saying unto Him, "Where wilt Thou that we prepare for Thee to eat the passover?" And He said, "Go into the city to such a man and say unto him, 'The Master saith: My time is at hand; I will keep the Passover at thy house with My disciples.'" And the disciples did as Jesus had appointed them, and they made ready the passover. (Matt. 26:17-19)

And the first day of Unleavened Bread, when they killed the passover, His disciples said unto Him, "Where wilt Thou that we go and prepare that Thou mayest eat the passover?" And He sendeth forth two of His disciples and saith unto them, "Go ye into the city, and there shall meet you a man bearing a pitcher of water; follow him. And wheresoever he shall go in, say ye to the goodman of the house, 'The Master saith: Where is the guestchamber where I shall eat the passover with My disciples?' And he will show you a large upper room furnished and prepared; there make ready for us." And His disciples went forth and came into the city and found as He had said unto them; and they made ready the passover. (Mark 14:12-16)

Then came the day of Unleavened Bread, when the passover must be killed. And He sent Peter and John saying, "Go and prepare us the passover, that we may eat." And they said unto Him, "Where wilt Thou that we prepare?" And He said unto them, "Behold, when ye are entered into the city, there shall a man meet you, bearing a pitcher of water; follow him into the house where he entereth in. And ye shall say unto the goodman of the house 'The Master saith unto thee: Where is the guestchamber, where I shall eat the passover with My disciples?' And he shall show you a large upper room furnished; there make ready." And they went and found as He had said unto them; and they made ready the passover. (Luke 22:7-13)

The first day of the Feast of Unleavened Bread was beyond question the fourteenth of Nisan, which that year was Thursday. It began when the first three stars appeared on Wednesday evening (see page 4).

"When the passover must be killed" refers to the lamb, so named for the feast of which it was the chief item. This statement fixes beyond a doubt the day when Jesus celebrated the Passover and instituted His Supper as the regular Passover, the same time as observed by the other Jews. The disciples take for granted that Jesus wants to celebrate the Passover with them, but they are concerned about the place where this would be done. They ask, "Where wilt Thou that we go and prepare for Thee?" Since none of the Apostles were residents of Jerusalem, they could not offer their homes. They may also have wondered whether Jesus would like to celebrate at Bethany, where He had quietly withdrawn Himself from all public appearance and teaching since Tuesday evening. That would have been within the regulations of the time, as Bethany was included in Jerusalem for that purpose by rabbinical authority. However, His plans were to celebrate the feast within the Holy City, and His command was, "Go into the city!"

GO INTO THE CITY

Peter, the disciple of quickest action, and John, the disciple of deepest feeling, were given the assignment to make the preparations. More were not necessary for the task; and, furthermore, only two were allowed to bring the lamb into the Temple court where it was killed. In addition to roasting the lamb, the necessary preparations included the obtaining or preparation of the unleavened bread, the wine, and other requisites of the feast, and the arrangement of the room, unless the room arrangement had been provided by the owner. The preparation would keep them busy until the time of the celebration, when Jesus would lead the others to the designated place.

The main attention of the two disciples was naturally given to the preparation of the lamb. The instructions to Israel were: "Your lamb shall be without blemish, a male of the first year" taken "in the tenth day of the month," and shall be killed in the evening of the fourteenth day (Exod. 12). The proper hour for the slaughter was supposed to be between three and five — the interval between the afternoon and evening services. As the atten-

THE PREPARATION OF THE LAMB

dance at the festival increased, this rite was begun at one o'clock, to give ample time for all to be ready for the feast. Originally the lamb was slaughtered by the father of the household, or by the person appointed by him; but since the time of Josiah the lambs were killed in the Court of the Priests in the Temple (cf. 2 Chron. 30 and Ylvisaker, p. 635). This was done by the worshiper himself, with the assistance of the priests, all twenty-four divisions of whom were on duty for the festival. For this purpose laymen were admitted to the Court of the Priests.

As the hour of the slaughter approached, the Temple courts were thronged with worshipers from all parts of the land, as well as from foreign countries far and near. At the given time there were admitted to the Court of the Priests as many as it would hold, and then the gates were closed. The rite took place with a threefold blast from the silver trumpets of the priests, and the Great Hallel (Ps. 113-118) was chanted by the Levites with responses by the people. The priests formed two lines. The Levites were in charge of the slaughter (2 Chron. 35:11), and the priests caught the blood of the Paschal lambs in golden vessels and passed them on down the line, emptying them at the base of the altar while the empty vessels were simultaneously returned. The tallow, kidneys, liver, and tail were burned as a sacrifice unto the Lord.

The lamb was then bound up in its own skin and carried to the house where the feast was prepared. There it was pierced with a pomegranate spit that passed through it from the mouth to the vent. Ordinarily a cross prong was also used, resulting in the form of a cross. The lamb was roasted intact over glowing embers in an oven. Care was taken that no bone should be broken.

Neither the house where the Passover was to be celebrated nor the owner were named, presumably to keep the information from Judas and to block his plans of betrayal for the time being. Not until Jesus had celebrated this last and important Passover, and had instituted the Holy Supper in peace and security, should the traitor be free to operate. But the directions which Jesus gave to Peter and John not only served to foil Judas; they also provided all of His disciples with a demonstration of His omniscience and authority. Once again it revealed His glory — and that just before His deepest humiliation. Jesus foretold exactly what the disciples would find and what the owner of the house would do in answer to Jesus' request. The same foreknowledge which was evident when His disciples were to make ready for His Palm Sunday entry into Jerusalem was shown here. We dismiss the suggestion (apparently designed to explain away the omniscience of Jesus) that He had made previous arrangements with this unnamed owner of the house. This explanation would be completely out of harmony with the message delivered by the two disciples.

JUDAS BLOCKED

Jesus gave these disciples their directions by means of a sign — one which they could hardly fail to notice. In Palestine the carrying of water was women's work. If men carried water, they generally used water skins. When the disciples would meet a man "bearing a pitcher of water," they were not to speak to him, but to follow him into the house, presumably into the open courtyard. There they should address themselves to the owner with a message from Jesus. To tell him that "the Master saith" implies that Jesus was his Master as well as the disci-

A MAN CARRYING WATER

13

ples'. That he was also one who was advanced in knowledge and faith is apparent from the message to be delivered to him and his anticipated reaction to it. The city of Jerusalem, over which Jesus had so recently uttered His bitter lament (Matt. 23:37), was not without its faithful followers.

Attempts to identify the owner of the house as Joseph of Arimathea, Nicodemus, the father of the Evangelist Mark, or even Mark himself, are pure speculation, even though some rather plausible arguments have been advanced, especially regarding the last two. We simply do not know who this man was.

Peter and John were instructed to tell the unnamed man, "My time is at hand." The word here used for time is not "*chronos*," the general Greek term for time, but "*kairos*," which always designates a short time. "My time" was the time which He had long foreseen and foretold. It was the time of His suffering and martyrdom. That time was "at hand." This was the final opportunity for Jesus to celebrate the Passover.

When Jesus said, "I will keep the Passover," He was using the ancient Jewish form for celebrating it. Jesus made it a practice to perform all the customary duties of the Law. He showed again that He had not come to destroy, but to fulfill. "At thy house" was not an ordinary request, nor does it seem to be acceptance of an offer previously made, but an expression of His right or authority to requisition it for His use, as He had requisitioned the colt for His entry into Jerusalem on Palm Sunday. What the Lord has need of, He claims by divine right. Claiming His right would not necessarily rule out the customary fee paid by pilgrims for the use of a room for the Passover: the skin of the paschal lamb and the vessels used for the meal.

THE RIGHT TO REQUISITION

The need for privacy is contained in the statement, "with My disciples." The extremely crowded conditions of Jerusalem during the Passover, when, according to Josephus, as many as 255,600 lambs were slain at one Passover feast, made privacy impossible for many celebrants. For the Master's purpose no outsiders, no disturbances, no sharing of the room with another party of celebrants would do. Even Mary, the mother of Jesus, though present at the feast, was not to be in this party.

WITH MY DISCIPLES

Jesus foretold exactly what the owner would do in answer to their request: "He shall show you a large upper room furnished and prepared." This would be no makeshift affair quickly pressed into service, but well suited for the Lord's purpose, fully adequate for the momentous occasion. It was an "upper room," reached by an outside staircase, to which entrance could be made without passing through any part of the house. Such upper rooms were used for retirement and quiet relaxation. Jesus said that it would be "large," or ample, for them. Jewish authorities, according to Dr. Edersheim, computed the average dining apartment at fifteen feet square. The room is described in the Greek as "*estromenos*" — literally, "having been strewn." Some translators take this to mean paved or tiled. Most of them, however, seem to agree with the KJV in rendering it "furnished." The expression undoubtedly means that the room was prepared for its intended use. That meant arranging couches around

AN UPPER ROOM

the table, except at its end, so that the supper could be eaten in a reclining position, indicating rest, safety, and liberty.

Peter and John found everything to be as Jesus had foretold it, and they made all the arrangements.

— E —
Strife At The Passover Meal

And in the evening, when the hour was come, He sat down, and the Twelve Apostles with Him. And He said unto them, "With desire I have desired to eat this passover with you before I suffer; for, I say unto you, I will not any more eat thereof, until it be fulfilled in the kingdom of God." And there was also a strife among them, which of them should be accounted the greatest. And He said unto them, "The kings of the Gentiles exercise lordship over them; and they that exercise authority upon them are called benefactors. But ye shall not be so; but he that is greatest among you, let him be as the younger; and he that is chief, as he that doth serve. For whether is greater, he that sitteth at meat, or he that serveth? Is not he that sitteth at meat? But I am among you as he that serveth. Ye are they which have continued with Me in My temptations. And I appoint unto you a kingdom, as My Father hath appointed unto Me; that ye may eat and drink at My table in My kingdom, and sit on thrones judging the twelve tribes of Israel." (TLL, p. 262)

Now when the even was come, He sat down with the Twelve. (Matt. 26:20)
And in the evening He cometh with the Twelve. (Mark 14:17)
And when the hour was come, He sat down, and the Twelve Apostles with Him. And He said unto them, "With desire I have desired to eat this passover with you before I suffer; for, I say unto you, I will not anymore eat thereof until it be fulfilled in the kingdom of God."
And there was also a strife among them, which of them should be accounted the greatest. And He said unto them, "The kings of the Gentiles exercise lordship over them; and they that exercise authority upon them are called benefactors. But ye shall not be so; but he that is greatest among you, let him be as the younger; and he that is chief, as he that doth serve. For whether is greater, he that sitteth at meat, or he that serveth? Is not he that sitteth at meat? But I am among you as he that serveth. Ye are they which have continued with Me in My temptations. And I appoint unto you a kingdom, as My Father hath appointed unto Me, that ye may eat and drink at My table in My kingdom and sit on thrones judging the twelve tribes of Israel." (Luke 22:14-16; 24-30)

When St. Mark reports that at even Jesus came "with the Twelve" to the Upper Room, we believe that he was not using the term in the strictly numerical sense, but

IN THE EVENING that it here signifies the Apostles, ten in number, who came with Jesus from Bethany to Jerusalem. While it is not impossible that Peter and John left the roasting of the lamb and the other preparations in the hands of others while they returned to Bethany, this appears most unlikely. It is more logical to assume that they personally took care of all arrangements and in the Upper Room waited for the arrival of the others. Of this we are certain, that there was no need for them to tell Jesus the place of the feast. He who was able to foretell all of the circumstances about engaging the room would also know where to find it. Then too, the absence of Peter and John from the company of the disciples at Bethany would better serve to prevent Judas from learning the location too soon (see page 13).

"When the hour was come" probably refers to the crucial hour when Jesus officially began His journey to the cross, rather than the hour for the feast to begin. Jewish writers frequently used the phrase for dying.

Though the translation in the KJV tells us that Jesus "sat down," He really reclined. The actual picture of the Lord's Supper is quite different from that made popular by Western artists, such as Leonardo da Vinci (see **HE SAT DOWN** page 14f.). At the original celebration of the Passover the meal was to be eaten while standing (Exod. 12:11); but later it became the custom to recline during the celebration, just as at any other festive meal. It is thought that this was to symbolize the freedom which Israel had obtained through the Exodus, since ordinarily only slaves stood while eating.

"With desire I have desired" is a Hebraism expressing great desire. We can readily understand that Jesus would eagerly look forward to celebrating this greatest and most meaningful of Jewish festivals with His own disci- **"WITH DESIRE"** ples. Added to this was His plan for the institution of a great sacrament for the New Testament Church. Yet He also desired it for another reason. It brought nearer His suffering, and with it the completion of His work of redemption (Luke 12:49,50).

The next Passover that Jesus will celebrate with His disciples, He tells them, will be in heavenly glory — "until it be fulfilled in the kingdom of God." What a pathetic spectacle, then, that on such a sacred occasion **STRIFE AMONG THEM** and at such a time, when the Master was weighed down with so great a burden, there should be "strife among them," and for such a vain reason: to decide "which of them should be accounted the greatest." We see here how deeply pride and the desire to gain distinction are rooted in every human heart.

We cannot determine exactly when the strife broke out or what its immediate cause may have been. The great importance which the Jews attached to rank in seating at festive meals may have had something to do with it, as may also the question of who, as lowliest, should perform the servant's task of washing the feet of the others. If these were the causes, then the strife must have broken out at the beginning of the feast. St. Luke, who places it after the institution of the Lord's Supper, frequently departs from the chronological order in reporting events.

Whatever the immediate cause, we know that it was an old difficulty which here flared up again. It had cropped up on the way to Capernaum (Mark 9:33,34). It reared its head again on the way to Jerusalem for this feast, when the mother of James and John requested the top honors for her sons (Matt. 20:20-24). The underlying cause was their fleshly and earthly conception of the kingdom of God, and of their place in this kingdom as rulers over other people. Instead of a well-deserved reprimand for their conduct, Jesus gives His disciples another lesson in the principles of true greatness. He virtually repeats what He had said to them a few days before (Matt. 20:25-28), reminding them with infinite patience that, paradoxically, true greatness is found in humility and service, rather than in rank and pride.

AN OLD DIFFICULTY

The pagan way to greatness is lording it over others, measuring that greatness in terms of power and authority. They and their flatterers might call them "benefactors" (Gr., *euergetai*), but to do good is much more honorable than to look great. Because the Apostles gave evidence of being animated by the same spirit of pride and craving for rank, Jesus admonishes, "But ye shall not be so." The kingdom of God is not like the kingdoms of this world. They were not Gentiles, pagans, but "a chosen generation." They were disciples of Jesus. They should follow His precepts and example, not putting themselves above others in lordly fashion, but always standing ready to give humble service.

"THE KINGS OF THE GENTILES EXERCISE LORDSHIP"

Among the Jews, where old age was highly honored and esteemed, the words of Christ, "let him be as the younger," were readily understood to mean that those who were truly spiritually great should cheerfully step down to the lower ranks. Expressed in another way, they should forget all about position and social standing and be "as he that doth serve." God is no respecter of persons (Acts 10:34). Jesus now uses the present situation to illustrate His teaching. If a man is being waited on and served by another while at dinner, all will know that he is the greater of the two. While the disciples were afraid of losing rank if they lowered themselves and acted like servants, He, their acknowledged Lord and Master and host at this Passover celebration, did not hesitate to serve. "I am among you as He that serveth." Obviously this was a reference to the footwashing, which Luke does not report. It was also true of His entire ministry. His lowly service did not make Him any less great, but it was rather the very evidence of His greatness.

"LET HIM BE AS THE YOUNGER"

From reproof the Lord now quickly passes to commendation. He was not forgetting their faithfulness and unwavering loyalty when countless others deserted and rejected Him. "Ye are they which have continued with Me in My temptation." Their mistakes and weaknesses are passed by, but their loyalty is gratefully remembered. And this loyalty He rewards generously. They had dreams of a kingdom, and a kingdom they shall have, not one of earthly might and glory as they had envisioned, but one far surpassing these expectations. He formally makes a covenant with them. "I appoint unto you a kingdom," He confidently asserts. The verb

A KINGDOM APPOINTED

diatithemai (to appoint) has the force of a covenant or testamentary appointment. He who was poor, homeless, and without armed support — who knew that He was about to be bound, tried, condemned, scourged and crucified — speaks with divine authority and majestic confidence concerning His ultimate triumph (Luke 1:32,33).

Another handsome reward is promised them for their loyalty: "that ye may eat and drink at My table in My kingdom." The choicest and best that heaven can provide will be theirs. They will be provided for at the royal table, just as Mephibosheth was at David's table (2 Sam. 9:7).

A ROYAL TABLE

They will be guests of honor at the heavenly feast, "the marriage supper of the Lamb" (Rev. 19:9.). They will have full satisfaction and will be partakers of His glory. We are reminded of the many passages of Scripture which speak of heaven as a magnificent feast.

They will also have great honor and authority, "and sit on thrones judging" with their beloved Lord and Master. Since they were nearest to Jesus during His earthly activity, so they will also be hereafter. As His Apostles, sent forth to proclaim salvation, they would also pronounce the verdict on man's response to that proclamation. When the question of reward came up on the final journey to Jerusalem (Matt. 19:28), Jesus had made the same promise of sitting upon thrones, there using the number twelve, which is here omitted. The number twelve was obviously omitted because of Judas. The previous use of the number twelve with reference to the thrones was made in anticipation of the fact that the apostolic chair, soon to be vacated by Judas, would again be filled. "The twelve tribes of Israel" includes the entire nation, from earliest days unto all future ages. Since the ten tribes had long before been absorbed into the Gentile nations, the judging would extend to the Gentiles as well.

ROYAL POWER AND HONOR

It is noteworthy that while Jesus had been instructing His disciples in service, He does not promise the kingdom as a reward for service, but for faithfulness, in complete harmony with the entire Scripture's teaching of salvation by grace.

The Arrangement of the Paschal Table[1]

"Imagination loves to reproduce the probable details of the solemn scene. And if we compare the notices of ancient Jewish customs with the fashions still existing in the changeless East, we can feel quite confident as to the general nature of the arrangements. These are, however, unlike those with which the genius of Leonardo da Vinci and other great painters have made us familiar. The couches, or cushions, each large enough to hold three persons, were arranged in the form of an elongated horseshoe around three sides of one or more low wooden tables, each one scarcely higher than a stool. The seat of honor was probably the central position on the first couch, to the right of the servants as they approached the open end of the table. The Talmud formulates the position of guests as follows: The worthiest lies down first, on his left side, with his feet stretching back. The next worthiest reclines behind him at his left hand. The third worthiest lies beside the one who had lain down first (at his right), so that the chief person is in the

---

[1] From *The Life of Christ* by Adam Fahling, copyright 1936 by Concordia Publishing House. Used by permission.

middle (between the worthiest guest at his left and the less worthy one at his right hand). From the Gospel narrative we know that John occupied a place to the right of Jesus, so that his head could at any moment be placed upon the breast of His Friend and Lord. He would therefore have received the second place of honor among the guests. At the left and back of Jesus lay the man of Kerioth, as we infer from a few details of the meal, that of dipping his hand into the dish with Jesus, receiving the sop directly from Him, and other indications which point to a position close to the Lord. According to the arrangement prescribed by the Talmud it seems that he really occupied a place at the Passover table first in honor. It is probable that he boldly claimed and obtained the chief seat at the table next to the Lord."

— F —
Jesus Washes The Disciples' Feet

Now before the feast of the Passover, when Jesus knew that His hour was come that He should depart out of this world unto the Father, having loved His own which were in the world, He loved them unto the end. And supper being ended, the devil having now put into the heart of Judas Iscariot, Simon's son, to betray Him — Jesus knowing that the Father had given all things into His hands, and that He was come from God, and went to God — He riseth from supper, and laid aside His garments; and took a towel, and girded Himself. After that, He poureth water into a basin, and began to wash the disciples' feet, and to wipe them with the towel wherewith He was girded. Then cometh He to Simon Peter; and Peter saith unto Him, "Lord, dost Thou wash my feet?" Jesus answered and saith unto him, "What I do thou knowest not now; but thou shalt know hereafter." Peter saith unto Him, "Thou shalt never wash my feet." Jesus answered him, "If I wash thee not, thou hast no part with Me." Simon Peter saith unto Him, "Lord, not my feet only, but also my hands and my head." Jesus saith to him, "He that is washed needeth not save to wash his feet, but is clean every whit; and ye are clean, but not all." For He knew who should betray Him; therefore said He, "Ye are not all clean." So after He had washed their feet, and taken His garments, and was set down again, He said unto them, "Know ye what I have done to you? Ye call Me Master and Lord, and ye say well; for so I am. If I then, your Lord and Master, have washed your feet, ye also ought to wash one another's feet. For I have given you an example, that ye should do as I have done to you. Verily, verily, I say unto you, the servant is not greater than his lord; neither he that is sent greater than he that sent him. If ye know these things, happy are ye if ye do them." (TLL, pp. 262-263; *John 13:1-17*)

The first verse is the prologue to John's story of the Upper Room (John 13-17). "He loved His own unto the end" is the dominant theme of the entire section. That

HE LOVED HIS OWN love was not hindered by the knowledge of His imminent departure from the world, but rather was intensified by it. At this critical time when His thoughts might have been centered upon Himself, "His own" were still His chief concern. This great love manifested itself in many ways: in His gentle admonitions and His charity toward their faults and weaknesses, in the foot-washing, in the institution of the Lord's Supper, in safeguarding the disciples from arrest, and in His prayers for them. The selfish quarreling of the disciples makes this great and abiding love stand out all the more by contrast.

Deipnou genomenou — "supper having arrived," rather than the KJV "Supper being ended." This is in agreement with the custom of the day, which called for foot-washing to remove the dust of the road before the meal, not during or after it. The suggestion that Jesus substituted foot-washing for a customary hand-washing during the course of the Passover meal is unrealistic. The presence of the betrayer at the feast was a most disturbing element in the celebration, for by this time Satan had taken full possession of his heart. So far it was known only to the omniscient Lord that the devil had "put into the heart of Judas Iscariot, Simon's son, to betray Him." To have unmasked Judas then and there would have created much greater disturbance than the strife over rank in seating (see page 16). The suggestion that it might even have roused the fiery spirits of Peter and John to bloodshed is probably not entirely impossible in view of Peter's attack upon Malchus (see page 63). To have had one grave disturbance on this sacred occasion was bad enough, without having another even greater, so Jesus includes Judas in the foot-washing. How marvelous is the love of Jesus, causing Him to humble Himself in this way before His betrayer.

AT SUPPERTIME

JESUS KNEW Jesus did not merely know that the hour was come that He should depart from this world unto the Father, but also that, even in this crucial hour, when Judas and the Sanhedrin were plotting the end of His career, complete triumph was His. He was conscious of His deity, "that the Father had given all things into His hands, and that He was come from God, and went to God." He was fully aware of His own elevation far above His enemies. If Jesus had been merely a great teacher, even then His humiliation would have been remarkable, but much more is it the case because of His deity. "That the Father had given all things into His hands" indicates complete and unrestricted authority. "All power is given unto Me in heaven and in earth" (Matt. 28:18). This, of course, refers to His human nature. His divine nature was already in possession of omnipotence from eternity. The hands into which the Father had placed all things from eternity are now engaged in the most menial task.

The Upper Room had been "furnished." Thus, in addition to the table and seating arrangements, the room was supplied with water, basin, and towel, to be used for the customary foot-washing. They were an invitation to anyone humble enough to use them.

Perhaps the disciples expected that the Master would designate one of their number to take over the duties of a servant, as He had designated Peter and John to make

THE DISCIPLES SHAMED the preparations for the feast. However, Jesus spared them the humiliation which they feared, of being marked as a servant forever after. When it was apparent that none of the disciples would offer his services, "He riseth from supper," laid aside His robe, and attired Himself like a servant assigned to the task of washing the feet, took the materials supplied for that purpose, and proceeded to carry out this humble task. The Twelve must have been astonished and deeply shamed when they realized His intentions, but still no one arose to offer himself for the task. No one interfered until Jesus came to Peter.

The claim that Jesus started with Peter is no doubt intended to bolster the primacy of Peter. But this claim finds no support in the text. It is not difficult to imagine Peter drawing his feet away from Jesus as he impetuously exclaims: "Lord, dost Thou wash my feet?" The refusal of Peter was probably due in part to reverence for Jesus, as Tholuck suggests. The idea that his Master, whom he had confessed to be the Christ, the Son of the Living God, should be on His knees washing his dirty feet, just did not seem right. But beside the reverence, there also appears to be a measure of guilt and shame and a rather strange self-will.

PETER OBJECTS

Jesus tells Peter that his objection was due to a lack of understanding of the real significance of His task. Jesus then predicts that in due time the meaning would be clear to him. "What I do thou knowest not now; but thou shalt know hereafter." He should trust the wisdom of his Master until He chose to explain. God often does things which we do not fully understand now, but He will make them plain to us later — if not in this life, then certainly in heaven. Then we shall understand how His ways with us were ways of divine love for our eternal good.

LACK OF UNDERSTANDING

Even then Peter is not satisfied and does not listen. In open contradiction to the Lord, Peter replies still more strongly, "Thou shalt never wash my feet." The strongest form of negation is used, "in no wise forever." The continued refusal of Peter was rank insubordination, and therefore Jesus was constrained to use stern reproof, lest persistence in disobedience should harm Peter's soul and exclude him from salvation. The attitude of Peter elicits the warning: "If I wash thee not, thou hast no part with Me." Significantly He does not say: "If thou wilt not let Me wash thy feet." More is implied than a mere external washing. He uses the term figuratively of an inward cleansing which removes sin and guilt.

RANK INSUBORDINATION

No part in Him? Shocked and frightened, Peter suddenly changes his line of thinking. Now he swings to the other extreme. He would have also his hands and head, all parts of his body not covered by clothing, washed so that his part in the Savior might be greater. He seems to submit to the will of Jesus, and yet his submission is not complete. He still wants to give directions to the Master. Once when he had done this Jesus called him "Satan" (Matt. 16:23).

"ALSO MY HANDS AND MY HEAD"

Once again it becomes necessary for Jesus to set His impulsive disciple straight. He tells him that the person who has bathed needs only to wash his feet to be clean all over. This was because he walked in the dust with open san-

CLEAN ALREADY dals. As believing disciples, they were clean by the redemption which He was even now providing for them. Through faith in Jesus' redemption, the disciples were spiritually cleansed from all sins, corresponding to the daily washing of feet in physical life. "And ye are clean," He says to His disciples.

But He is compelled to make an exception. He adds the words " . . . but not all." There was one who was not clean because he had spurned Christ's redemption and denied the faith. Even though Judas had lost his faith, and

"BUT NOT ALL" was a disciple only by pretense, Jesus, by these words, once more appeals to his conscience in order to deter him from his purpose. Nothing is left undone to try to win back the erring disciple.

No one else dared to object or to interrupt the Master as He finished the menial task. Then He put on His robe and went back to His place at the table as "the head of the household." Now He asked, "Know ye what I have done

AN EXAMPLE to you?" The action of Jesus was too plain for them not to have comprehended something of the meaning. By so humbling Himself Jesus rebuked their pride and shamed them for their quarreling over positions of rank and power in a future kingdom. This they already keenly felt, and nothing needed to be said on that score. But He had also given them an example of true love. This He would explain and impress upon their hearts so that they might become more like Him. By His example He accomplished what could not have been done so well merely by instruction or reproof. Skillfully He turned a quarreling, bickering, jealous group of men into a chastened and united company of disciples.

"Ye call Me Master and Lord," that is, "*the* Teacher and *the* Lord." The disciples called Him that when they spoke about Him, not merely using it as a title of respect when they addressed Him. "And ye say well," Jesus

MASTER AND LORD commended them. Jesus asserted His full right to bear these names. Then He made this deduction: if He, whom they so honored, did not think it beneath His dignity to perform this most humble service, could they, who were all equal, refuse to do the same among themselves?

"Ye also ought to wash one another's feet." These words are commonly accepted to be figurative, teaching humble and modest service to one another. Jesus did not make foot-washing an ordinance. He called it "an exam-

FOOT-WASHING ple." Some, however, have insisted on a literal interpretation, and have instituted various customs and practices. Bernard of Clairvaux even sought to have it recognized as a sacrament of the Church, but he did not succeed. In such foot-washing ceremonies usually a few selected and prepared old paupers had their feet washed with much display in a holy show. The fact is that the Lord wanted reciprocal foot-washing among all His followers rather than a one-sided washing of inferiors by superiors as a demonstration of a spurious humility. Jesus was aware of the temptation to pride and self-elevation. Therefore He bade His disciples to remember that they were servants and ambassadors rather than lords in the church. Emphatically He told them that servants cannot be above their master, or ambassadors above him who sent them. If anyone should think himself too great or important to stoop to menial tasks, he should remember that such an attitude is self-elevation over the Master. Let him recall Jesus' own words, "I am meek and lowly of heart" (Matt. 11:29). Jesus did not make an exhibition of His humility, but He gave the disciples a revelation of His inmost self.

He concluded with the earnest reminder that the mere knowledge of the will of the Lord is not enough. It must be translated into action to bring blessing and happiness.

— G —
Treason Present Among The Twelve

And He took the cup, and gave thanks, and said, "Take this, and divide it among yourselves; for, I say unto you, I will not drink henceforth of this fruit of the vine, until that day when I drink it new with you in My Father's kingdom. I speak not of you all; I know whom I have chosen: but that the Scripture may be fulfilled, 'He that eateth bread with Me hath lifted up his heel against Me.' Now I tell you before it come, that, when it is come to pass, ye may believe that I am He. Verily, verily, I say unto you, he that receiveth whomsoever I send receiveth Me; and he that receiveth Me receiveth Him that sent Me." (TLL, pp. 263-264)

"But I say unto you, I will not drink henceforth of this fruit of the vine until that day when I drink it new with you in My Father's kingdom." (Matt. 26:29)

"Verily I say unto you, I will drink no more of the fruit of the vine until that day that I drink it new in the kingdom of God." (Mark 14:25)

And He took the cup and gave thanks and said, "Take this and divide it among yourselves; for, I say unto you, I will not drink of the fruit of the vine until the kingdom of God shall come." (Luke 22:17,18)

"I speak not of you all. I know whom I have chosen; but that Scripture may be fulfilled, 'He that eateth bread with Me hath lifted up his heel against Me.' Now I tell you before it come, that, when it is come to pass, ye may believe that I am He. Verily, verily, I say unto you, he that receiveth whomsoever I send receiveth Me; and he that receiveth Me receiveth Him that sent Me." (John 13:18-20)

"Take this and divide it among yourselves." This was obviously not the cup of the institution of the Lord's Supper, but one of the cups of the Passover meal. But which one? Some commentators hold that it was the first by which the feast was opened. The reason for this position is that Luke has placed his account of it next to the Lord's expression of desire for the Passover meal, and before his

AND HE TOOK THE CUP

record of the institution of the Sacrament. On the other hand, others suggest that it was the fourth or fifth cup of the Passover feast because of the position given the accompanying words by Matthew and Mark. It is possible, but not probable, that the Lord's accompanying statement was used with two cups, as a similar statement had been used by Jesus in connection with His expression of desire for the feast (Luke 22:15). If all three of the Evangelists refer to the same cup, it is safe to say that it was one of the cups at the end of the feast, since Luke frequently combines statements that have the same general thought, while Matthew and Mark hold closer to the chronological order.

With verity and authority Jesus states, "I will not drink henceforth of this fruit of the vine." He will not eat another Passover meal, nor will He drink another cup of this wine. Implied is His death at this Passover (see page 3). There will not be another cup of "this fruit of the vine," but only *oxos,* the cheap wine (vinegar) of the soldiers to moisten His lips on the cross (see page 161f.) and the bitter cup of suffering. To this sad announcement Jesus adds a most glorious promise to lift the hearts of the disciples to the contemplation of the great things to come. He will drink it new with them in His Father's kingdom — in heaven. They will be reunited under happier circumstances.

THE PROMISE OF A HEAVENLY FEAST

Jesus makes a second allusion to Judas, this one stronger than the first (John 13:10). The glorious promise of blessing could not apply to all of them because one of their number had excluded himself (see page 22). The heart of Judas was already hardened. It is true that Judas was not one of the elect, even though he had been chosen as an Apostle (and our full comprehension of this must wait until the knowledge in part shall be made perfect in heaven). However, this is evidently not what Jesus means when He says, "I know whom I have chosen." The eleven did not know the true character of one of the chosen Twelve. Jesus informs them that He knows. He knows the significance of Judas' action. We dare not conclude that Judas was a hypocrite when he was chosen by Jesus, but even in his diabolical plan, against his will he was compelled to do the will of God and to fulfill the Scriptures, which foretold that the Messiah should be betrayed by a trusted friend. The passage from Psalm 41:9 is not quoted literally. For "my bread" Jesus substitutes, "he that eateth bread with Me." Eating bread with someone was an expression of intimate friendship and confidence, as it is even now in all countries. In that Psalm David pictured the treachery of Ahithophel, who betrayed the king's confidence and cast his lot with Absalom. Both David and Jesus were friends to traitors who had much in common, both of whom even hanged themselves after their treachery (2 Sam. 17:23).

I SPEAK NOT OF YOU ALL

Jesus does not mention Judas by name, but the very way in which He speaks shows Judas that he is not in any way deceiving the Lord. At the same time, it is another appeal to the heart and conscience of Judas before it is too late. "Now I tell you" — literally, "from now on," intimating that He will tell them repeatedly. They should know that nothing was being hidden from them — so that

A WORD OF ASSURANCE

when the tragedy occurs they will have no reason to think that He was deceived by Judas or that He was the helpless victim of events that were hidden from Him. He tells them what will come to pass, "that ye may believe that I am He." Through this demonstration of divine knowledge their faith, which might otherwise suffer shipwreck, should be increased and strengthened. Thereupon Jesus adds a word of assurance for the eleven. The defection of Judas would not affect their commission in the least. With an oath He reassures them that "he that receiveth whomsoever I send, receiveth Me." Whatever Judas may do, the work of Jesus will go on.

CHAPTER TWO
Jesus' Agony Of Soul In Gethsemane

— A —

The Shadow Of The Betrayal

When Jesus had thus said, and as they sat and did eat, He was troubled in spirit, and testified, and said, "Verily, verily, I say unto you, one of you which eateth with Me shall betray Me. But behold, the hand of him that betrayeth Me is with Me on the table." And the disciples were exceeding sorrowful and looked one on another, doubting of whom He spoke. And they began to enquire among themselves, which of them it was that should do this thing, and to say unto Him one by one, "Is it I?" and another, "Is it I?" And He answered and said unto them, "It is one of the Twelve, that dippeth with Me in the dish — the same shall betray Me. The Son of Man indeed goeth, as it is written of Him; but woe to that man by whom the Son of Man is betrayed! Good were it for that man if he had never been born." (TLL, p. 264)

And as they did eat, He said, "Verily, I say unto you that one of you shall betray Me." And they were exceeding sorrowful, and began every one of them to say to Him, "Lord, is it I?" And He answered and said, "He that dippeth his hand with Me in the dish, the same shall betray Me. The Son of Man goeth as it is written of Him; but woe unto that man by whom the Son of Man is betrayed! It had been good for that man if he had not been born." (Matt. 26:21-24)

And as they sat and did eat, Jesus said, "Verily, I say unto you, one of you which eateth with Me shall betray Me." And they began to be sorrowful and to say unto Him one by one, "Is it I?" And another said, "Is it I?" And He answered and said unto them, "It is one of the Twelve, that dippeth with Me in the dish. The Son of Man indeed goeth, as it is written of Him; but woe to that man by whom the Son of Man is betrayed! Good were it for that man if he had never been born." (Mark 14:18-21)

"But behold, the hand of him that betrayeth Me is with Me on the table. And truly the Son of Man goeth, as it was determined; but woe unto that man by whom He is betrayed!" And they began to inquire among themselves which of them it was that should do this thing. (Luke 22:21-23)

When Jesus had thus said, He was troubled in spirit and testified and said, "Verily, verily, I say unto you, that one of you shall betray Me." Then the disciples looked one on another, doubting of whom He spoke. (John 13:21,22)

"As they sat and did eat" makes it certain that the exposure of Judas took place during the actual eating of the meal and not after the institution of the Sacrament (see p. 33). Luke 22:21-23 again disregards the exact order of time. Being troubled in spirit was more than the physical compassion which Jesus showed so frequently. His spirit was filled with horror, and the disturbance caused by it probably showed itself in His face and in the tone of His voice. The cause of the inner disturbance was Judas Iscariot, who was blinded by Satan, teetering on the edge of eternal destruction, rejecting every appeal to the conscience,

HE WAS TROUBLED IN SPIRIT

spurning proffered grace, and with brazen hypocrisy keeping up the pretense of discipleship. The sight of such arrogant spurning of His great love and grace by one who had been so highly favored must have severely tempted Jesus to turn His back on the whole human race.

Suddenly the disciples were made aware of the cause of Jesus' agitation. Like a stroke of lightning flashing across the darkened sky came the Master's startling words, "Verily, verily, I say unto you, one of you which eateth bread with Me shall betray Me." He speaks with absolute certainty. The betrayal was no mere surmise, no hearsay. "Behold, the hand that betrayeth Me is with Me on the table." Purposely Jesus omits the name of the traitor, saying only, "one of you." He was one of His guests, eating with Him.

THE BETRAYAL ANNOUNCED

Now it was the disciples' turn to be troubled. They were "exceeding sorrowful." First they "looked one on another," wondering who could be guilty of such an atrocity. It was a tense moment as they were scrutinizing each other. Judas too came under the scrutiny of the other disciples. The pressure upon him must have been terrific, but he showed himself a very skillful actor by escaping suspicion of guilt. After some moments of mute astonishment, when the disciples could detect no telltale sign of guilt upon the faces of the others, their own feeling of innocence began to waver in the face of the positive assertion of Jesus. With dismay one after the other of them asked, "Is it I?" Deep in their hearts they knew that it could be any one of them, for by nature the imaginations of the heart are evil indeed.

"IS IT I?"

These anxious questions of the eleven (Judas also asked, to avoid suspicion) were not answered directly. They should have helped to stir up the conscience of Judas. From them he could observe that the eleven were certain that Jesus knew the identity of the betrayer. Instead of naming him, Jesus once more indicates that he will come from the circle of the Apostles — "It is one of the Twelve." Yet another expression is used by Jesus to show that the traitor was present at this very time as His guest at the feast. He is one "that dippeth with Me in the dish." This can hardly have been meant as a mark of identification, since all of the guests dipped into the bowl containing the *charoseth,* a reddish-brown sauce prepared from figs, dates, apples, nuts and spices. The *charoseth* served as a reminder of the burning of bricks in Egypt. This dipping into the bowl was done according to the custom of the feast and is to be understood in the same way as eating bread with Him.

"ONE OF THE TWELVE"

Lest anyone should think that Jesus was at the mercy of any wicked person, He tells the disciples that the counsel of God concerning the redemption of mankind will be carried out according to the divine plan. "The Son of Man goeth, as it is written of Him." His course, including the suffering and shame to the bitter end, was mapped out in Scripture (see Acts 2:23). But that does not remove the guilt or responsibility from the traitor, nor make him any less guilty. Sin never originates with God. It comes from man's own evil heart,

ACCORDING TO DIVINE PLAN

and man must bear the consequences of his sin, even when God uses the evil to serve His divine purpose.

Jesus needed no sympathy. That should be saved for the traitor who had separated himself from his Savior. When Jesus pronounces His woe upon the betrayer He calls him "that man." He was no longer one of His own. Separation from Christ also meant separation from eternal life. Therefore the Lord sadly says: "Good were it for that man if he had never been born." Yes, better for anyone never to have seen the light of day than to have such an end!

"THAT MAN!"

— B —
The Traitor Is Exposed

Now there was leaning on Jesus' bosom one of His disciples, whom Jesus loved. Simon Peter therefore beckoned to him, that he should ask who it should be of whom He spoke. He, then, lying on Jesus' breast, saith unto Him, "Lord, who is it?" Jesus answered, "He it is, to whom I shall give a sop, when I have dipped it." And when He had dipped the sop, He gave it to Judas Iscariot, the son of Simon. Then Judas, which betrayed Him, answered and said, "Master, is it I?" He said unto him, "Thou hast said." And after the sop, Satan entered into him. Then said Jesus unto him, "That thou doest, do quickly." Now no man at the table knew for what intent He spoke this unto him. For some of them thought, because Judas had the bag, that Jesus had said unto him, "Buy those things that we have need of against the feast," or that he should give something to the poor. He, then, having received the sop, went immediately out; and it was night. (TLL, pp 264-265)

Then Judas, which betrayed Him, answered and said, "Master, is it I?" He said unto him, "Thou hast said." (Matt. 26:25)

Now there was leaning on Jesus' bosom one of His disciples, whom Jesus loved. Simon Peter therefore beckoned to him that he should ask who it should be of whom He spoke. He, then, lying on Jesus' breast, saith unto Him, "Lord, who is it?" Jesus answered, "He it is, to whom I shall give a sop, when I have dipped it." And when He had dipped the sop, He gave it to Judas Iscariot, the son of Simon. And after the sop Satan entered into him. Then said Jesus unto him, "That thou doest, do quickly." Now no man at the table knew for what intent He spoke this unto him. For some of them thought, because Judas had the bag, that Jesus had said unto him, "Buy those things that we have need of against the feast," or that he should give something to the poor. He, then, having received the sop, went immediately out; and it was night. (John 13:23-30)

To explain what follows, John finds it necessary to indicate his position at the table. He "was leaning on Jesus' bosom." He lay upon the same wide couch, or

THE DISCIPLE WHOM JESUS LOVED

cushion, to the right of Jesus, as they rested upon the left side and elbow. Thus in leaning back to talk with Jesus his head would fall back against the Master. Deep humility caused John never to mention his own name in the Gospel which he wrote. Whenever he found it necessary to refer to himself, he used the description, "whom Jesus loved." To be loved by Jesus was far more desirable to him than to have his name proclaimed. It is probable that the designation was first used by others who observed the close attachment. Jesus loved all His disciples (see page 19ff.), but there was a special attachment between Him and John, the youngest of the Apostles, then about 22 years of age. Of all the disciples, John was nearest and understood the mind of the Master the best. John, with his brother James, and Peter formed the inner circle of the disciples. They alone were permitted a premature glimpse of the Master's glory at the Transfiguration and to witness His deep humiliation in Gethsemane. Of the Twelve, John alone was present under the cross, and to him Jesus committed the care of His mother.

Peter takes the initiative to learn the identity of the traitor, and yet he lacks the boldness to ask for himself. He recognizes the advantageous position of John and motions to him that he should ask. Spurred by Peter's request, and anxious to know for himself, John asks Jesus, "Who is it?" Even now the Lord does not yet give the name of the traitor. Instead He takes an action designed to give the traitor another opportunity to repent, and failing to do so, to reveal himself. "The sop" ("morsel," NASB; "piece of bread," NIV, Beck) was a small portion, or mouthful, of food, probably bread.

"HE IT IS TO WHOM I SHALL GIVE THE SOP"

Even when there could no longer be any doubt in the mind of Judas that Jesus knew, he still attempts to put on a bold front. Brazenly he tries to bluff by challenging Jesus, "Master, is it I?" Where others had used "Lord" he uses "Rabbi," and thereby inadvertently betrays his real estimate of Jesus. Judas had rejected Jesus as the promised Messiah. Jesus instantly sweeps away the pretense of Judas by answering, "Thou hast said." This was the common Jewish way of using the questioner's own statement to answer.

"SURELY, NOT I, RABBI?"

"After the sop, Satan entered into him" — not by means of the sop, but after he had deliberately taken the morsel and opened the door for Satan. This was not bodily possession, but something far worse, namely, "complete spiritual possession." Judas had become the hopeless victim of Satan. Previously Satan had put it into the heart of Judas to betray Christ (Luke 22:3; see also page 8). Now he took full possession of him. This is a tragic example of the saying: "Give the devil a finger, and he will take your whole hand."

SATAN ENTERED INTO HIM

Since Judas had hardened his heart against the influence of the Lord and had yielded it to the will of Satan, Jesus abandons His former disciple and sends him out into the night. He commands him, "That thou doest, do quickly." Judas may think that Jesus is in his hands, but Jesus is still directing the turn of events. As the plan of the Jewish leaders not to destroy Jesus at the feast (see page 7) was overruled by the Lord, so Judas must carry out his evil design when Jesus allows it, and not when he feels like doing it.

All of the disciples had undoubtedly heard the command of Jesus, but none of them, including John, who by this time knew the identity of the betrayer, realized what He meant by it. It did not enter their minds that the betrayal was so imminent — only a few crucial hours away. There were some guesses, probably not openly expressed in the Upper Room, but brought out later when the events of the evening were discussed. Because Judas was the treasurer for the group, they assumed that he was to attend to some business matter, either purchases to be made for the feast, or alms to be given to the poor. It is noteworthy that even in His poverty Jesus remembered the poor with alms.

NOT COMPREHENDED

Some expositors take the guess of the disciples, that Judas was sent out to "buy those things that we have need of against the feast," as evidence that Jesus was not celebrating the regular Passover on that night. What they overlook is that this was an eight-day feast, one day for the Passover itself and seven days for the Feast of Unleavened Bread (see page 4). Furthermore, the night following the 14th, and ushering in the 15th, of Nisan was full of activity.

"Having received the sop," Judas "went immediately out." He felt out of place there and did not further participate in the Passover meal. Thus I believe that we here have an answer to the question that has puzzled so many — as to whether or not Judas was present at the institution of the Lord's Supper. The instruction, "do quickly," may well have been motivated in part by the determination that Judas should not partake of the Sacrament. "And it was night" — there is something haunting about this statement. It is obviously more than a mere designation of time. It also shows the terrible spiritual condition in the soul of the traitor. It makes us shudder to see this former Apostle going out into the night in the service of the powers of darkness, to accomplish a deed fit only for the blackest night. The hour for the power of darkness had come (Luke 22:53). Judas now belongs to those who love darkness rather than light. "And it was night," eternal night. Never again would the day break for him or the light of grace shine upon his way.

AND IT WAS NIGHT

AND IT WAS NIGHT

"And it was night" when the traitor departed,
Night when he spurned what the Savior had said,
Night when the Tempter was luring him onward,
Night that grew darker and darker ahead.

"And it was night" when he thought of the silver,
Night when his plotting must not go amiss,
Night when he guided the troops to the Garden,
Night when he gave them the sign of a kiss.

"And it was night" when his conscience accused him,
Night when he spoke of the innocent blood,
Night when the priests of the temple forsook him,
Night that came in with the force of a flood.

"And it was night" when he cast down the silver,
Night with no thought of forgiveness and grace,
Night of remorse, of despair, and destruction,
Night when he went to his self-chosen place.

"And it was night!" What a definite warning
Rings from these words as the ages unroll!
If all the world had been gained by the traitor,
What could he give in exchange for his soul?

Jesus is keeping the doorway wide open;
Let no one linger in sin or in doubt!
Trusting His promise and pleading for mercy,
No one that cometh is ever cast out.

W. M. Czmanske, *Concordia Pulpit*, 1943, p. 114

— C —
The Son Of Man Glorified

Therefore, when he was gone out, Jesus said, "Now is the Son of Man glorified, and God is glorified in Him. If God be glorified in Him, God shall also glorify Him in Himself, and shall straightway glorify Him." (TLL, p. 265; *John 13:31,32*)

The departure of Judas seems to have cleared the atmosphere. A great weight appears to have been lifted from the heart of Jesus, and He can breathe more freely again. With the disturbing element removed, serenity and gladness return to the feast. The conversation takes on a different tone. No sooner had the traitor left the room than Jesus begins to speak of triumph and glory. The defection of one who was trusted did not detract anything from the glory of His ultimate victory.

THE ATMOSPHERE CLEARED

With spirit raised Jesus declares, "Now is the Son of Man glorified." The idea that Jesus only views a glory which shall be His after His life-work is accomplished overlooks the "now." Indeed, He was aware and confident of the coming glory, of His triumph over the spirits in hell, His resurrection, ascension, and session at the right hand of the Father — in other words, of His exaltation; and this raised His spirits. "Who for the joy that was set before Him endured the cross, despising the shame, and is set down at the right hand of the throne of God" (Heb. 12:2). But He was also being glorified by the passion itself, the decisive part of His redemptive work which was set in motion by the depar-

GLORIFIED

ture of the betrayer. "And God is glorified in Him." The glorification must also pertain to the glory of the Father, especially because it was derived from obedience to the Father's will. The present glory of the passion would shortly be followed by the other glory of His exaltation, for "God shall also glorify Him straightway."

This message of Christ's glory, like the vision on the Mount of Transfiguration, was given for the comfort and consolation of the disciples in view of the sorrows and tribulations which would soon engulf them.

— D —
The Lord's Supper Instituted

And as they were eating in the night in which He was betrayed, Jesus took bread and gave thanks and broke it and gave it unto His disciples, saying, "Take, eat, this is My body, which is given for you; this do in remembrance of Me." Likewise also He took the cup after supper, and when He had given thanks, He gave it to them, saying, "Drink ye all of it; this cup is the New Testament in My blood, which is shed for you and for many for the remission of sins. This do, as often as ye drink it, in remembrance of Me." And they all drank thereof. (TLL, p. 265)

And as they were eating, Jesus took bread and blessed it and broke it and gave it to the disciples and said, "Take, eat; this is My body." And He took the cup and gave thanks and gave it to them, saying, "Drink ye all of it; for this is My blood of the New Testament, which is shed for many for the remission of sins." (Matt. 26:26-28)

And as they did eat, Jesus took bread and blessed and broke it and gave to them and said, "Take, eat; this is My body." And He took the cup, and when He had given thanks, He gave it to them; and they all drank of it. And He said unto them, "This is My blood of the New Testament, which is shed for many." (Mark 14:22-24)

And He took bread and gave thanks and broke it and gave unto them, saying, "This is My body which is given for you; this do in remembrance of Me." Likewise also the cup after supper, saying, "This cup is the New Testament in My blood, which is shed for you." (Luke 22:19,20)

The Lord Jesus, the same night in which He was betrayed, took bread; and when He had given thanks, He broke it and said, "Take eat; this is My body, which is broken for you; this do in remembrance of Me." After the same manner also He took the cup, when He had supped, saying, "This cup is the New Testament in My blood; this do ye, as oft as ye drink it, in remembrance of Me." (1 Cor. 11:23b-25)

THE NIGHT IN WHICH HE WAS BETRAYED

It is St. Paul who supplies us with the expression, "in the night in which He was betrayed." The Evangelists have no need for specifying the time, since they simply include the institution of the Lord's Supper in their record of the events of Thursday evening. Considerable interest centers on the specific time in the Passover celebration during which the Sacrament was instituted. This would be the key as to whether or not Judas also partook of it.

"As they were eating," as expressed by both Matthew and Mark, indicates that the institution occurred during the supper, considered as a whole, before the feast was concluded. St. Luke is more specific when he says, "likewise also the cup after supper," when the supper (in the narrow sense) was at an end. By that time Judas had left (see page 33). By inserting the institution of the Sacrament into the framework of the Passover, Jesus fixed the character of His supper as a feast, rather than a sacrifice. As the Passover feast was preceded by a sacrifice, so the feast for the soul in the Lord's Supper rests upon Christ's sacrifice, rather than being a sacrifice in itself.

A FEAST

"Jesus took bread," the representative food (the unleavened bread of the Passover meal) "and gave thanks." The words of blessing and thanksgiving have not been preserved for us. It has been suggested that they corresponded to the giving of thanks for the bread and wine for bodily sustenance at the beginning of the feast and that they enlightened the disciples, preparing them for the intelligent reception of the Sacrament. These, however, are only conjectures.

THE EUCHARIST

After giving thanks Jesus "broke" the bread. This was the natural thing to do to reduce it to the proper size for eating. Unleavened bread could not be baked in loaves, but it was rather baked in thin sheets and customarily broken for eating. The breaking was only incidental and had no symbolical significance. The body of Jesus was not broken on the cross, and thereby the Scripture was fulfilled, "A bone of Him shall not be broken" (John 19:36).

THE BREAKING OF BREAD

"And He gave it to His disciples." How He gave the bread, and later the cup, whether by personally putting it to their lips or by passing it around, is not indicated, though Passover custom would suggest the latter. With the distribution Jesus gave the simple and natural instruction, "Take eat . . . take drink ye all of it." There is not the slightest suggestion that any other use of the Sacrament, whether for display, adoration, or sacrifice, ought to be approved or tolerated.

THE DISTRIBUTION

As Jesus distributes the bread, He says, "This is My body." This bread which He was now giving to them He declares to be His body which was to die on the cross for the salvation of sinners. The bread and the body were present in the most intimate union. The words are simple and clear. It is only our human reason that threatens to confuse the matter by rationalizing and by trying to discover how this can be so.

"THIS IS MY BODY"

> He is the Word that spake it;
> He took the bread and brake it;
> And what His Word did make it,
> That I believe and take it.
>   Donne

"This do in remembrance of Me," the Lord commands. What they saw and heard from Jesus, without any tampering whatsoever, they were to practice. Participation in the Sacrament should recall Jesus to us, especially the great sacrifice which He made for us. As the Passover was a memorial to Israel, so the Lord gave His Church a new and greater memorial in the Lord's Supper. The words, "as often as," indicate repetition of this feast of remembrance, without indicating a prescribed time of frequency. In its repetition this Sacrament differs from Baptism.

"IN REMEMBRANCE"

"Likewise, also, He took the cup." Jesus used one cup for the institution and distribution of the Sacrament, and He invited them all to drink out of that one cup. The content of the cup was the "fruit of the vine" that is, wine (Matt. 26:29). For the Passover celebration the wine was diluted with water. This cup was prepared for general distribution to all the celebrants. Jesus commands, "Drink ye all of it," and St. Mark reports, "They all drank of it." To receive the Sacrament properly, all who ate were also required to drink.

THE CUP

"After supper" reminds us that Jesus and His disciples had been feasting, and not fasting, before the celebration of the Lord's Supper. The practice of fasting in connection with the Sacrament has no historical basis as far as the first observance is concerned. The great importance of the Sacrament is established by Jesus when He says, "This cup is the New Testament in My blood." A new era was opened and a new covenant established by the shedding of His precious blood. The wall of separation between the holy God and sinful mankind was removed. Because this Sacrament is a *testament* it cannot be altered without invalidating it.

"THE NEW TESTAMENT"

His blood, present in the Sacrament, was "shed for you and for many." It was for His own, the eleven, that Jesus would sacrifice Himself and shed His priceless blood on the cross. He died, not only for them, but also "for many," for the unlimited number of mankind. Jesus' blood was shed "for the remission of sins." In this Sacrament Jesus reassures the disciples of the forgiveness He has secured for them. The forgiveness is doubly sure because it is a term of a divine testament.

"SHED . . . FOR THE REMISSION OF SINS"

— E —
Peter Is Warned

"Little children, yet a little while I am with you. Ye shall seek Me; and as I said unto the Jews: Whither I go, ye cannot come; so now I say to you. A new commandment I give unto you, that ye love one another; as I have loved you, that ye also love one another. By this shall all men know that ye are My disciples, if ye have love one to another." Simon Peter said unto Him, "Lord, whither goest Thou?" Jesus answered him, "Whither I go, thou canst not follow Me now; but thou shalt follow Me afterwards." Peter said unto Him, "Lord, why cannot I follow Thee now? I will lay down my life for Thy sake." Jesus answered him, "Wilt thou lay down thy life for My sake? Simon, Simon, behold, Satan hath desired to have you, that he may sift you as wheat; but I have prayed for thee, that thy faith fail not; and when thou art converted, strengthen thy brethren." And he saith unto Him, "Lord, I am ready to go with Thee, both into prison, and to death." And He said, "Verily, verily, I tell thee, Peter, the cock shall not crow this day before that thou shalt thrice deny that thou knowest Me." (TLL, p. 266)

And the Lord said, "Simon, Simon, behold, Satan hath desired to have you, that he may sift you as wheat; but I have prayed for thee, that thy faith fail not; and when thou art converted, strengthen thy brethren." And he said unto Him, "Lord, I am ready to go with Thee both into prison and to death!" And He said, "I tell thee, Peter, the cock shall not crow this day before that thou shalt thrice deny that thou knowest Me." (Luke 22:31-34)

"Little children, yet a little while I am with you. Ye shall seek Me; and as I said unto the Jews: Whither I go, ye cannot come; so now I say to you. A new commandment I give unto you, that ye love one another as I have loved you, that ye also love one another. By this shall all men know that ye are My disciples, if ye have love one to another." Simon Peter said unto Him, "Lord, whither goest Thou?" Jesus answered him, "Whither I go, thou canst not follow Me now; but thou shalt follow Me afterwards." Peter said unto Him, "Lord, why cannot I follow Thee now? I will lay down my life for Thy sake." Jesus answered him, "Wilt thou lay down thy life for My sake? Verily, verily, I say unto thee, the cock shall not crow, till thou hast denied Me thrice." (John 13:33-38)

Jesus had told His disciples about His glorification, beginning in His passion and extending into the final step of His exaltation (see page 34f.). This would mean an early withdrawal of His visible presence from them.

A TENDER WARNING   For this He proceeds to fortify them. He addresses them with the diminutive "little children" (Gr., *teknia*), a term of affection and endearment, but also implying their immaturity. "Yet a little while," really only a few hours, and they would be left without their beloved Master. With the words, "as I said unto the Jews," Jesus refers to what He had told the Jews at the Feast of the Tabernacle (John 7:34). He would leave them, and they would seek Him in vain. Jesus then applies this to the eleven. Significantly omitted was the warning to the Jews, that they would die in their sins (John 8:21). The familiar associations which they had hitherto enjoyed would be ended forever, and they would keenly miss Him. "Whither I go, ye cannot come." That applies in their case only for the present (John 13:36). In due time they should follow Him to heavenly glory, but for the present they had a task to carry out.

With His visible presence removed, it would be all the more important that they should be closely attached to each other by love. To unite them more perfectly He

"A NEW COMMANDMENT"

continues, "A new commandment I give unto you, that ye love one another." This is a precept for them to follow, rather than a legal mandate to obey in a servile way. The commandment of love is not new in time (Gr., *nea*), in the sense that it had never existed before. "Thou shalt love thy neighbor as thyself" (Lev. 19:18) was well known since the days of Moses. Rather, it was new in kind or quality (Gr., *kainos*). Instead of using their own love of self as a standard, they were to use the purer and nobler love of Christ for them as a standard. "As I have loved you" means to love with unselfish, self-sacrificing love. The disciples knew that they had often failed their Lord Jesus, that they had often disappointed Him, and yet He had continued to love them sincerely and deeply in spite of their shortcomings. "As" refers to the pattern of love, not the measure. To love as much as Jesus loved would be utterly impossible for us sinners.

This love is to be the distinguishing mark of the disciples, the test of true discipleship. "By this shall all men know that ye are My disciples." Where true brotherly love exists it must also show itself in such a way that it is also recognized by others. St. John declares, "We know that we have passed from death unto life, because we love the brethren" (1 John 3:14). The early Christians measured up to this expectation. Marcus Minucius Felix testified, "They love each other even without being acquainted with each other." And Lucian scoffed, "Their lawgiver has persuaded them that they are all brethren."

THE MARK OF DISCIPLESHIP

In Peter's mind the idea of Jesus going away evidently overshadows the Master's precept of brotherly love. He reacts by asking, "Whither goest Thou?" The answer of Jesus indicates that it was more anxiety than curiosity that had prompted the question. Jesus does not reply regarding His destination. Peter should know that, for Jesus had spoken often enough about His going to the Father. Instead Jesus says, "Whither I go, thou canst not follow Me now." The suggestion that Peter was not "ripe" for such a journey is reading something into the words of Jesus that is not there. There was work for Peter and the others to do. That is why they had been called to the apostleship. That work must be done first. "But thou shalt follow Me afterwards." In due time Peter would follow His Lord and Master into suffering and death by crucifixion.

"WHITHER GOEST THOU?"

Peter is not satisfied by what Jesus has said. He does not honor the words of Jesus and does not shrink from setting himself in opposition to them: "Why cannot I follow Thee now?" In his zeal he protests, "I will lay down my life for Thy sake." Peter had greatly overestimated himself, and Jesus is constrained to issue His first warning of the impending denial, a warning repeated on the way to Gethsemane (see page 45). "Wilt thou lay down thy life for My sake?" Peter might think so, but Jesus knows better. He foresees the cowardly conduct of His disciple. He knows how near at hand his fall is. Indeed, were it not for the intervention of Jesus, this night would see proud Peter utterly overwhelmed and destroyed. Solemnly, mingling affection with distress, the Savior says, "Simon, Simon," — doubling the name, as He did on other occa-

PETER PROTESTS

sions, when He said, "Martha, Martha," or "Jerusalem, Jerusalem." Thereby He serves notice that He has something serious and important to discuss. He doesn't say "Peter, Peter," that new name that portrays him as a "rock-man," but He uses the old name, Simon, to remind him of his frailty.

Satan had already seduced Judas, but that did not satisfy him. Satan wanted all of the disciples. The "you" here is plural. The audacity of Satan surpasses imagination.

SATAN RESTRICTED He desires, yes, lays claim upon and demands from God, the very ones whom Jesus had called to be His own. They represent the Church. Through them the Church was to live and grow. The goal of Satan was to destroy the Church through the destruction of the Lord's Apostles. Satan had never been able to prevail against Jesus, though he did not shy away from attacking Him. Jesus was the Sinless One. But against the disciples he could press the claim that they were sinners, and that the wages of sin is death. Frantic as Satan was in the final hour before the consummation of man's redemption, he still could not assail the disciples at will. He could try them only with God's permission, and then only within the bounds set by God, as in the case of Job. For the comfort of all Christians we have been given the promise, "God is faithful, who will not suffer you to be tempted above that ye are able; but will with the temptation also make a way to escape, that ye may be able to bear it" (1 Cor. 10:13).

"That he may sift you as wheat." Whether the figure of sifting was used by Satan in filing his claim upon the disciples, thereby implying that they will be found chaff, or whether the figure belongs to Jesus, it vividly portrays the turbulence of this night. The disciples would be shaken back and forth violently as wheat when it is shaken in a sieve. But while men toss grain in a sieve to cleanse it, Satan sifts to destroy faith.

Peter is now addressed personally, with the rest as attentive listeners. It is not that Jesus failed to pray for all of the disciples (cf. John 17), but impetuous Peter was in

"BUT I HAVE PRAYED FOR THEE" special need of the Lord's intercession. Jesus did not ask that the sifting might stop. It was necessary and wholesome for Peter, that he might learn to know himself and discover the depth of his own depravity and weakness. The sifting of Satan could and should become a lasting blessing to Peter by curing him of his pride and self-sufficiency. Therefore the intercession of Jesus was not for the removal of the trial, but for strength to sustain him — "that thy faith fail not."

Jesus foreknows that Peter's faith will not perish permanently and accordingly instructs him, "And when thou art converted, strengthen thy brethren." After he had once again recovered he should consider his brethren and

AFTER RECOVERY strengthen them, since they would also be sifted by Satan. Peter is singled out because he fell most deeply and thus also experienced the fullest measure of divine grace. How Peter later did as Jesus here instructs we see in Acts, as well as in his own Epistles. His own experience is reflected in the words, "Ye are kept by the power of God through faith unto salvation" (1 Peter 1:5).

But Peter refuses to take the warning of Jesus seriously. He contradicts the positive statement of Christ and repeats his readiness to die for Him. "Lord, I am ready to go with Thee, both into prison and to death." Jesus did not need to worry about him! He could rely on Peter's loyalty! No doubt Peter meant it, but Jesus knew that, instead of dying, Peter would lie and deny in order to save his own life.

PETER CONTRADICTS THE LORD

With emphasis, "Verily, verily," Jesus tells Peter how quick and great his fall will be. "The cock shall not crow this day, before thou shalt thrice deny that thou knowest Me." Contrary to his grand words, Peter would completely disown his Lord and Master, not by silence, but by three loud and forceful declarations. How short the time before Peter's downfall is indicated by the crowing of the cock — ere day should break again! Here we also see the Savior's great concern for His own. With the designation of the cock's crow as the time limit, Jesus also supplies an aid to bring Peter to repentance (see page 76).

BEFORE THE COCK CROWS

— F —
Jesus Warns Of Coming Danger

And He said unto them, "When I sent you without purse, and scrip, and shoes, lacked ye anything?" And they said, "Nothing." Then said He unto them, "But now, he that hath a purse, let him take it, and likewise his scrip: and he that hath no sword, let him sell his garment, and buy one. For I say unto you, that this that is written must yet be accomplished in Me: 'And He was reckoned among the transgressors'; for the things concerning Me have an end." And they said, "Lord, behold, here are two swords." And He said unto them, "It is enough." (TLL, pp. 266-267; *Luke 22:35-38*)

From Peter the attention of Jesus returns to the circle of the disciples. Once more He speaks of things to come. Greatly changed circumstances were awaiting them. To explain how different things will be, He recalls an experience of the past. On the mission tour through Galilee Jesus had sent His disciples out empty-handed to teach them complete trust in the Sender. He asks, "Lacked ye anything?" They are compelled to answer, "Nothing." But in the future the situation would be entirely different. Earlier they had been instructed, "Go not into the way of the Gentiles, and into any city of the Samaritans enter ye not; but go rather to the lost sheep of the house of Israel" (Matt. 10:5,6). There the great fame of their Master had preceded them and they were among friends. Hospitality was to be expected. That was quite different from the great commission He was soon to give them, to go into all the world as messengers of His Gospel. Then they would often find themselves in foreign and hostile countries. The Lord would still take care of

THINGS WILL BE DIFFERENT

them, but the manner of doing so would be different. They would not immediately and everywhere find believers ready to provide for them. Therefore they would need money, clothes, and even a sword for self-defense. "But now, he that hath a purse, let him take it, and likewise his scrip, and he that hath no sword, let him sell his garment and buy one."

The reason for this sharp contrast lay in the fact that when the disciples would go out again, they would not be looked upon as disciples of a great and popular, miracle-working hero, but followers of one who had been rejected and disowned by His people, executed as a criminal by crucifixion, and whose name would produce scorn, mockery, and opposition. This, however, would not be due to an unforeseen calamity caused by the hostility of man, but was part of the divine plan of redemption, clearly foretold in the Scriptures. "This that is written must yet be accomplished in Me: 'And He was reckoned among the transgressors' " (cf. Isa. 53:12). This reckoning among the transgressors would be one of the last things fulfilled concerning Him, "for the things concerning Me have an end." The final impression would be deep and lasting. To this day Jesus is known as "the hanged one" among the Jews. Paul wrote, "We preach Christ crucified, unto the Jews a stumbling block, and unto the Greeks foolishness" (1 Cor. 1:23).

AN UNPOPULAR CAUSE

Once again the words of Christ were misunderstood. The disciples did not grasp the real meaning — that He was referring to the future. Thinking only of the present, the disciples thought they should equip themselves for an emergency. "They said, 'Lord, behold, here are two swords.' " Where they came from, whether concealed under their outer garment after the manner of their countrymen, or whether they were hanging right there in the upper room, we cannot say. All that we know is that one of them showed up later in the Garden in the hands of Peter (see page 63). The reply of Jesus, "It is enough," did not refer to the number of swords but simply indicated that He wanted that discussion to cease. This was not the time to reason with them. Later they would understand how preposterous it was to offer two swords against the might of the world, hell, and death, all of which were united to defeat Him.

"TWO SWORDS"

— G —
Peter's Second Warning

When Jesus had spoken these words, and when they had sung a hymn, He came out and went forth, as He was wont, over the brook Cedron, to the Mount of Olives; and His disciples also followed Him. Then saith Jesus unto them, "All ye shall be offended because of Me this night; for it is written, 'I will smite the Shepherd, and the sheep of the flock shall be scattered abroad.' But after I am risen again, I will go before you into Galilee." Peter answered and said unto Him, "Though all men shall be offended because of Thee, yet will I never be offended." Jesus said unto him, "Verily, I say unto thee, that this night, before the cock crow twice, thou shalt deny Me thrice." Peter spoke the more vehemently, "Though I should die with Thee, yet will I not deny Thee in any wise." Likewise also said all the disciples. (TLL, p. 267)

And when they had sung a hymn, they went out into the Mount of Olives. Then saith Jesus unto them, "All ye shall be offended because of Me this night; for it is written, 'I will smite the Shepherd, and the sheep of the flock shall be scattered abroad.' But after I am risen again, I will go before you into Galilee." Peter answered and said unto Him, "Though all men shall be offended of Thee, yet will I never be offended." Jesus said unto him, "Verily, I say unto thee that this night, before the cock crow, thou shalt deny Me thrice." Peter said unto Him, "Though I should die with Thee, yet will I not deny Thee." Likewise also said all the disciples. (Matt. 26:30-35)

And when they had sung a hymn, they went out into the Mount of Olives. And Jesus saith unto them, "All ye shall be offended because of Me this night, for it is written, 'I will smite the Shepherd, and the sheep shall be scattered.' But after that I am risen, I will go before you into Galilee." But Peter said unto Him, "Although all shall be offended, yet will not I." And Jesus saith unto him, "Verily, I say unto thee, that this day, even in this night, before the cock crow twice, thou shalt deny Me thrice." But he spoke the more vehemently, "If I should die with Thee, I will not deny Thee in any wise." Likewise also said they all. (Mark 14:26-31)

And He came out and went, as He was wont, to the Mount of Olives; and His disciples also followed Him. (Luke 22:39)

When Jesus had spoken these words, He went forth with His disciples over the brook of Cedron. (John 18:1a)

When Jesus had completed His discourses with His disciples and had prayed His high-priestly prayer, the feast was concluded with the singing of "a hymn." There is something very touching in the report that in this very hour,

JESUS SINGS when the powers of darkness were assembling to prepare an all-out attack against the Anointed of the Lord, the voice of singing was issuing from His lips. As we reflect on this, we wonder at the origin of modern customs which would seal the lips of Christians against songs of faith and hope in times when their emotions are deeply moved by affliction and sorrow.

What kind of songs came from the lips of Jesus and His disciples? It was the custom to sing a group of inspired Psalms, known as the "Hallel," in connection with the celebration of the Passover. These were Psalms

THE HALLEL 113-118. Sometimes also Psalms 130-136, or just Psalm 136, were sung. Although these same words had been sung, and were being sung, by countless others, never were they sung with the same force and meaning as they were during these crucial hours in the Upper Room. For others these were the hymns of Israel, expressions of gratitude and trust, of faith and hope, written for them by divine inspiration. For Christ, the eternal Word, it was the Author singing His own Psalms, whose prophecies were being fulfilled in Himself.

"He came out and went forth" into the city streets, which on this festive night were far from deserted. The gates of the Temple would be thrown open at midnight. Everywhere people were on their way up to the Holy Place, or getting ready to go. But instead of going to the Temple, Jesus led His disciples out of the city "over the brook Cedron."

This winter stream, or *wady*, was a dry ravine most of the year, but it turned into a torrent in the rainy season. It was also known as Kedron, or Kidron. From its source about a mile and a half northeast of Jerusalem it flowed past the city through a deep gorge in the Valley of Jehoshaphat, between Mount Moriah and Mount Olivet. After cutting across the wilderness of Judea it emptied directly into the Dead Sea. The name Cedron means "black" or "turbid." The brook's naturally dark and turbid waters were darkened even more when the blood of the sacrifices of the Temple worship flowed into it. The Cedron is mentioned frequently in the annals of Israel. Notable was the crossing of the brook by King David, following his betrayal by Ahithophel, a member of his bodyguard, during the uprising of his son Absalom (2 Sam. 15:23). This was more than a thousand years before great David's greater Son led His disciples on the road that led to the Mount of Olives on the night in which He was betrayed.

THE BLACK TORRENT

This was no flight to escape personal danger, but a deliberate going forth to carry out the will of the heavenly Father. Jesus' crossing of the Cedron has been called infinitely more momentous than Ceasar's crossing of the Rubicon. However, for the disciples that evening there appeared to be nothing unusual or decisive in the way they were going, for He led them this way "as He was wont" (accustomed). Of previous visits to the Mount of Olives and the Garden of Gethsemane we know very little, except that they had taken place. This visit was destined to be both completely different and also fully recorded.

CROSSING THE CEDRON

Before they had gone far, another discussion between the Master and His disciples takes place. Jesus begins with a prediction: "All ye shall be offended because of Me this night." This night was to be a fateful one for them. Impending events would cause all of them, without exception, to stumble. They would be ashamed to be known as disciples of Jesus.

Jesus shows His disciples that His suffering was not contrary to the Old Testament predictions, but rather a fulfillment of them. It was the Prophet Zechariah (13:7) who foretold, "I will smite the Shepherd, and the sheep of the flock shall be scattered abroad." Jesus applies the words of this Prophet to His own death and its effects upon the disciples. As a flock deprived of its shepherd will scatter abroad and flee in all directions, so they would be shepherdless, and their flight would be without purpose and direction.

IT IS WRITTEN

But Jesus immediately adds the promise of bringing the scattered sheep together again. "But after I am risen again, I will go before you into Galilee." Jesus had repeatedly announced His resurrection to His disciples, but here He adds the comforting assurance that He would gather His scattered flock again. The place where He would collect them would be the region in Galilee, from where He had originally gathered most of His flock.

Peter felt that this warning of Jesus threatened his own pledge of loyalty unto death which he had made in the Upper Room. Therefore he hastened, from his point of view, to set the record straight. Peter let no modesty interfere in comparing himself with the other disciples and to his own great advantage. "Though all men shall be offended because of Thee, yet will I never be offended," he said. Jesus met this self-conceit of Peter by repeating in almost the same words the warning which He had uttered in the Upper Room earlier in the evening: "This night, before the cock crow twice, thou shalt deny Me thrice" (see pages 39-41). The second crowing was just before dawn. But Peter cast aside this second warning even more determinedly than the first. Instead of being sobered by the words of Jesus he "spoke the more vehemently." With all possible force he emphasized his self-confidence, ignoring all the warnings of Jesus.

PETER PROTESTED

Carried away by the claims and promises of Peter, the rest of the disciples "said likewise." Jesus was silent. Further words now would be useless. The time would soon come when Peter would remember, and thereby be led to repentance. It was enough.

— H —
Jesus Enters Gethsemane

Then cometh Jesus with them unto a place called Gethsemane, where was a garden, into the which He entered, and His disciples. And Judas also, which betrayed Him, knew the place; for Jesus ofttimes resorted thither with His disciples. And when He was at the place, He saith unto the disciples, "Sit ye here, while I go and pray yonder. Pray that ye enter not into temptation." (TLL, p. 267)

Then cometh Jesus with them unto a place called Gethsemane, and saith unto the disciples, "Sit ye here, while I go and pray yonder." (Matt. 26:36)
And they came to a place which was named Gethsemane; and He saith to His disciples, "Sit ye here, while I shall pray." (Mark 14:32)
And when He was at the place, He said unto them, "Pray that ye enter not into temptation." (Luke 22:40)
Where was a garden, into the which He entered, and His disciples. And Judas also, which betrayed Him, knew the place; for Jesus ofttimes resorted thither with His disciples. (John 18:1b,2)

The specific destination of this nocturnal trek to the Mount of Olives was the Garden of Gethsemane. The name signifies "oil press," and St. John calls the place

THE GARDEN OF GETHSEMANE

"a garden." It was appropriate that in a garden Jesus began His intense suffering to atone for sin, which was first committed in a garden — the Garden of Eden. This Garden of Gethsemane appears to have been a grove of olive trees which also had the equipment for making olive oil. Probably surrounded by a stone wall, it offered a place of quiet retreat and seclusion. A traditional site with eight olive trees, surrounded by a stone wall, is pointed out today as the sacred spot, but there is no way of determining the accuracy of the claim. The trees, of course, cannot be the same ones under which the Savior sorrowed. Those which the passage of time did not destroy, Titus, the Roman general, prematurely cut down during the siege of Jerusalem in the year 70.

The owner of the garden remains unknown, but the free access which Jesus and His disciples enjoyed gives weight to the suggestion that he was a friend and follower of the Lord.

Lest it be thought that Jesus went into the garden to hide Himself, it is added, "and Judas also, which betrayed Him, knew the place, for Jesus ofttimes resorted thither with His disciples." Judas was familiar with the

JUDAS KNEW THE PLACE

Master's habits and His place of retreat and prayer. The "ofttimes" indicates the frequency of meeting here without giving any indication when that was. The opinion has been expressed that the nights between Monday and Maundy Thursday were spent by Jesus and His disciples in Gethsemane, rather than at Bethany, and that for this reason the place was known unto Judas. It must be said, however, that "the Mount of Olives" (Luke 21:37), cited as proof, could refer to Bethany as well as to Gethsemane, since Bethany was on the eastern slope of the Mount of Olives.

Eight of the disciples were left near the entrance of the garden with the instruction, "Sit ye here, while I go and pray yonder." Only the three who had been witnesses of His glory on the Mount of Trans-

"WHILE I GO AND PRAY YONDER"

figuration were taken along. Now they could see the conflict of His soul in His deep humiliation. There was nothing more natural for Jesus to do under the circumstances than to converse with His heavenly Father in prayer. But before He went "yonder" He exhorted His disciples to pray also, not that they might escape the ordeal of this night, but that they might "enter not into temptation."

DARK GETHSEMANE

"It was night, and the olive trees made the garden darker with their shadows, despite the shining of the full moon at this Passover season. But there were other things that contributed to the darkness of this Garden, a darkness such as had fallen upon no other garden in all the world. To our hymn writer's mind came a darker foe than Judas, who was on his way to the Garden. He saw the Prince of Darkness coming to match his power with the very Son of God. The old evil foe was lurking, gathering his forces for a decisive attack upon the second Adam, to do with Christ what he had succeeded in doing in the Garden of Eden."

Czmanske, *Concordia Pulpit*, Vol. 14, p. 117

— I —

The Agony In The Garden

And He taketh with Him Peter and James and John, the two sons of Zebedee, and began to be sorrowful, and very heavy. And saith unto them, "My soul is exceeding sorrowful, even unto death. Tarry ye here and watch with Me." (TLL, pp. 267-268)

And He took with Him Peter and the two sons of Zebedee, and began to be sorrowful and very heavy. Then saith He unto them, "My soul is exceeding sorrowful, even unto death. Tarry ye here and watch with Me." (Matt. 26:37,38)

And He taketh with Him Peter, James and John, and began to be sore amazed and to be very heavy and saith unto them, "My soul is exceeding sorrowful unto death. Tarry ye here and watch." (Mark 14:33,34)

On other occasions Jesus preferred to be alone in His devotions, but in this fateful hour He felt the need to have someone with Him. Exhorting the eight to watchful prayer, "He taketh with Him Peter and James and John" and went deeper into the Garden with them.

HE YEARNS FOR COMPANIONSHIP

These three, called "pillars" by St. Paul in Galatians 2:9, had been singled out by Jesus before (cf. Mark 5:37), having been witnesses of His greatest earthly glory at the sight of the Transfiguration. Now they were also to witness His deep humiliation. The contrast between the Upper Room and the Garden is strikingly sharp: In the Upper Room Jesus GIVES — gives strength, courage, and hope; gives Himself in the blessed Sacrament to His disciples — to those present and to all unto the end of days. Here in the Garden He is suddenly weak and helpless, and has need for RECEIVING. Yet He receives so little, except from the angel of God. Many times the disciples had depended upon Jesus, so often He had given comfort and confidence to them in times of trouble. Now in His great distress He felt the urgent need of the presence of His trusted friends to comfort, encourage, and support Him with their prayers.

Even before He spoke, it was apparent to the three that He "began to be very sorrowful, and very heavy." The mighty worker of miracles was crushed. The tremendous load of the sin of all mankind had beaten Him down. Mark tells us that He was "sore amazed." What He had known all along and had plainly told His disciples regarding the course He must follow now swept over Him with devastating fury. He confided His anguish to His companions. "My soul is exceeding sorrowful, even unto death." He was overwhelmed with sorrow, anguish, and the terror of death to a degree that surpasses our comprehension. Although He was untainted by sin and death, He was now burdened by the combined weight of all men's transgressions. "One should need to have been

SORROWFUL AND VERY HEAVY

in hell for some time in order to understand what it is that is tearing Jesus apart in the garden" (Schilder).

The anguish mounts. Filled with terror, Jesus pleads, "Tarry ye here and watch with Me." He urgently desires that comfort which the nearness of those He loved most might offer. He expects them to watch with Him in His distress, for they were the very three who had most fervently proclaimed their love and loyalty to Him. The sons of Zebedee had so confidently professed their ability to drink His cup (cf. Matt. 20:22), and Peter had assured Him of his loyalty even if it meant death (see page 45).

"WATCH WITH ME"

— J —
Jesus Prays For The Removal Of The Cup

And He was withdrawn from them, and went forward a little, about a stone's cast, and kneeled down, and fell on the ground, on His face, and prayed that, if it were possible, the hour might pass from Him. And He said, "Abba (Father), all things are possible with Thee; take away this cup from Me; nevertheless, not what I will, but what Thou wilt; not My will, but Thine, be done." (TLL, p. 268)

And He went a little farther, and fell on His face and prayed, saying, "O My Father, if it be possible, let this cup pass from Me; nevertheless not as I will, but as Thou wilt." (Matt. 26:39)

And He went forward a little, and fell on the ground and prayed that, if it were possible, the hour might pass from Him. And He said, "Abba (Father), all things are possible unto Thee; take away this cup from Me; nevertheless, not what I will, but what Thou wilt." (Mark 14:35,36)

And He was withdrawn from them about a stone's cast, and kneeled down and prayed, saying, "Father, if Thou be willing, remove this cup from Me; nevertheless, not My will, but Thine be done." (Luke 22:41,42)

The solitude of Christ in Gethsemane was steadily deepening. Counterbalancing the suffering Savior's need for companionship with His most intimate disciples was the desire to be alone in His conflict. No human eye should witness His agonizing struggle except through the shadows cast by the gnarled olive trees. No human being could share in the conflict in which He must engage. As He was alone in His first conflict with Satan in the wilderness (cf. Matt. 4:1-11), so He must now also tread the winepress alone (Isa. 63:3). "And He was withdrawn from them, and went forward a little." St. Luke speaks of being "withdrawn from them about a stone's cast," that is, about fifty or sixty feet. There are those who feel that this distance refers to His removal from the eight whom He had left at the entrance of the garden. This opinion may be in-

TREADING THE WINEPRESS ALONE

fluenced by the limited dimensions of the traditional site being shown today as Gethsemane. "A stone's cast" would still leave the Savior within hearing of His disciples, since His prayers were uttered "with strong crying and tears" (Heb. 5:7).

Through the shadows the disciples observed that Jesus "kneeled down, and fell on the ground on His face." Nowhere else does Scripture record that Jesus fell on His face during prayer, but nowhere else was His anxiety so great, His battle so hot, or His prayer so intense as here. He lay on the ground like a worm (Ps. 22:6).

Through the very agony endured by Jesus, prayer is wrung from His heart and lips. Trembling and fearful, yet perfectly obedient, He makes a fervent plea for relief from His suffering. Without the slightest indication of murmuring He asks that "the hour pass." It is not a prayer to be absolved from doing the Father's will, but a question as to whether or not another way might be found to accomplish the redemption, without His passing through that hour. It is Christ the man who is speaking. Crushed by the incomprehensible burden, He pleads, "Take away this cup from Me." He prays that He might be spared the agonizing death by crucifixion and that He might be delivered from the terrors confronting Him! It was a bitter cup, filled with the concentrated wrath of God against the iniquity of a rebellious world.

A PLEA FOR RELEASE

In His great need He turns to His heavenly Father, addressing Him as "Abba" (Father). He prays with the trust and confidence that is appropriate for a dear Son asking His dear Father. He recognizes that the cup was pourex m the Father and that His suffering was determined by Him. "God spared not His own Son" (Rom. 8:32). Jesus continues, "All things are possible unto Thee." He reminds His Father of His omnipotence, which His Father could use on His behalf.

From the very outset the prayer of Christ was offered in the spirit of perfect submission and absolute surrender to the Father's will. "Not what I will, but what Thou wilt." Never for a moment would He place His will, according to His human nature, ahead of the Father's will. He was still abiding by the principle, "My meat is to do the will of Him that sent Me, and to finish His work" (John 4:34). The Father's will was still also His will. By contrast, how often aren't we tempted to dictate to God the time, place, and manner of His response.

"NOT MY WILL, BUT THINE, BE DONE"

— K —

The Disciples Sleep During The Master's Agony

And He cometh unto the disciples, and findeth them asleep for sorrow, and saith unto Peter, "Simon, sleepest thou? What, could ye not watch with Me one hour? Watch ye and pray, lest ye enter into temptation. The spirit truly is ready, but the flesh is weak." He went away again the second time, and prayed, saying, "O My Father, if this cup may not pass away from Me, except I drink it, Thy will be done." And when He returned, He found them asleep again (for their eyes were heavy), neither wist they what to answer Him. And He left them and went away again, and prayed the third time, saying the same words. And there appeared an angel unto Him from heaven, strengthening Him. And being in an agony, He prayed more earnestly; and His sweat was as it were great drops of blood falling down to the ground. (TLL, p. 268)

And He cometh unto the disciples and findeth them asleep, and saith unto Peter, "What, could ye not watch with Me one hour? Watch and pray, that ye enter not into temptation; the spirit indeed is willing, but the flesh is weak." He went away again the second time and prayed, saying, "O My Father, if this cup may not pass away from Me, except I drink it, Thy will be done." And He came and found them asleep again, for their eyes were heavy. And He left them and went away again and prayed the third time, saying the same words. (Matt. 26:40-44)

And He cometh and findeth them sleeping, and saith unto Peter, "Simon, sleepest thou? Couldest not thou watch one hour? Watch ye and pray, lest ye enter into temptation. The spirit truly is ready, but the flesh is weak." And again He went away and prayed and spoke the same words. And when He returned, He found them asleep again, for their eyes were heavy; neither wist they what to answer Him. (Mark 14:37-40)

And there appeared an angel unto Him from heaven, strengthening Him. And being in an agony He prayed more earnestly; and His sweat was as it were great drops of blood falling down to the ground. And when He rose up from prayer and was come to His disciples, He found them sleeping for sorrow, and said unto them, "Why sleep ye? Rise and pray, lest ye enter into temptation." (Luke 22:43-46)

Jesus derived little comfort and support from the nearness of His disciples. Rising from prayer "He cometh to His disciples and findeth them asleep for sorrow." His yearning for even a word of comfort and sympathy from their lips went unsatisfied. It has baffled a great many people that the disciples should be able to sleep under these circumstances, and some have even questioned the accuracy of the report. However, the fact is clearly stated, and St. Luke offers us the divinely inspired explanation that they were sleeping "for sorrow." The tension had proven too great. They were utterly exhausted from the strain that they had been under since coming to Jerusalem. The repeated declarations of Jesus concerning His imminent death had greatly depressed them. Jesus charitably attributes the drowsiness of the disciples to the weakness of the flesh: ". . . but the flesh is weak." We should also not overlook the contribution which the powers of darkness were making toward the disappointing behavior of the disciples. Satan was not only making an all-out attack upon the Savior during these crucial hours, but he also "desired to sift" the disciples (see page 40).

LITTLE COMFORT

The anguish in the Master's heart as He roused the slumbering disciples is apparent in His mild rebuke to them, addressed particularly to Peter, "Simon, sleepest thou? What, could ye not watch with Me one hour?" Peter had been most ardent in his pledge of loyalty and most vehement in his protest against the Lord's warning about

NOT ONE HOUR?

taking offense, and he was in greatest danger. "One hour" has been called a proverbial expression. Here it seems to be used in the literal sense of the duration of His first conflict. It was a small thing that Jesus asked of His disciples — only an hour of watching and praying. How inconsiderate and heartless their yielding to drowsiness appears!

After His gentle rebuke Jesus renews the admonition, "Watch ye and pray." This time He does not say, "with Me." They were to do it for themselves, "lest ye enter into temptation." Their own soul's welfare is at stake. They are to rouse themselves from their indifference and to safeguard themselves by being ready for the onslaught of Satan, by availing themselves of divine assistance through prayer. His own great burden does not hinder Jesus from helping His disciples to bear their burdens also.

"WATCH YE AND PRAY"

Jesus had warned His disciples of the severity of the temptation while they were in the Upper Room (see page 40). Only through watchful prayer could they hope to withstand the fierce onslaughts upon them, for "the spirit truly is ready, but the flesh is weak." According to the "new man," they had the desire and inclination to do the will of God and to follow His directions. But because of their "flesh," the "old man," they lacked the strength and endurance for the hard fight, and would be ready to give up when the battle intensified. By failing to be on their guard — giving way to sleep — they were yielding to the flesh.

"THE FLESH IS WEAK"

Left "in the lurch" by His disciples, "He went away again the second time and prayed." The second prayer was similar to the first, with a few changes in the wording. Driven to and fro by distress too great to be controlled, He returned again to His disciples and found that they had paid no heed to His warning. They were even drowsier than the first time and were unable to give Him an intelligent answer: "neither wist they what to answer Him." Shame probably helped to tie their tongues. But the entire scene calls to mind the words of the Psalmist: "Reproach hath broken My heart; and I am full of heaviness; and I looked for some to take pity, but there was none; and for comforters, but I found none" (Ps. 69:20).

THE SECOND TIME

A third time He went to plead with His heavenly Father. The intensity of His agony increased, and "He prayed more earnestly," but the prayer remained the same, "saying the same words." So severe was the agony, so intense the struggle, that "His sweat was as it were great drops of blood falling down to the ground." Although the night was so cold that the soldiers built a fire of coals to warm themselves (cf. John 18:18), perspiration was oozing from the pores of Jesus' body. It was the product of fear and anguish. So great was the anguish that the sweat was mingled with blood forced through tiny ruptured blood vessels of the skin. They then formed into clots, which dropped to the ground. Only in the rarest cases do we find human beings reacting this way. Medical history records such bloody sweat as a rare phenomenon, caused by severe mental distress and strain.

AGONY AND BLOODY SWEAT

The blood spilt upon the ground in Gethsemane was sacrificial blood, as well as that which poured forth from His wounds on Calvary.

When the human system is put under severe strain, it may cause some part of the circulatory system to rupture or break, causing sudden death. But the Father did not want Jesus to die this way. Jesus was not to succumb before it was time, before He could bear the full measure of the wrath of God. So the Father provided relief to alleviate the anguish. "And there appeared an angel unto Him from heaven, strengthening Him." His fervent prayers had been heard by the Father. The disciples may sleep and be indifferent to His sorrows, but heaven is still concerned about Him. He is not forgotten in His Father's house.

STRENGTHENED BY AN ANGEL

When the people assigned to the task of strengthening their Lord fell short of their high privilege and duty, withholding the comfort from Him that they should have given, the task was given to an angel to perform. The angel not only brought comfort, but he also gave further evidence of Christ's humiliation. The Creator needed to be strengthened by a creature. So great was His weakness, so deep was His poverty! The Father did indeed send the strength, but a creature brought it. "Thou madest Him a little lower than the angels" (Heb. 2:7).

ALSO HUMILIATION

The nature of the strengthening, whether spiritual or physical, is not indicated. Artists especially like to picture the Lord receiving refreshment for His exhausted body. Others hold that the strengthening was spiritual in nature, giving Him encouragement and spiritual stimulation. Both are probably true. His worn and tired body was in need of physical strengthening to keep it alive for the taxing ordeal of the following day. But His spirit likewise was weary and in need of invigoration. Picturing the glorious results of His substitutionary suffering, the great host of believers who would do homage to Him could well have served in this spiritual strengthening.

PHYSICAL OR SPIRITUAL?

The contention that this act of strengthening occurred between Christ's first and second prayer is only a conjecture which is not shared by all scholars.

— L —

Rise, Let Us Be Going!

And He cometh the third time to His disciples and found them sleeping and saith, "Sleep on now, and take your rest. Behold! the hour is at hand, and the Son of Man is betrayed into the hands of sinners. Rise, let us be going; behold, he is at hand that doth betray Me." (TLL, p. 268)

Then cometh He to His disciples and saith unto them, "Sleep on now, and take your rest. Behold! the hour is at hand, and the Son of Man is betrayed into the hands of sinners. Rise, let us be going; behold, he is at hand that doth betray Me." (Matt. 26:45,46)

And He cometh the third time and saith unto them, "Sleep on now, and take your rest; it is enough; the hour is come. Behold! the Son of Man is betrayed into the hands of sinners. Rise up, let us go; lo, he that betrayeth Me is at hand." (Mark 14:41,42)

When Jesus returns from His third period of prayer, He finds His three disciples, who had promised so much, still deep in slumber. They had utterly failed their Master in His hour of need. Now He no longer needs their aid or sympathy, for the agony of this hour is over. He now displays a different attitude, and there is a different tone in His voice as He chides His disciples for their sleepiness. "Sleep on now and take your rest," He tells them. These words have been variously called a question, an exclamation, or an expression of pain. The fact that He does not permit the disciples to go on sleeping would indicate that His words were meant ironically.

JESUS CHIDES HIS DISCIPLES

Any thought of further sleep is driven away by the two momentous announcements which Jesus now makes. He draws their attention to the importance of what He has to say to them by introducing it with "behold!" or "lo!" St. Mark adds the words, "It is enough." Previously the enemies could lay no hand on Him because His hour had not yet come (cf. John 7:30; 8:20). Now His hour is at hand. He leaves no doubt what hour He means by adding, "and the Son of Man is betrayed into the hands of sinners." In Matthew 26:18 He called it "My time." He had earnestly prayed for the removal of this hour. (On the title "Son of Man" see page 4)

"THE HOUR IS AT HAND"

"Rise!" He commands. In that posture they could better shake off their drowsiness. "Let us be going," not to seek escape in hiding, but to meet the enemy (see page 58f.). He knows what lies ahead. Yet of His own free will, without flinching, He calmly and deliberately faces death. He is fully obedient to His heavenly Father. If there were still any drowsiness left in the disciples, it must have taken quick flight with the second announcement, "Behold! he is at hand that doth betray Me."

"LET US BE GOING"

He of whom Jesus had spoken as the traitor (see page 30f.) was approaching. While they had heedlessly slumbered on, the traitor and his confederates had been very watchful. They had plotted and toiled at their hellish scheme, and now they were ready to strike.

CHAPTER THREE
Jesus Before The Sanhedrin

— A —
Jesus Meets The Multitude

And immediately, while He yet spoke, lo, Judas, one of the Twelve, came, and with him a great multitude with swords and staves and lanterns and torches and weapons, from the chief priests and the scribes and the elders of the people. And Judas went before them. Jesus therefore, knowing all things that should come upon Him, went forth, and said unto them, "Whom seek ye?" They answered Him, "Jesus of Nazareth." Jesus said unto them, "I am He." And Judas also, which betrayed Him, stood with them. As soon then as He had said unto them, "I am He," they went backward, and fell to the ground. Then asked He them again, "Whom seek ye?" And they said, "Jesus of Nazareth." Jesus answered, "I have told you that I am He; if therefore ye seek Me, let these go their way," that the saying might be fulfilled which He spoke, "Of them which Thou gavest Me have I lost none." (TLL, p. 269)

And while He yet spoke, lo, Judas, one of the Twelve, came, and with him a great multitude with swords and staves, from the chief priests and elders of the people. (Matt. 26:47)

And immediately, while He yet spoke, cometh Judas, one of the Twelve, and with him a great multitude with swords and staves, from the chief priests and the scribes and the elders. (Mark 14:43)

And while He yet spoke, behold a multitude, and he that was called Judas, one of the Twelve, went before them. (Luke 22:47a)

Judas then, having received a band of men and officers from the chief priests and Pharisees, cometh thither with lanterns and torches and weapons. Jesus therefore, knowing all things that should come upon Him, went forth and said unto them, "Whom seek ye?" They answered Him, "Jesus of Nazareth." Jesus said unto them, "I am He." And Judas also, which betrayed Him, stood with them. As soon then as He had said unto them, "I am He," they went backward and fell to the ground. Then asked He them again, "Whom seek ye?" And they said, "Jesus of Nazareth." Jesus answered, "I have told you that I am He; if therefore ye seek Me, let these go their way," that the saying might be fulfilled which He spoke, "Of them which Thou gavest Me have I lost none." (John 18:3-9)

No respite was granted to Jesus in His passion. Scarcely had the first wave passed over Him, when the next one struck. No sooner had the agony of soul let up, when bodily torture was intensified.

JUDAS IN THE CAMP OF THE ENEMY "Immediately, while He yet spoke" — before the disciples even had time to comprehend that the traitor about whom Jesus had so earnestly spoken in the Upper Room must be the absent disciple, they saw Judas Iscariot in the camp of the enemy. When he left the company of the disciples, at least some of them supposed that he was on an errand for the Master (see page 33). Now they could see what he had been up to since his departure.

"Lo, Judas, one of the Twelve, came" to Gethsemane. As a disciple, he knew of this quiet retreat. He, who had once been called to lead people to Christ for their salvation, and now was leading a band to Him to destroy Him, had no scruples about violating the Master's sanctuary of prayer. (On "one of the Twelve" see page 8f.)

"And with him a great multitude" came, consisting of the cohort of Roman soldiers, the Temple police, some servants of the chief priests, and perhaps some voluntary followers. The fear of an uprising had prompted the Jewish leaders to decide against disposing of Jesus at the Passover (see page 7). When their timing was overruled by divine counsel, and they decided to avail themselves of the offer of Judas, this fear still persisted. It prompted them to enlist the assistance of the Roman soldiers garrisoned just off from the Temple court in the tower of Antonia.

A GREAT MULTITUDE

St. John called the detachment of soldiers that took part in the arrest "the cohort," referring to this one stationed in Jerusalem. A cohort was the tenth part of a legion, and it normally consisted of 600 men — although we are told that the number might run as high as a thousand, or might be considerably less than six hundred. It is unlikely that the entire garrision was used for this expedition. Only a sizable portion of the garrison would have warranted the language employed by the Apostle, or would have been under the personal command of the chiliarch (officer of a thousand) or tribune (John 18:12). There is no indication that Pilate was consulted. The chief officer of a garrison, stationed in a trouble spot like Jerusalem for the very purpose of preventing or quelling uprisings, certainly had the authority to make such a decision.

THE COHORT

It was indeed a formidable band that came out to capture one unarmed rabbi. The Sanhedrists were playing it safe. They had probably not forgotten the disappointing experience which they had previously had with their own police (John 7:45,46), and they were thinking of the possibility of violence. The multitude came well armed, "with swords and staves." The swords were the weapons of the soldiers, and the staves were the weapons of the Temple police. They were also equipped "with lanterns and torches." Thus they were prepared to subdue any resistance, or to beat the bushes and to search out the dark corners in pursuit of a fugitive.

PLAYING IT SAFE

Judas went ahead of them, reaching the Lord before the band. Hypocritically he probably wanted to give the impression that he did not belong to the band, and that he had come to warn his beloved Master or to sympathize with Him. How blind a person can become! How blind for "one of the Twelve" who had witnessed so many examples of the Lord's omniscience, and had seen his own traitorous plans exposed in the Upper Room, to imagine that Jesus could be deceived so easily! Sin is not isolated. One sin gives birth to another. In Judas, covetousness led to hypocrisy and willful rejection of Christ.

JUDAS WENT BEFORE THEM

St. John calls attention to the omniscience of Jesus by saying, "Jesus therefore, knowing all things that should come upon Him, went forth." He knew exactly where is no reason to assume that some had already laid hands on the disciples when Jesus gave these orders.

This shielding of the disciples, St. John explains, was in fulfillment of part of Jesus' high-priestly prayer (see John 17:12). In 18:9 John wrote: "That the saying might be fulfilled which He spoke: 'Of them which Thou gavest Me have I lost none.'" Some have called this verse an interpolation, because they see a conflict between the prayer of Jesus, which speaks of perishing eternally, and the escape from arrest. While it is true that in His prayer Jesus pleads that His disciples might not be lost in the eternal sense, arrest here might have had that effect. It could have plunged them into spiritual temptations beyond their ability to endure.

FULFILLMENT

— B —

Jesus Betrayed With A Kiss

Now he that betrayed Him had given them a token, saying, "Whomsoever I shall kiss, that same is he; take him, and lead him away safely." And as soon as he was come, he goeth straightway to Him, and drew near unto Jesus to kiss Him, and said, "Hail, Master," and kissed Him. And Jesus said unto him, "Friend, wherefore art thou come? Judas, betrayest thou the Son of Man with a kiss?" (TLL, p. 269)

Now he that betrayed Him gave them a sign, saying, "Whomsoever I shall kiss, that same is he; hold him fast." And forthwith he came to Jesus and said, "Hail, Master," and kissed Him. And Jesus said unto him, "Friend, wherefore art thou come?" (Matt. 26:48-50a)

And he that betrayed Him had given them a token, saying, "Whomsoever I shall kiss, that same is he; take him, and lead him away safely." And as soon as he was come, he goeth straightway to Him and saith, "Master, Master," and kissed Him (Mark 14:44,45)

Judas . . . drew near unto Jesus to kiss Him. But Jesus said unto him, "Judas, betrayest thou the Son of Man with a kiss?" (Luke 22:47b,48)

The expedition to arrest Jesus was not a disorderly mob, but an orderly band with a responsible leader. They had agreed upon a definite plan of action. This required that the victim be positively identified. Judas had agreed to do this and had given a sign of identity.

THE SIGN OF BETRAYAL

"Now he that betrayed Him had given them a token, saying, 'Whomsoever I shall kiss, that same is he.'" While Judas himself had devised the sign, the shamelessness of it suggests the influence of Satan, who had entered into his heart. The kiss, universal symbol of love, friendship, and fidelity, and in the East a sign of discipleship, was to be the sign of betrayal. A less offensive sign, such as pointing Him out with a finger, would have been just as effective for the betrayal, but we can hardly conceive of a sign that would reveal Satan's rule in the

JESUS WENT FORTH and when He must suffer. This was proof of His divinity. He "went forth" with His disciples to meet the multitude, perhaps in front of the Garden. He could have sidestepped the cross, but He would not leave us to be lost. "He does not conceal Himself, for He knows neither the sense of guilt nor the sense of fear" (Schilder).

Standing in the light of the lanterns and torches, Jesus addressed the leaders with unmistakable authority, "Whom seek ye?" His challenge was answered with the reply, "Jesus of Nazareth." Presumably the answer was **"WHOM SEEK YE?"** given by the chiliarch as the chief officer and commander of the expedition. As a Roman he may not have recognized Jesus, but the majestic authority of Jesus would have required an answer regardless. "Of Nazareth" (the Nazarene) was added to the name Jesus (Heb., *Jeshua* or *Joshua*) to distinguish Him from others who bore that honored and beloved name. "I am He," came the majestic reply, thereby brushing aside any need of identification by the traitor.

The position of Judas showed on which side he really belonged. He had gone over to the camp of the enemy. It could appear from the account of St. John that the Judas-kiss had already been given, and that, after **JUDAS STOOD WITH THEM** his exposure by Jesus, the traitor had returned to the company he had led there. However, opinions differ on this point. John has also another reason for telling us that Judas stood with the enemy. He thereby includes him in the incident which immediately followed. When Jesus identified Himself by saying, "I am He," they went backward and fell to the ground. This whole band, numbering in the hundreds, a large portion of them trained, combat-ready Roman soldiers, were thrown to the ground by the omnipotent word of Jesus. They were helpless before Him. There is no question that the soldiers were greatly surprised. God gave them this miraculous evidence that a mighty power was on the side of this unarmed man confronting the armed mob. By this miracle, the eternal "I am" (Exod. 3:14), standing before the representatives of human authority, clearly showed both His enemies and His disciples that He was not overpowered and could not be overpowered. He would surrender Himself unto them out of His own free will.

After the multitude had struggled to their feet again, Jesus repeated His question with the same authority. Still they were blindly determined to carry out their purpose, in spite of Jesus' demonstration of majesty **"LET THESE GO THEIR WAY"** and power. Jesus had even compelled the officer to repeat his instructions. They were to take *Him*. That was all. In this way the point was brought out that they had no instructions to take the disciples. Jesus then commanded them to abide by their instructions and not to take His disciples. "If therefore ye seek Me, let these go their way." He would permit Himself to be captured, but His disciples must go free. If any of the mob had been inclined to go beyond their instructions, this command effectively stopped them. Jesus had trained these disciples to carry on His work after His death, and He did not forget their safety now, even in the hour of His own great peril. There heart of the traitor as effectively as this one. None other would so effectively demonstrate hypocrisy.

By giving a sign, Judas showed that the act which followed was one of deliberation, and not of sudden impulse. The traitor seemed anxious that there should be no slip in the plan after he had done his part. Therefore he instructed the band, "Take him and lead him away safely." The bargain called for delivery to the council, not merely to the troops; that way there would be no escape or rescue.

"And as soon as he was come he goeth straightway to Him." Opinions differ as to whether this was before Jesus had identified Himself, or after (see page 59). Pretending that he was overjoyed to find Jesus, "he said, 'Hail, Master,' and kissed Him." As in the Upper Room, Judas again calls Him only "Rabbi" instead of "Lord" (see page 32). Foolishly the traitor overplays his part. As if to disarm Jesus and to hold Him inactive as long as possible, Judas kisses Him repeatedly; he showers, or smothers, Him with kisses. Neither the bruising blows of servants or priests, nor the spittle, sweat, and blood that marred the holy face of Jesus in the hours ahead, matched the indignity heaped upon His face by the kisses of betrayal.

WITH KISSES

Jesus tolerated this indignity. When He spoke, it was not in scorn or anger, but in words of wounded love. He showed as much patience and restraint here as He later would before Caiaphas and Pilate. At the same time He also showed that He was not deceived by the pretense of Judas. Jesus made a final appeal to his conscience. He penetrated the pretense of His former disciple and addressed him as "friend." Though not the much more intimate *phile*, the Greek word, *etaire*, which means "fellow" or "comrade," which is in our text, is a reminder of the close fellowship which existed between them. For many months they had traveled together through the land on their mission to proclaim the kingdom of God.

"FRIEND"

"Why art thou come?" Jesus knew well why he had come, but He wanted to make Judas realize what he is doing. To make him ashamed and terrified at his own deed, Jesus exposed Judas' sin in all its ugliness. "Judas, betrayest thou the Son of Man with a kiss?" Base and vile as the betrayal was in itself, it became despicable beyond all others in history, because the One betrayed was the Son of Man. But this last plea of Jesus also went unheeded. Judas had sold himself to Satan.

"WHY HAVE YOU COME?"

WITH A KISS

Of all perversions one of the worst is the selling of the Lord by Judas to those who would put Him to death, with a kiss, tenderest token of human affection. Hypocrisy here gives birth to its most hideous child. Human nature here reveals itself in its most horrible capacity for evil. If Judas had pointed out the Lord by striking Him with a stick, it would have been far more appropriate for the situation, and a truer expression of his own foul heart. But to give the Lord away to mistreatment and death with a kiss is indeed testimony to an abyss of human degradation of, we might say, an inhumanity, which no plumbline has ever been able to fathom.

Anonymous

— C —
Peter Strikes With The Sword

Then came they and laid hands on Jesus and took Him. When they which were about Him saw what would follow, they said unto Him, "Lord, shall we smite with the sword?" And behold, one of them which were with Jesus, Simon Peter, having a sword, stretched out his hand and drew his sword, and smote the high priest's servant and cut off his right ear. The servant's name was Malchus. And Jesus answered and said, "Suffer ye thus far." And He said to Peter, "Put up again thy sword into the sheath; for all they that take the sword shall perish with the sword. The cup which My Father hath given Me, shall I not drink it? Thinkest thou that I cannot now pray to My Father, and He shall presently give Me more than twelve legions of angels? But how then shall the Scriptures be fulfilled, that thus it must be?" And He touched his ear, and healed him. (TLL, pp. 269-270)

Then came they and laid hands on Jesus and took Him. And behold, one of them which were with Jesus stretched out his hand and drew his sword, and struck a servant of the high priest and smote off his ear. Then said Jesus unto him, "Put up again thy sword into his place; for all they that take the sword shall perish with the sword. Thinkest thou that I cannot now pray to My Father, and He shall presently give Me more than twelve legions of angels? But how then shall the Scriptures be fulfilled, that thus it must be?" (Matt. 26:50b-54)

And they laid their hands on Him and took Him. And one of them that stood by drew a sword and smote a servant of the high priest and cut off his ear. (Mark 14:46,47)

When they which were about Him saw what would follow, they said unto Him, "Lord, shall we smite with the sword?" And one of them smote the servant of the high priest and cut off his right ear. And Jesus answered and said, "Suffer ye thus far." And He touched his ear and healed him. (Luke 22:49-51)

Then Simon Peter, having a sword, drew it and smote the high priests's servant and cut off his right ear. The servant's name was Malchus. Then said Jesus unto Peter, "Put up thy sword into the sheath; the cup which My Father hath given Me, shall I not drink it?" (John 18:10,11)

After Jesus had made Himself known to the multitude, "came they and laid hands on Jesus and took Him." One would think that after the Lord's demonstration of divine power, no one would have dared to lay his hands on Jesus, for fear of what might happen to him. But so depraved is the

THEY LAID HANDS ON JESUS

sinful heart of man, that this miracle did not at all deter His enemies from their determination to capture Him. By causing the multitude to fall to the ground, Jesus had demonstrated to the band that its armed might was useless. Now, by giving Himself into their hands and submitting to arrest without the slightest show of resistance, He showed them that all their precautions and preparations were unnecessary.

"They which were about Him" were the eleven who had been with their Master in the Garden. While one of the Twelve had defected and had gone over to the camp of the enemy, these had remained loyal to Jesus and did not hesitate to show where they stood.

THE ELEVEN HAD REMAINED LOYAL

"When they saw what would follow" — that Jesus was being placed under arrest and being turned over to His bitter enemies without a struggle — they were stirred to sudden, though misguided, action. The moment seemed opportune to make good their pledge of unending loyalty, for their Master had just demonstrated His divine might by casting the whole multitude to the ground in confusion (see page 59).

Eagerly the disciples offered their services to the Master, asking, "Lord, shall we smite with the sword?" It was indeed proper that the disciples should ask the Master for His directions in this decisive moment, but they should also have waited for His command. However, Simon Peter was much too impulsive to wait. Only John identifies Peter. He could safely do so, for he wrote his Gospel after the death of Peter. The other Evangelists, writing while Peter was still living, perhaps might have endangered him if they had revealed his identity.

"LORD, SHALL WE SMITE WITH THE SWORD?"

Peter "drew his sword and smote the high priest's servant and cut off his right ear." Peter wanted to make up for his failure to watch and pray. Peter wanted Jesus to know that he meant it when he declared himself willing to lay down his life for Jesus. Possession of the sword tempted Peter to use it in a rash manner. With deadly intent he fell upon the high priest's servant. Either because he was unskilled with the sword, or upset by the series of events, Peter's aim was poor, and he succeeded only in cutting off the servant's ear. It is not indicated whether this servant had given any provocation by an offensive attitude or by first laying hands on Jesus, or whether he simply happened to be the nearest one to Peter when he started swinging. But Peter's action was unjustified under any circumstances.

PETER TRIES TO REDEEM HIMSELF

All accounts call the servant a "doulos," a bondservant or slave. It is interesting to note that Caiaphas, the highest religious leader in the land, was in possession of a bondservant, especially since at that time the sect of the Essenes was prodding the national conscience and the church's conscience with its teaching that slavery was out of harmony with religious ethics and should be prohibited. Caiaphas sent a slave to help capture Him who would free us from the slavery of sin.

THE HIGH PRIEST'S SLAVE

It is John who identifies the servant as Malchus. We would like to think that this experience at Gethsemane caused Malchus to see the Messianic light, and that John mentioned his name as one that was known among the Christians as one of their number, but that would only be speculating. John's acquaintance with the high priest (John 18:15) probably accounts for knowing his bondservant's name.

Jesus quickly restrains His disciples with the command, "Suffer ye thus far!" Enough of this! Let them have their way! Peter's ill-considered assault gave the impression that Jesus and His disciples were ordinary rioters, placing the Lord in a very difficult position. By His decisive action, Jesus removes the reflection on Him and His disciples, and at the same time holds back the enemy from retaliation. His authority was respected by friend and foe alike.

"ENOUGH OF THIS!"

Having spared Peter from swift retribution for his folly, Jesus now administers a well-deserved public reprimand to His impulsive desciple. "Put up again thy sword into the sheath!" Thereby Jesus disclaims any part of or sympathy for Peter's action in drawing blood. The disciples should learn that the "weapons of our warfare are not carnal" (2 Cor. 10:4). The sword belongs to the government to preserve law and order (Rom. 13:1-4). When others, like Peter, usurp its use for themselves, they invite just retribution. Jesus confirms an ancient law (Gen. 9:6), "All they that take the sword shall perish with the sword."

A WELL-DESERVED REPRIMAND

Besides being foolhardy, Peter's rash action was an unwitting attempt to interfere with the divine plan of salvation. "The cup which My Father hath given Me, shall I not drink it?" Peter was trying to tear the cup from the lips of Jesus. This was the cup which the heavenly Father had placed there, and which in His prayer Jesus had sacredly bound Himself to drink. Nevertheless, Jesus' reprimand of Peter is much milder than one He spoke at another time, when he had similarly tried to interfere with the Lord's plans and was called "Satan" (Mark 8:33).

INTERFERENCE WITH THE DIVINE PLAN

The Lord has no need for such help. Not only is He well able to defend Himself, but He also has the unlimited resource of prayer. By His request the heavenly Father would put an invincible host at His disposal. "Thinkest thou that I cannot now pray to My Father, and He shall presently give Me more than twelve legions of angels?" A legion normally numbered six thousand soldiers. This meant there would be more than a legion of the heavenly host for each one of the Apostles. This power from the boundless resources of heaven, instantly available, would made inexpressibly overwhelming odds against the one cohort of Roman soldiers, the Temple guard, and the motley band allied with them. Alongside this kind of help, how puny was the power of Peter!

NO NEED FOR SUCH HELP

"But how then shall the Scriptures be fulfilled, that thus it must be?" This frightening possibility is set aside by the divine "must." The Scripture passages con-

THE SCRIPTURES MUST BE FULFILLED

cerning the suffering Messiah, such as Psalm 22, Isaiah 53, and Zechariah 13:7, needed to be fulfilled. Therefore Jesus lays aside the use of His omnipotence as well as any service of angels or of men. Voluntarily Jesus puts the cup to His lips and drinks. No more shall there be any doubt concerning the fulfillment of all Scriptures.

Jesus is no respecter of persons. A slave received as much consideration from Him as a king. The damage done by Peter should be made good. "And He touched his ear and healed Him." This was the last miracle Jesus performed in the state of His humiliation, and, as far as we know, the only one which He performed unrequested. It likewise shows us that faith is not an absolute requirement for being healed. The miracles of Jesus were not conditioned by the faith of the recipient. They were never performed for mere display, but to serve His mission of ministering to man's ultimate need — of leading people to salvation.

JESUS HEALS THE EAR OF MALCHUS

— D —
Jesus Rebukes The Multitude

In that same hour Jesus answered and said to the multitude, unto the chief priests, and captains of the Temple, and the elders, which were come to Him, "Are ye come out as against a thief, with swords and staves for to take Me? I sat daily with you teaching in the Temple, and ye stretched forth no hands against Me; but this is your hour and the power of darkness. But all this was done, that the Scriptures might be fulfilled." Then all the disciples forsook Him and fled. (TLL, p. 270)

In that same hour said Jesus to the multitudes, "Are ye come out as against a thief with swords and staves for to take Me? I sat daily with you teaching in the Temple, and ye laid no hold on Me. But all this was done, that the Scriptures of the Prophets might be fulfilled." Then all the disciples forsook Him and fled. (Matt. 26:55,56)

And Jesus answered and said unto them, "Are ye come out, as against a thief, with swords and with staves to take Me? I was daily with you in the Temple teaching, and ye took Me not; but the Scriptures must be fulfilled." And they all forsook Him and fled. (Mark 14:48-50)

Then Jesus said unto the chief priests, and captains of the Temple, and the elders, which were come to Him, "Be ye come out, as against a thief, with swords and staves? When I was daily with you in the Temple, ye stretched forth no hands against Me; but this is your hour and the power of darkness." (Luke 22:52,53)

After Jesus had called His over-zealous disciple to order and had repaired the damage which he had done, He turned His attention to the band which was closing

JESUS CHIDES THE JEWISH LEADERS in to arrest Him. The religious leaders in the multitude, "the chief priests, and captains of the Temple, and the elders" had pressed to the front so that they would not miss anything, and so they could lend encouragement to their servants. Jesus chided them, "Are ye come out as against a thief, with swords and staves for to take Me?" They were treating Him as a dangerous criminal and a fugitive from justice. That was a grave injustice and an insult to Him. Jesus had a right to resent it, and to reproach them for it; He was no bandit who needed to be hunted with swords and staves.

It was also ridiculous. He had never hidden from them. His conduct was open and fearless. "I sat daily with you teaching in the Temple, and ye stretched forth no hands against Me." If there were any reason for arresting Him, RIDICULOUS why had they not done so when He was freely and openly walking among them and publicly teaching in the Temple? They had not dared to cast Him into prison as had been done with John the Baptist. They had certainly tried hard enough to find some reason to stop His activity, but His behavior and speech had been without reproach; He remained free to go and to speak until this hour.

This protest should have shamed them, if they were still capable of shame, but it had no effect upon these shameless leaders. Their positions should have made them champions of right and justice, instead of instigators of evil.

Let them have no illusion that they had taken Him captive because of their great cunning or their overpowering might! Any notion of this kind which they might have is promptly deflated by the observation of Jesus: THE HOUR OF DARKNESS "But this is your hour, and the power of darkness." If God had not given them this hour to perform their devilish deed, they could have done nothing. However, Jesus charges, it was not only THEIR hour, but also that of the powers of darkness. It was the hour, determined in the eternal counsels of God, in which the devils should loose their full fury upon the Champion of sinners. These leaders had placed themselves into the employment of Satan, the Prince of Darkness. They were being used, only to be tossed aside later, as they themselves were about to do with Judas Iscariot. The deeds which they were performing were fit only for darkness, for they sprang from hate-filled and sin-darkened hearts.

But this was no unlimited surrender to the powers of darkness. God had set very definite limits for Satan. It was to be only an "hour" that darkness should have free course. Implied is the promise that the light would soon NO SURRENDER again prevail and shine forth in glorious brightness. God permitted this evil for only one purpose, "that the Scriptures of the Prophets might be fulfilled." Even now the enemies of Christ were unwittingly helping to carry out the prophetic plan.

The last ray of hope that Jesus would somehow free Himself from the hands of His captors was quenched in His disciples by the Master's last words to the Jewish

ALONE leaders. "Then all the disciples forsook Him and fled." When they realized that His announcements about His capture had to be taken literally, and that He would not even attempt to escape, they reacted just as He had said (see page 44). Jesus was left entirely alone. The isolation constituted intense suffering for Him, whose heart yearned for fellowship and understanding.

Jesus had ordered for His disciples the right to go their way unharmed (see page 59f.), but they did not simply go their way calmly and peacefully; they fled in terror, leaving Him to His fate. He was to tread the winepress alone (Isa. 63:3). If even one of His disciples had stuck with Him and suffered martyrdom, he would sooner or later have been credited by some with participation in the redemption of man, and that could not be.

The disciples had relied too much on their own strength and had neglected the warnings of Jesus. Full of confidence they promised: "Though we should die with Thee, yet will we not deny Thee," but they withdrew from the combat long before it came to dying. They were so easily overcome because they kept their eyes fixed upon their enemies instead of fastening them upon their Lord and Master. They forsook Him with their hearts before they ran away from Him. "What folly, to flee, for fear of death, from Him who is the fountain of life!" stated Lactantius in the early fourth century!

THE FOLLY OF SELF-CONFIDENCE

To a lesser degree Paul later shared the experience of the Lord, causing Paul to write, "All men forsook me; I pray God that it may not be laid to their charge" (2 Tim. 4:16).

— E —
Jesus Is Bound

Then the band and the captain and the officers of the Jews took Jesus, and bound Him, and led Him away. And there followed Him a certain young man, having a linen cloth cast about his naked body; and the young men laid hold on him; and he left the linen cloth and fled from them naked. (TLL, pp. 270-271)

And there followed Him a certain young man, having a linen cloth cast about his naked body; and the young men laid hold on him, and he left the linen cloth and fled from them naked. (Mark 14:51,52)

Then the band and the captain and officers of the Jews took Jesus and bound Him. (John 18:12)

His hands had scarcely finished their service of healing, when they "took Jesus, and bound Him" as though He were a dangerous criminal. They tied His hands, which had done only good and had bestowed untold blessings. When King Ahaziah wanted to capture Elijah (2 Kings 1), God

NO DIVINE INTERVENTION

came to his rescue. He endorsed His prophet with fire from heaven. When the king of Syria sought to apprehend Elisha, God smote the Syrians with blindness (2 Kings 6:18). But when the enemies of Christ stepped forward to lay hands on Him, there was no divine intervention. The Father willed that He should be put in bonds.

Yet Jesus could be bound only because He permitted Himself to be bound, showing His complete submission to the Father's will. Hands so powerful as His could not have been held in bonds if He had chosen to use His power. Had He made use of His omnipotence He could have broken these bonds more easily than Samson tore off his ropes (Judg. 16:12). He was restrained from using His omnipotence by the power of His love.

The binding of Jesus was done jointly by the Roman and Jewish authorities. "The band and the captain and the officers of the Jews" all participated in the indignity.

JESUS IN BONDS

But two of the disciples, each in his own way, had also contributed their part to insure bonds for the Master: Judas, by his instruction, "take Him and lead Him away safely," and Peter, with his wild swordsmanship. Ultimately we all, by our transgressions, share responsibility for the bonds of Jesus.

The bonds of Jesus were an offense to His disciples. They are still an offense to many. Our reason rebels at the thought of the Creator being bound by the creature. Only the Spirit can make His bonds beautiful by portraying His amazing love, which permitted Him to be bound in order to free us from the bonds of sin and Satan.

Having placed Jesus in bonds, they "led Him away." His captors led the submissive Jesus back to the city. They had no need to drag Him, for He went willingly. "He is brought as a lamb to the slaughter" (Isa. 53:7).

When the disciples forsook Jesus and fled, it seemed that He was now entirely alone with the enemy. Yet it was not quite so. His isolation was not yet complete.

A CERTAIN YOUNG MAN

"There followed Him a certain young man." This young man revealed his interest in Jesus by taking the risk of following Him without having been invited, even though he had apparently witnessed the arrest of Jesus and the flight of the disciples. Because this youth was recognized in some manner as a follower of Jesus "the young men laid hold on him." The "young men" evidently were not soldiers, or members of the Temple guard, but others who belonged to the multitude. Their attack upon this follower of Jesus revealed their hostile disposition and helped to emphasize the Lord's authority, since they had not dared to lay hold on the disciples after He had forbidden them. The youthful follower avoided capture and possible violence only by slipping out of the linen cloth in which he had wrapped himself and by fleeing.

From the circumstance that only Mark reports this incident, it is quite generally assumed that Mark himself was that "young man." Some have added embellishments to the idea, such as ascribing ownership of

COMPLETELY ISOLATED

the Upper Room to Mark's parents, suggesting that Judas returned there with the multitude before going to Gethsemane, etc. While the identification of this courageous young man with Mark is quite plausible, the fact remains that we do not know who he was, nor is it important that we know his name. What is important is to see how even this lingering companion was snatched from Jesus, leaving Him entirely cut off and alone. There was simply no one to strengthen and to reassure Him, no one to shield and to comfort Him. He stood completely alone to face the power and curse of sin and the onslaughts of Satan.

— F —
Jesus Before Annas and Caiaphas

And they that had laid hold on Jesus led Him away to Annas first, for he was father-in-law to Caiaphas, which was the high priest that same year. Then led they Jesus away bound to Caiaphas, where all the chief priests and the scribes and the elders were assembled. Now Caiaphas was he which gave counsel to the Jews, that it was expedient that one man should die for the people. (TLL, p. 271)

And they that had laid hold on Jesus led Him away to Caiaphas, the high priest, where the scribes and the elders were assembled. (Matt. 26:57)
And they led Jesus away to the high priest; and with him were assembled all the chief priests and the elders and the scribes. (Mark 14:53)
Then took they Him and led Him and brought Him into the high priest's house. (Luke 22:54a)
And led Him away to Annas first, for he was father-in-law to Caiaphas, which was the high priest that same year. Now Caiaphas was he which gave counsel to the Jews that it was expedient that one man should die for the people. Now Annas had sent Him bound unto Caiaphas, the high priest. (John 18:13,14,24)

"They that had laid hold on Jesus" were the representatives of church and state, "the band and captain and the officers of the Jews" (see page 68). The second stage of Christ's suffering began when they "led Him away." Up to that point He had governed the situation. But now He suffered the indignity of yielding the direction of events to His bitter foes.

To assemble the Sanhedrin in the middle of the night required some time. While messengers scurried through the darkened streets to gather the members, Jesus was brought before Annas. The words of John suggest no sinister motive or even secret reason for bringing the prisoner "to Annas first." Neither is there any indication that Annas had issued the order for Jesus' arrest. The only reason which John offers is a personal one, "for he was father-in-law to Caiaphas." Annas and Caiaphas, however, were of one mind and spirit in this matter, and they probably lived in different parts of the same high priestly palace. Besides being father-in-law to the high priest, Annas was himself a former high priest and head of the most prominent family of priests.

TO ANNAS FIRST

ANNAS — Annas was a man who held sway over the national affairs of Israel over a long period of time. Yet his place in history depends chiefly on his connection with the trial of Jesus. He was high priest in the years 6-15 A.D. After he was deposed by Valerius Gratus, five of his sons, a son-in-law, and a grandson held the office. Most of them were high priest during his own lifetime, so that one may almost speak of the "dynasty" of Annas. All were appointed by the Romans. At the time of the trial of Jesus the high-priestly office was occupied by Annas' son-in-law, Caiaphas. However, Annas also bore the title of the office, even as we ususally call former occupants of an office (such as professor, pastor, or senator) by the title of that office. Annas, at seventy, was still a member of the Sanhedrin and still wielded great influence.

A SADDUCEE — The Sadducees, the sect to whom Annas belonged, had long been infuriated by the teachings and activities of Jesus. Jesus' warning to beware of the leaven of the Sadducees (Matt. 16:6), as well as their being humiliated in their encounters with Jesus, accounted for their loss of influence and prestige among the people. Their leaders were afraid of losing all that they held dear in this life (and Sadducees had no belief in another life after death) if the ministry of Jesus were not halted. What a cause of grim delight for crafty old Annas to have that feared and hated rabbi before him, bound and under heavy guard!

THE HIGH PRIESTHOOD — Behold the High Priest "after the order of Melchizedek" (Heb. 5:10) standing captive before the unworthy representative of the Aaronic priesthood! Throughout the years the high priesthood was an office held for life. In its declining years it was degraded to a political instrument of the Roman governors, who appointed and deposed high priests at will. For this reason there were several "high priests" in the Sanhedrin at this time. The desecration of the office is also reflected in the expression: "high priest that same year."

By conducting an informal pretrial examination, Annas would make productive use of the time required for the Sanhedrin to assemble and to get ready for their extraordinary session.

TO CAIAPHAS — "Then led they Jesus away bound to Caiaphas." Jesus was led away to Caiaphas as He had been brought to Annas — "bound." "Now Caiaphas was he which gave counsel to the Jews, that it was expedient that one man should die for the people." This is a parenthetical remark showing that no justice could be expected from this man who had already condemned Jesus before the trial began. Cynical Caiaphas had bluntly recommended the judicial death of Jesus as the lesser of two evils. Unwittingly Caiaphas uttered a significant prophecy about the sacrificial death of Jesus (see page 6).

NEVER MIND THE TECHNICALITIES — "Where all the chief priests and scribes and the elders were assembled." It was the council, the Sanhedrin (Matt. 26:59), that assembled in this nocturnal hour. If *Mishna* rules were then in force, the meeting was illegal because of the hour of assembly. That it violated the rules pertaining to the Festival is not questioned. People of this stripe were not the ones to bother about technicalities when they saw their opportunity to do away with their hated rival. So what if they needed to break some regulations in their haste to have it done before the Festival Sabbath, and before the people should realize what was happening! This meeting was held in "the high priest's house," instead of their regular meeting place on the Temple mount (see page 5f.). While the world slept, they perpetrated their judicial inquiry and finished it in hardly an hour.

— G —
Peter Enters The High Priest's Palace

And Simon Peter followed Jesus afar off unto the high priest's palace, and so did another disciple. And that disciple was known unto the high priest and went in with Jesus into the palace of the high priest. But Peter stood at the door without. Then went out that other disciple, which was known unto the high priest, and spoke unto her that kept the door and brought in Peter. And the servants and officers stood there, who had made a fire of coals, for it was cold; and they warmed themselves; and Peter went in and sat with the servants, to see the end. (TLL, p. 271)

But Peter followed Him afar off unto the high priest's palace and went in and sat with the servants to see the end. (Matt. 26:58)
And Peter followed Him afar off, even into the palace of the high priest; and he sat with the servants and warmed himself at the fire. (Mark 14:54)
And Peter followed afar off. And when they had kindled a fire in the midst of the hall and were set down together, Peter sat down among them. (Luke 22:54b,55)
And Simon Peter followed Jesus, and so did another disciple. That disciple was known unto the high priest and went in with Jesus into the palace of the high priest. But Peter stood at the door without. Then went out that other disciple, which was known unto the high priest, and spoke unto her that kept the door and brought in Peter. And the servants and officers stood there, who had made a fire of coals, for it was cold; and they warmed themselves; and Peter stood with them and warmed himself. (John 18:15,16,18)

After the first panic caused by Christ's arrest had subsided, two of the fleeing disciples halted, and soon recovered enough to follow Jesus "afar off." Love caused them to follow, but fear made them careful to keep well out of sight of the multitude. Simon Peter is named. The other, though unnamed, most certainly was John, the "disciple whom Jesus loved." Peter was acting in his characteristic, self-willed way by following after Jesus and His captors. That was not the kind of following that Jesus wanted from His disciples. Jesus had warned Peter: "Whither I go, thou canst not follow Me now" (John 13:36; see also

FOLLOWING JESUS AFAR OFF

page 38). He should have stayed away from here. It is folly willfully and deliberately to place oneself into grave danger.

These two disciples went to the very court of the high priest's palace. There they parted when "the other disciple," John, "went in with Jesus into the palace of the high priest." John mustered up enough courage to enter in with the crowd. His own explanation of how this was possible was that he "was known to the high priest." John entered as an acquaintance of the high priest, and not as a disciple of Jesus. How he had come to know the high priest, as well as certain of his servants, is not mentioned. Statements that have been made regarding that are probably no more than guesses. Among them we find one by the Egyptian scholar Nonnus (ca. 400 A.D.), stating that John had been delivering the choice fish of Lake Galilee to the house of Annas, and so was known to the doorkeeper.

JOHN WENT INTO THE PALACE

"Peter stood at the door without." Perhaps John saw Peter through the gate. Intending to do Peter a favor, John "spoke to her that kept the door and brought Peter in." (As it turned out, it was no favor to him, and John confesses his part in the fall of Peter. Without John's aid Peter could not have entered the palace.) After Peter had been brought in, the two disciples parted again. John went in where Jesus had been taken, while "Peter went in, and sat with the servants" around "a fire of coals." The atmosphere of the courtyard was hostile toward Christ, but Peter cast prudence aside and acted as though he belonged there. The overconfidence which had cropped out earlier in the evening (see page 45) had returned to him.

PETER ENTERS

Peter entered "to see the end." He was not there to confess Jesus. Jesus had told him what the end would be. Did Peter doubt the word of Jesus and still expect a different turn of events? Or was he merely there as a curious spectator?

We hear no more of the Roman cohort. Evidently it returned to the barracks after delivering the prisoner to the palace.

— H —
Peter's First Denial

Then one of the maids of the high priest, the damsel that kept the door, when she saw Peter as he sat by the fire warming himself, earnestly looked upon him and said, "And thou also wast with Jesus of Nazareth. Art not thou also one of this man's disciples?" But he denied before them all, saying, "Woman, I know him not, neither understand I what thou sayest." (TLL, p. 271)

Now Peter sat without in the palace, and a damsel came unto him, saying, "Thou also wast with Jesus of Galilee." But he denied before them all, saying, "I know not what thou sayest." (Matt. 26:69, 70)

And as Peter was beneath in the palace, there cometh one of the maids of the high priest; and when she saw Peter warming himself, she looked upon him and said, "And thou also wast with Jesus of Nazareth." But he denied, saying, "I know not, neither understand I what thou sayest." (Mark 14:66-68a)

But a certain maid beheld him as he sat by the fire, and earnestly looked upon him and said, "This man was also with him." And he denied Him, saying, "Woman, I know him not." (Luke 22:56,57)

Then saith the damsel that kept the door unto Peter, "Art thou also one of this man's disciples?" He saith, "I am not." (John 18:17)

Peter's downfall came from an entirely unexpected source. Had he been called upon to assume a hero's role in the defense of Jesus, he might even now have responded as eagerly as he wielded the sword in Gethsemane. But Satan was much too clever to attack Peter where his strength lay. He employed "one of the maids of the high priest, the damsel that kept the door," to launch the attack where Peter least expected it. "She saw Peter as he sat by the fire warming himself" and "earnestly looked upon him." The fire of coals not only shed heat, but it also cast light upon the group around it. Peter would have been better concealed if he had avoided the light of the fire. His presence there gave the servant girl, or slave woman (Gr., *paidiske*), an opportunity to size him up.

UNDONE BY A MAID

The maid could see that Peter was out of place in the company which he had chosen. She may also have wondered whether she had done the right thing in admitting him into the palace. With womanly intuition the maid perceived where he belonged. She saw an opportunity to make herself important. Therefore she came to him, and in the presence of the group of servants who were busily talking about Jesus, said, "And thou also wast with Jesus of Nazareth. Art thou also one of this man's disciples?" It was only a servant that asked the question, but its force was intensified because it was asked in the presence of others.

At other times Peter would have been proud to acknowledge discipleship, but in this night he had already denied His Master in act, and was now about to do so in word. The very suddenness and unexpectedness of the exposure left no time for reflection or weighing of words. It required an instantaneous answer. Caught off guard, Peter was upset and began to quail. He felt the need to repulse the attack. The only way out that he could see was to lie, "and he denied before them all, saying, 'I know him not.'"

CAUGHT OFF GUARD

Such is the frailty of man and the power of fear! Only a few hours after the most intimate fellowship in the Upper Room, culminating in participation in the first Lord's Supper, Peter cowardly denied any knowledge of his beloved Master. Faintheartedly he rejected his God and his salvation. Whether the maid's question was asked out of curiosity, jokingly, in ridicule, unsuspectingly, contemptuously, or compassionately (all contentions have been made for it by someone), it effectively swept the proud boaster off his feet and brought him to an inglorious fall.

THE POWER OF FEAR

— I —
Peter's Second And Third Denials

And Simon Peter stood and warmed himself. And after a little while (after the first denial), as he went out into the porch, the cock crowed. And another maid saw him and began to say to them that stood by, "This fellow was also with Jesus of Nazareth." They said, therefore, unto him, "Art not thou also one of his disciples?" And another said, "Thou art also of them." And again he denied it with an oath, saying, "Man, I am not; I do not know the man." After a little while, about the space of one hour, another confidently affirmed, saying, "Of a truth this fellow also was with him; for he is a Galilean." Then came they that stood by and said to Peter, "Surely thou art one of them, for thou art a Galilean, and thy speech agreeth thereto and betrayeth thee." One of the servants of the high priest, being his kinsman, whose ear Peter cut off, saith, "Did not I see thee in the garden with Him?" Then began he to curse and to swear, saying, "I know not this man of whom ye speak." And immediately, as he yet spake, the cock crowed the second time. And the Lord turned, and looked upon Peter. And Peter remembered the word that Jesus said unto him, "Before the cock crow twice, thou shalt deny Me thrice." And he went out and wept bitterly. (TLL, pp. 271-272)

And when he was gone out into the porch, another maid saw him and said unto them that were there, "This fellow was also with Jesus of Nazareth." And again he denied with an oath, "I do not know the man." And after a while came unto him they that stood by and said to Peter, "Surely thou also art one of them; for thy speech betrayeth thee." Then began he to curse and to swear, saying, "I know not the man." And immediately the cock crew. And Peter remembered the word of Jesus which said unto him, "Before the cock crow, thou shalt deny Me thrice." And he went out and wept bitterly. (Matt. 26:71-75)

And he went out into the porch; and the cock crew. And a maid saw him again and began to say to them that stood by, "This is one of them." And he denied it again. And a little after, they that stood by said again to Peter, "Surely thou art one of them, for thou art a Galilean, and thy speech agreeth thereto." But he began to curse and to swear, saying, "I know not this man of whom ye speak." And the second time the cock crew. And Peter called to mind the word that Jesus said unto him, "Before the cock crow twice, thou shalt deny Me thrice." And when he thought thereon, he wept. (Mark 14:68b-72)

And after a little while another saw him and said, "Thou art also of them." And Peter said, "Man, I am not." And about the space of one hour after, another confidently affirmed, saying, "Of a truth this fellow also was with him, for he is a Galilean." And Peter said, "Man, I know not what thou sayest." And immediately, while he yet spoke, the cock crew. And the Lord turned and looked upon Peter. And Peter remembered the word of the Lord, how He had said unto him, "Before the cock crow, thou shalt deny Me thrice." And Peter went out and wept bitterly. (Luke 22:58-62)

And Simon Peter stood and warmed himself. They said therefore unto him, "Art not thou also one of his disciples?" He denied it and said, "I am not." One of the servants of the high priest, being his kinsman whose ear Peter cut off, saith, "Did not I see thee in the garden with him?" Peter then denied again; and immediately the cock crew. (John 18:25-27)

Peter did not leave the fire immediately lest he should draw attention to himself, but his conscience did not allow him to remain there long. Peter "went out into the porch" (Gr., *pulon*), the narrow passageway which led from the court unto the street. He evidently wanted to leave the palace, but before he could get away he was drawn into the second denial. At this point "the cock crowed" the first time, but in his agitated condition Peter did not hear it.

AFTER A LITTLE WHILE

Unsolved is the question whether St. John's statement, "and Simon Peter stood and warmed himself," refers to this "little while," or whether the disciple returned to the fire once more just before the third denial.

Peter was unable to slip out unnoticed. "And another maid saw him" and pointed Peter out to "them that stood by," accusing him of being a follower of Jesus. "They said, therefore, unto him, 'Art not thou also one of his disciples?' " The theme was quickly taken up by another bystander. He pounced upon the hapless disciple with the charge: "Thou art also one of them," meaning that he surely belonged to that notorious gang. The attention which Peter was getting was most embarrassing. The accusations came from all sides. Poor Peter! Trying to lie himself out of a difficult situation, he had only gotten himself in deeper. It was no longer merely a question of confessing Christ, but of exposing his own falsehoods as well, and he lacked the courage to come clean. He tried the age-old trick of covering up a lie with another and more emphatic lie, and for double emphasis he also added "an oath." It is mere assumption to say that by resorting to an oath Peter was reverting to an old habit from his fishing days.

THE PROBE RESUMED

When Peter denied the charge of discipleship by saying, "I am not," he actually ceased to be a disciple. With his oath he completely severed himself from his Master. He called upon God as a witness that he did not belong to Him. Insult was added to injury by the use of the scornful designation, "I know not the man." Yet, in a way, Peter played his role well. How can a person better show that he does not belong to Christ than by resorting to cursing and by denying Him?

"I KNOW NOT THE MAN"

Peter's vehement denial, sealed with an oath, took the accusers off his back for a while, and he was left in peace. He decided to stay in the courtyard. But just when he was beginning to feel secure, the attack upon him resumed. It was after "about the space of an hour." This time the charge is pressed with greater determination than before: "Of a truth this fellow also was with him." In spite of his vehement denials, the suspicions of the bystanders had not been completely allayed, and they confronted Peter regarding his telltale

THE NET IS DRAWN TIGHTER

Galilean accent, or brogue, somewhat broader and more harsh than the Judean pronunciation. They baited him by suggesting this as proof that he "was with him." If Peter could only have kept his mouth shut, his danger would have been less. To climax the charges that Peter had been lying, a relative of Malchus (see page 63f.) identified Peter as having been in the Garden with Jesus. "Did I not see thee in the Garden with him?" Now Peter was really on the spot.

Silence to these accusations would condemn him as a disciple and as a liar, and might seriously endanger him. Terror-stricken he casts all discretion aside and rejects the charges with all the power at his command. "Then began he to curse and to swear, saying, I know not the man of whom ye speak." He does not hesitate to perjure himself in order to save himself from discovery. Cowardice had overcome the once staunch disciple.

Before his accusers could resume the attack upon Peter, two events took place which changed the picture completely: First we read, "And immediately the cock crowed the second time." This time Peter heard

THE PICTURE CHANGED the crowing of the cock, but that alone was not enough to rouse him out of his sin. Secondly, as the cock crowed, Jesus was led past, either on His way from Annas to Caiaphas, or from Caiaphas to a place of detention to await the formal trial before the Sanhedrin. "And the Lord turned and looked upon Peter." That was the only means of communication possible between Jesus and Peter at this time, but it was enough. That look struck home.

"And Peter remembered the word that Jesus said unto him." Suddenly he saw the enormity of his sin. But he also recalled the Savior's loving warning, and he was led to repentance. "And he went out." He could no longer

PETER REMEMBERED remain on the scene of his sin and shame. It seems that he had no difficulty getting out of the courtyard. His exit may have been facilitated by the increased activity while the guards were moving the Prisoner from one courtroom to another. Once outside, Peter's pent-up emotions broke loose and "he wept bitterly." He made no attempt to excuse his sin or to cover it. He was overwhelmed by its enormity and repented of it. Peter's repentance can in no way be ascribed to any act of his own. It was due alone to divine grace.

The portrait of Peter's fall and repentance is so interesting and instructive, that there is grave danger to become so absorbed in Peter's conduct, or even in the Savior's look, that the effect of the denial on

BITTER AGONY FOR JESUS the suffering of Jesus is forgotten. We need to remind ourselves again that Christ must always remain the central figure in our study of His passion. Peter's denial was as much a part of Jesus' suffering as the agony in Gethsemane and the pain which He endured in the judgment hall and upon the cross. It was a conscious and deliberate rejection by one of His own, by one from the most intimate circle of His disciples. What shame and disgrace! First Judas connived with the enemy, and now Peter disowns Jesus publicly, where His enemies observe it and are given cause to mock Him for it. What kind of a Master must He be to have such faithless disciples? Jesus was not even permitted to view the repentance of His renegade disciple, for their meeting in the courtyard was only momentary; then each went his own way. Jesus knew that it would happen. He had foretold it and had warned Peter, but now Jesus was experiencing it, tasting the bitterness of it. These base denials were stabbing into the heart and soul of the Savior.

Nor should it be overlooked that the maids and the Temple guards were adding their considerable part to the suffering of Jesus by smiting Him with their tongues.

— J —
Jesus Questioned By The High Priest

The high priest then asked Jesus of His disciples and of His doctrine. Jesus answered him, "I spoke openly to the world. I ever taught in the synagog, and in the Temple, whither the Jews always resort; and in secret have I said nothing. Why askest thou Me? Ask them which heard Me, what I have said unto them; behold, they know what I said." And when He had thus spoken, one of the officers which stood by struck Jesus with the palm of his hand, saying, "Answerest thou the high priest so?" Jesus answered him, "If I have spoken evil, bear witness of the evil; but if well, why smitest thou Me?" Now Annas had sent Him bound unto Caiaphas, the high priest, where all the chief priests and the elders and the scribes were assembled with him. And the chief priests and the elders and all the council sought for false witness against Jesus to put Him to death; and found none. Yea, though many false witnesses came and bore false witness against Him, yet they found none; their witness agreed not together. (TLL, pp. 272-273)

Now the chief priests and elders and all the council sought false witness against Jesus to put Him to death, but found none. Yea, though many false witnesses came, yet found they none. (Matt. 26:59,60a)

And they led Jesus away to the high priest; and with him were assembled all the chief priests and the elders and the scribes. And the chief priests and all the council sought for witness against Jesus to put Him to death, and found none. For many bore false witness against Him, but their witness agreed not together. (Mark 14:53,55,56)

The high priest then asked Jesus of His disciples and of His doctrine. Jesus answered him, "I spoke openly to the world; I ever taught in the synagogue and in the Temple, whither the Jews always resort; and in secret have I said nothing. Why askest thou Me? Ask them which heard Me, what I have said unto them; behold, they know what I said." And when He had thus spoken, one of the officers which stood by struck Jesus with the palm of his hand, saying, "Answerest thou the high priest so?" Jesus answered him, "If I have spoken evil, bear witness of the evil; but if well, why smitest thou Me?" Now Annas had sent Him bound unto Caiaphas, the high priest. (John 18:19-24)

"The high priest" in this instance is Annas, not Caiaphas, as some interpreters claim (see page 69f.). He conducted the pretrial examination. The reason that he was chosen for this is explained in John 18:13. It was not the fact of a pretrial hearing that was reprehensible, for preliminary hearings and investigations nearly always precede the regular trial, but its conduct was blameworthy. Jesus recognized its validity by answering the high priest. The object of this hearing was to extort some information from Jesus which could be used at the trial to formulate specific charges against Him, or which might ensnare or incriminate Him. The possibility of the innocence of the prisoner did not come into consideration at all. The determination to put Him to death had been arrived at some time before (see page 5f.).

THE PRETRIAL EXAMINATION

While hurried preparations for the ecclesiastical trial were under way, Annas "asked Jesus of His disciples and His doctrine." Two related questions were addressed to Him: The first was "of His disciples." What kind of an organization did He head? Who were His followers? The question seemed to imply that Jesus was heading a subversive organization, engaged in sedition or conspiracy. No direct answer was given to this question. As far as the identity of His disciples was concerned, He would not bring them into the discussion. This was a case regarding Him, and the disciples should not be involved. Let Annas not confuse the issue! Secondly, His right to have disciples was subject to question only if His doctrine were false or subversive. The second question pertained to this subject, "His doctrine":

TWO QUESTIONS

Under somewhat similar circumstances the Apostle Paul burst into sudden anger (Acts 23:3), but Jesus did not allow Himself to be inflamed or to lose His temper, nor did He make any move toward revenge. With calm and dignity "Jesus answered him, 'If I have spoken evil, bear witness of the evil; but if well, why smitest thou Me?'" Assuming that Jesus had spoken evil, the proper way to correct it would have been testimony to that effect, specifying what the evil was. On the other hand, if His speech had been proper, why then this abuse? Smiting instead of answering the argument is the defense of the ignorant or unprincipled man.

THE SMITING REPROVED BY JESUS

The reply of Jesus was not only a rebuke for the underling who had struck Him, but for Annas as well, who condoned it. By allowing the blow of the servant to go unpunished, the lawful rights of Jesus, Himself the Lawgiver, were denied. He was treated as one who had no rights under the law. That kind of treatment can cause suffering more intense than physical pain.

DENIED THE RIGHTS OF THE LAW

The proceedings before Annas were ended, and he dismissed Jesus in bonds. The NIV deserves preference with its translation, "Then Annas sent Him, still bound, to Caiaphas, the high priest." Jesus was now sent "unto Caiaphas, the high priest, where all the scribes were assembled with him." The place of meeting was the palace

UNTO CAIAPHAS

of the high priest. The regular place of meeting in the Temple was closed at night. With Caiaphas was the Sanhedrin (see pages 5f. and 70), over which he presided as the regular high priest. Outwardly it was an elite group before whom Jesus was to stand trial. It was also a group that was blinded by prejudice against Him.

The trial, convened at an illegal hour (see page 70f.), began with a pretense of justice. The outcome was a foregone conclusion. "All the council sought false witness against Jesus to put Him to death." "All" means all who were present. Since Nicodemus and Joseph of Arimathea had not consented to the purpose and deed of the council (Luke 23:51, see page 176), it may be inferred that they were not present during this trial. Jesus had challenged Annas to ask those who had heard Him. At this time there would have been many witnesses in Jerusalem who had heard Him and who would gladly have given testimony, but that would not have served their evil purposes. They could not trust testimony honestly and freely given. They had already, without indictment, witness, or trial, determined that Jesus should be put to death. But unscrupulous as they were, they clung to a show of legal formality. They needed some outward show of right upon which to base the death sentence. The only way that they could manage that was by perjured testimony.

FALSE WITNESSES SOUGHT

Where evildoers rule, there unscrupulous people will always be found to curry their favor and do their bidding for some kind of personal gain or advantage. Such instruments of iniquity were not lacking in this case either. But "their witness agreed not together;" therefore it was worthless. "At the mouth of two witnesses, or three witnesses, shall he that is worthy of death be put to death; but at the mouth of one witness he shall not be put to death" (Deut. 17:6).

THEIR WITNESS DID NOT AGREE

The lament of David could be echoed by David's greater Son: "For the mouth of the wicked and the mouth of the deceitful are opened against me; they have spoken against me with a lying tongue" (Ps. 109:2).

Concern for the doctrine that was being taught was, not only the right, but the duty of the leaders of the church. When John the Baptist created a great stir among the people with his preaching, the Sanhedrin sent a delegation to investigate (John 1:19-27). Annas and Caiaphas should have been the first really to investigate the teachings of Jesus, and to try to understand what manner of kingdom He had come to establish. It is the course which Annas was pursuing that Jesus found necessary to correct.

A DUTY TO BE CONCERNED

Annas inferred that the doctrine of Jesus had been promulgated secretly. Jesus rejected this inference. "I spoke openly to the world; I ever taught in the synagog and in the Temple, whither the Jews always resort; and in secret have I said nothing." There was no secrecy in the propagation of Jesus' doctrine. He had nothing to hide. False prophets like to surround their teachings with an aura of mystery to make them

NOTHING TO HIDE

attractive and appealing to their followers. But Jesus' teaching was so public that anyone who wanted to know it, could. Yes, all the world might, and indeed should, know it. No secret hideouts, but the most public places, including synagogues and the Temple at Jerusalem, were the scenes of His teaching. Others, like the Sanhedrin, might conspire in secret, but not Jesus.

"Why askest thou Me? Ask them which heard Me." Deftly Jesus uncovers the real motive of the questions, to trap Him into saying something which might be misused against Him. If Annas really wants to know what Jesus taught, these multitudes who had heard Him should be called to testify. "Behold, they know what I said." Jesus testifies to the effectiveness of His teaching. He had presented it plainly, and clearly, and intelligibly so that His hearers could grasp and understand His doctrines and would be able to testify about them. Jesus' hands may have been bound, but His tongue and His spirit were not bound. The Word of God cannot be bound.

ASK THEM WHICH HEARD ME

It was most embarrassing to the high priest that he had to be reminded that according to Hebrew law a charge should be proved by witnesses. Shrewd old Annas was effectively foiled by the quiet, fearless logic of Jesus. He was left without a foot on which to stand. One of his henchmen observed his embarrassment and came to his rescue. He "struck Jesus with the palm of his hand, saying, 'Answerest Thou the high priest so?' " A quick new turn was given to the hearing by this underling, who probably tried to curry favor with his superior by abusing Jesus. When people find the content of the message unanswerable they like to find fault with the form in which it is given. This servant professed indignation, as though the high priest were being treated with disrespect, and he treated the Son of God with vulgar brutality. Before a single official charge had been brought against Him "punishment" was meted out — and by one who had no authority.

JESUS STRUCK BY THE SERVANT

— K —
Jesus Placed Under Oath By The High Priest

And there arose at last two, and bore false witness against Him, saying, "We heard this fellow say, 'I am able to destroy the Temple of God, and to build it in three days. I will destroy this Temple, that is made with hands, and within three days I will build another made without hands.' " But neither so did their witness agree together. And the high priest arose and stood up in the midst and asked Jesus, saying, "Answerest thou nothing? What is it these witness against thee?" But Jesus held His peace and answered nothing. Again the high priest asked Him and said unto Him, "Art thou the Christ, the Son of the Blessed? I adjure thee by the living God, that thou tell us whether thou be the Christ, the Son of God." Jesus said unto him, "Thou hast said; I am. Nevertheless, I say unto you, hereafter shall ye see the Son of Man sitting on the right hand of power and coming in the clouds of heaven." Then the high priest rent his clothes, saying, "He hath spoken blasphemy! What further need have we of witnesses? Behold, now ye have heard his blasphemy. What think ye?" And they all condemned Him and said, "He is guilty of death!" (TLL, pp. 273-274)

At the last came two false witnesses and said, "This fellow said, 'I am able to destroy the Temple of God and to build it in three days.'" And the high priest arose and said unto Him, "Answerest Thou nothing? What is it which these witness against thee?" But Jesus held His peace. And the high priest answered and said unto Him, "I adjure thee by the living God, that thou tell us whether thou be the Christ, the Son of God." Jesus saith unto him, "Thou hast said; nevertheless, I say unto you, hereafter shall ye see the Son of Man sitting on the right hand of power, and coming in the clouds of heaven." Then the high priest rent his clothes, saying, "He hath spoken blasphemy! What further need have we of witnesses? Behold, now ye have heard his blasphemy. What think ye?" They answered and said, "He is guilty of death!" (Matt. 26:60b-66)

And there arose certain and bore false witness against Him, saying, "We heard him say, 'I will destroy this Temple that is made with hands, and within three days I will build another made without hands.'" But neither so did their witness agree together. And the high priest stood up in the midst and asked Jesus, saying, "Answerest thou nothing? What is it which these witness against thee?" But He held His peace and answered nothing. Again the high priest asked Him and said unto Him, "Art thou the Christ, the Son of the Blessed?" And Jesus said, "I am: and ye shall see the Son of Man sitting on the right hand of power and coming in the clouds of heaven." Then the high priest rent his clothes and saith, "What need we any further witnesses? Ye have heard the blasphemy. What think ye?" And they all condemned Him to be guilty of death. (Mark 14:57-64)

FALSE WITNESSES

It took many attempts until approximate agreement was finally reached by two witnesses. They referred to a statement which Jesus had made almost three years before in answer to a demand that He furnish a sign of His authority for the first cleansing of the Temple. They garbled His answer, a prophecy concerning His resurrection (John 2:19). Although it appears that they resorted to collusion, when the witnesses testified separately as the law required, ''neither so did their witness agree together." Only truth will produce true agreement among witnesses.

THE JUDGE TURNS ACCUSER

By this time it was as plain as the nose on the high priest's face that they were getting nowhere by this procedure. Moreover, the silence of Jesus to all this was most disconcerting, since it was recognized as a fitting answer to the hollow charges against Him, rather than as an admission of guilt. The feeling of helplessness and frustration had reached the breaking point in Caiaphas, and he was unable to contain himself any longer. He forgot the dignity of his office and his position as judge, and he turned accuser. ''And the high priest arose and stood up in the midst and asked Jesus, saying, 'Answerest Thou nothing? What is it that these witness against Thee?' " He demanded that Jesus should defend Himself against all the accusations which were brought against Him. The strategy of the high priest was to goad Jesus into a retort that could be twisted into a corroboration of the testimony given by the witnesses.

The high priest lost his poise, but not Jesus. He did not allow Himself to be goaded into a rejoinder. "But Jesus held His peace and answered nothing." His only reply was a calm and dignified silence. There was no need for Him to speak. His silence was more eloquent than words could have been. His accusers knew that it laid bare their unholy motives and the utter falseness of their charges. After all, when the witnesses disagree with one another, what is there to defend?

JESUS HELD HIS PEACE

The silence of Jesus forced the high priest to abandon his attempt to convict Jesus by means of the testimony of witnesses. With a bold and dramatic stroke, he finally presented the real issue — the doctrine of Jesus about Himself. Who really was He?

JESUS PLACED UNDER OATH

To break the silence, Caiaphas put Jesus under oath: "I adjure thee by the living God that thou tell us whether thou be the Christ, the Son of God." The oath was the last resort. Its use here was also an admission that there had been no certainty until this time. By adjuring Him the high priest was demanding that Jesus should stand in the presence of the most high God and present His testimony with God as a witness. To be so placed under oath was deeply humiliating for Christ. The word of the holy and sinless Son of God, in whose mouth there was no guile (1 Peter 2:22), was deemed untrustworthy except under oath.

Under oath Jesus was to declare who He is — whether or not He is indeed the Son of God. That was the contention the Jewish leaders objected to most of all. Coupled with it was, of course, the claim that He was "The Christ," the promised Messiah. While Jesus seldom used this title, because of its political and nationalistic implications in the popular usage of that day, He did not repudiate it (John 4:25,26). The question of the high priest was conceived with great cunning, and it was aimed at the destruction of Jesus. If He should answer in the negative He would stand before the people as an imposter and deceiver. If His answer would be in the affirmative, they would, in their view, have cause to condemn Him to death for blasphemy.

THE SON OF GOD?

"Jesus said unto him, 'Thou hast said; I am.' " To have remained silent now would have been a denial of the truth, and it would have been construed as a withdrawal of what He otherwise had acknowledged. He made a clear confession in two short words: "I am" — just what you say I am. Caiaphas had come to the point. We could almost thank him for this, since we have received the benefit of Jesus' answer. The testimony of Jesus agreed fully with that of the Father (Ps. 2:7, Matt. 3:17; 17:5). By answering, Jesus acknowledged the authority of the high priest to put Him, who was "made under the Law," under oath. It is also noteworthy that the answer of Jesus to the high priest is identical with the name by which the eternal God identified Himself to Moses at the burning bush. "Thus shalt thou say unto the children of Israel, '*I AM* hath sent me unto you' " (Exod. 3:14).

"I AM"

Now Caiaphas was His judge, but the time would come when the tables would be reversed. "Nevertheless I say unto you, hereafter shall ye see the Son of Man sitting on the right hand of power and coming in the clouds of heaven." Christ prophesies in the midst of the Sanhedrin and thereby publicly and clearly asserts Himself according to His deity. They themselves would see His Messianic glory before their own eyes. (On "Son of Man" see page 4) This "seeing" of Christ is not limited to the final appearing of the Lord. "Hereafter" means "from this time forth" and it includes Christ's whole state of exaltation. The death of Jesus, which the Sanhedrin would cause by its own decree and its pressure upon Pilate, must result in Christ's glorification.

THE TABLES WILL BE TURNED

If they would not heed nor honor Him now they must do so in the future. The lowliness which they saw before them would in due time give way to divine glory. Then He would be "sitting at the right hand of power," exercising divine power. After His ascension He would, also according to His human nature, rule over and fill all things. "And coming in the clouds of heaven" is taken from Daniel 7:13. This expression ascribes divine glory to the Messiah. The Sanhedrin should realize just whom they are about to condemn to death.

FROM LOWLINESS TO GLORY

The testimony of Jesus caused the storm to break. Caiaphas gave a public exhibition of horror over the words of Christ. With a cry of "blasphemy!" he rent his clothes as a sign of intense grief. He wanted to have those present feel that these words were a defilement of God's honor. This was a theatrical ploy on the part of the high priest. He was concealing his joy, not expressing his grief. The priest was not permitted to rend his clothes in mourning, not even for a death within the family (Lev. 10:6). As an office-bearer, his attention was to be constantly fixed upon the living God. Blasphemy, however, was considered sufficient provocation for such conduct (2 Kings 18:37).

THE HIGH PRIEST RENT HIS CLOTHES

Caiaphas has what he wants, and now is determined to bring the case to a quick conclusion. "What need have we of further witnesses?" Involuntarily the high priest admits the failure to get suitable witnesses by false testimony. "What think ye?" Caiaphas disregards the legal procedure in capital cases, which specified that the verdict arrived at in a prescribed formal way could be passed only at a second session of the court, which was never to be convened on the same day. He presses for an immediate verdict. "And they all condemned Him and said, 'He is guilty of death.' " There is not a voice of protest at this procedure, nor a vote for the acquittal of the Prisoner. The verdict had been determined before the trial began. The excuse for the predetermined verdict is declared to be blasphemy. But in the land where the people had long been taught to wait expectantly for the Messiah, the Messianic claim should not have been pronounced to be blasphemy until it had been

A QUICK CONCLUSION

carefully and painstakingly investigated and found false. The hasty judgment of the high priest was an offense against justice.

God also declared Jesus to be guilty of death, not because of blasphemy, but because He had taken upon Himself the guilt of all people, who by their sins had blasphemed God.

— L —
Jesus Mocked By The Servants

And the men that held Jesus mocked Him, and some began to spit on Him and to cover His face and to buffet Him; and others smote Him with the palms of their hands, saying, "Prophesy unto us, thou Christ! Who is he that smote thee?" And many other things blasphemously spoke they against Him. (TLL, p. 274)

Then did they spit in His face and buffeted Him; and others smote Him with the palms of their hands, saying, "Prophesy unto us, thou Christ! Who is he that smote Thee?" (Matt. 26:67,68)

And some began to spit on Him and to cover His face and to buffet Him and to say unto Him, "Prophesy!" And the servants did strike Him with the palms of their hands. (Mark 14:65)

And the men that held Jesus mocked Him and smote Him. And when they had blindfolded Him, they struck Him on the face and asked Him, saying, "Prophesy! Who is it that smote thee?" And many other things blasphemously spoke they against Him. (Luke 22:63-65)

COURT RECESS PRODUCES GRUESOME MOCKERY

The irregular and illegal night session of the council had produced the predetermined verdict. To give this verdict the appearance of legality the court recessed until dawn. Jesus remained in the custody of the Temple guard. The fanatical hatred toward Jesus shown by the Jewish leaders was also transmitted to the underlings. To while away their time they made sport of their Prisoner. "And the men which held Jesus mocked Him." Whether the actual mockery and abuse was confined to the underlings, or, as Matthew seems to imply, was joined in by the Sanhedrists themselves, the council was not blameless in this outrage. If the Sanhedrists did no more, they did condone these personal indignities. In any event, Jesus was here grossly mistreated by His own people.

The atmosphere that filled the courtroom during the recess eloquently describes the tenor of the trial itself. If the council had been truly conscientious and unprejudiced in its judgment, the seriousness of condemning a man to death would have cast an air of solemnity which would not have been so quickly dispersed.

The brutal mockery took on such varied forms as their imagination was capable of devising. "And some began to spit upon Him." Being spit upon was considered an

THEY SPAT UPON HIM expression of utmost contempt among the Jews (Deut. 25:9; Num. 12:14). By this insult they showed what they thought of Him and His Word. This spitting upon the holy face of Jesus was most likely done right after His condemnation. Thereby the prophecy of Isaiah 50:6, as well as His own prophecy in Luke 18:32, was literally fulfilled. This was the climax of personal insult. By this they showed what they thought of "the Son of God" who was about to sit at the right hand of power, and who would return in the clouds of heaven.

The abuse of Jesus can only be described as devilish in character. With cowardly brutality His tormentors struck Him with the palms of their hands. His molesters especially gratified their coarse sense of humor by covering **DEVILISH ABUSE** His face during this buffeting and saying, "Prophesy unto us, thou Christ! Who is he that smote thee?" With cruel banter they made a joke of His office and ridiculed His works and words. That was their answer to His prophecy before the Sanhedrin. Jesus had not been without honor among the people, but here His honor was ruthlessly trodden underfoot.

As had already happened before Annas (see page 78), Jesus was treated as one outside of the law. The place of justice was converted into a place of injustice for Him. The abuse which Jesus endured is reported with great restraint. **BLASPHEMY** The Evangelists do not care to dwell upon the details at all. Instead they sum up briefly, "and many other things blasphemously spoke they against Him." His enemies had vainly tried to pin the charge of blasphemy on Jesus, and now they neatly turned the tables and became guilty of blaspheming Him themselves.

All of this scorn, mockery, and abuse were borne without complaint and with a patience that must always stand before His followers as an example to emulate when they suffer injustice. His power to strike back in vengeance was held in check and His tongue was restrained from issuing rebuke. Was not this the cup which the Father had given Him to drink? The pledge of submission to the Father's will which He had made in the Garden was being fulfilled.

CHAPTER FOUR
Jesus Sent From Caiaphas To Pilate

— A —

The Morning Session Of The Sanhedrin

And straightway when the morning was come, as it was day, all the chief priests, scribes, and the elders of the people, together with all the council, took counsel against Jesus to put Him to death; and led Him into their council, saying, "Art thou the Christ? Tell us." And He said unto them, "If I tell you, ye will not believe: and if I also ask you, ye will not answer Me, nor let Me go. Hereafter shall the Son of Man sit on the right hand of the power of God." Then said they all, "Art thou then the Son of God?" And He said unto them, "Ye say that I am." And they said, "What need we any further witness? For we ourselves have heard of his own mouth." (TLL, p. 274)

When the morning was come, all the chief priests and elders of the people took counsel against Jesus to put Him to death. (Matt. 27:1)

And straightway in the morning the chief priests held a consultation with the elders and scribes and the whole council. (Mark 15:1a)

And as soon as it was day, the elders of the people and the chief priests and the scribes came together, and led Him into their council, saying, "Art thou the Christ? Tell us." And He said unto them, "If I tell you, ye will not believe; and if I also ask you, ye will not answer Me nor let Me go. Hereafter shall the Son of Man sit on the right hand of the power of God." Then said they all, "Art thou then the Son of God?" And He said unto them, "Ye say that I am." And they said, "What need we any further witness? For we ourselves have heard of his own mouth." (Luke 22:66-71)

"And straightway when the morning was come, as soon as it was day" the Sanhedrin met again to ratify the action which had been taken in the night session.

THE SANHEDRIN REASSEMBLED This meeting presumably was held in the regular council chamber which would now be open again. They were extremely anxious to maintain a semblance of legality, and for this reason reassembled the council after sunrise. "All the chief priests," etc., indicates that this was a meeting of the full council, just as the one during the night had been (see page 79). It is obvious that there was no intention to retry the case. Their objective was to confirm the death sentence which had previously been passed, and to do this as quickly as possible, before the public should become aware of what was going on. They were afraid of causing an uproar among the people who were in Jerusalem for the feast (see page 7).

The demand of the Sanhedrin was rude and short. "Art thou the Christ? Tell us." This was but a part of the question put by Caiaphas in the night session. That is why

"ART THOU THE CHRIST?" Jesus did not answer it in the same way. During the night session the high priest expressly asked if He were the Son of God. This they would rather delete in the charge before Pilate. The term "Messiah" was much better suited for their purpose, since it had acquired a nationalistic, highly political, purely earthly meaning.

"And He said unto them, 'If I tell you, ye will not believe.' " If He were to explain to them in what sense He was the Messiah, they would not accept His word. They had amply demonstrated that in the past. "And if I also ask you, ye will not answer Me" — as when He had formerly asked them with reference to John the Baptist (Luke 20:4). They would not be ready to discuss with Him the Scriptures regarding the Messiah, thereby establishing proof of His Messiahship. "Nor let Me go." He exposes this whole trial procedure as a frame-up. They would not even consider the possibility of His release through establishment of His innocence. Still Jesus does not neglect to give them a clear warning and testimony of His identity. "Hereafter shall the Son of Man sit on the right hand of the power of God." He repeats what He had said in the night session regarding His exaltation to Messianic power and glory (see page 83).

THE FARCE EXPOSED

Now the other half of the original question is shouted at Jesus. "Then said they all, 'Art thou then the Son of God?' " This time it is not just Caiaphas who demands the answer, but the whole Sanhedrin gets into the act. They had correctly construed the answer of Jesus as a claim to divinity. Without equivocation "He said unto them, 'Ye say that I am.' " Jesus employed the customary form for giving an affirmative answer to a question. This is evident from the acceptance of His answer by the Sanhedrin.

THE DECISIVE QUESTION

With this answer the Sanhedrin declares that it can dispense with further testimony. "What need we any further witness?" As if they had any! They had not had any at the night session, and they had none now, and they knew it.

The formality of voting and of pronouncing the verdict is not mentioned. In the atmosphere that prevailed the result was obvious.

— B —
Jesus Delivered To Pilate

And the whole multitude of them arose, and when they had bound Christ, they led Him from Caiaphas unto the hall of judgment and delivered Him to Pontius Pilate, the governor; and it was early. (TLL, p. 274)

And when they had bound Him, they led Him away and delivered Him to Pontius Pilate, the governor. (Matt. 27:2)
And bound Jesus and carried Him away and delivered Him to Pilate. (Mark 15:1b)
And the whole multitude of them arose and led Him unto Pilate. (Luke 23:1)
Then led they Jesus from Caiaphas unto the hall of judgment; and it was early. (John 18:28a)

A new phase in Christ's suffering begins. He is transferred from the ecclesiastical authorities to the civil authorities, from His own people to the Gentiles. The ecclesiastical court had pronounced Jesus guilty of death. Most gladly would the Jews have carried out this sentence themselves, but they were prohibited from doing so. The scepter had departed from Judah (Gen. 49:10). The Romans had reserved the *"jus gladii,"* the right of inflicting the death penalty, for themselves. According to the Talmud, the Jews lost this right forty years before the destruction of Jerusalem, that is, only a few years before the death of Jesus. It was, therefore, necessary to deliver Jesus to the Roman governor for sentencing.

TRANSFERRED TO THE CIVIL AUTHORITIES

"When they had bound Him" indicates that the bonds which had been put on Jesus in Gethsemane had been removed from Him during the trial before the Sanhedrin. In preparation for the march to another part of the city, they were again put on Him.

"From Caiaphas" need not mean from the palace of Caiaphas. It can also, and here probably does, mean from the jurisdiction of Caiaphas, who as high priest presided over the Sanhedrin. St. Mark identifies the hall of judgment with the Praetorium (Mark 15:16). A praetorium was a governor's residence. The regular residence of the Roman governors, or procurators, was at Caesarea, on the seacoast. However, when they came to Jerusalem to guard the peace, which was their custom at the time of the Passover, an official residence or praetorium was established for the duration of their visit. The location of such a praetorium at this time cannot be positively fixed. Herod himself was in Jerusalem at this time and would therefore occupy the palace that bore his name. The Tower of Antonia, adjoining the Temple area and garrison for the Roman cohort, has most to recommend itself as the praetorium of our account. This would also fit with the record of Josephus, who placed Gabbatha between the Tower of Antonia and the western corner of the Temple, directly before the judgment hall.

TO THE HALL OF JUDGMENT

"And delivered Him to Pontius Pilate, the governor." Pilate represented the Roman government. The whole Roman empire stood back of him and acted through him. On the way to Jerusalem Jesus had foretold: "And they shall condemn Him to death, and shall deliver Him to the Gentiles" (Mark 10:33). Israel, through its religious leadership, rejected its long sought for Messiah and turned to the world for assistance in destroying Him. And "the world," with Pilate's help, complied. Since that day, to his everlasting infamy, the Christian Church everywhere regularly confesses that Jesus "suffered under Pontius Pilate."

DELIVERED TO THE GENTILES

"And it was early." Roman courts were open from dawn to sunset, so there was nothing unusual about Pilate's presence at this hour.

— C —
Judas' Remorse And End

Then Judas which had betrayed Him, when he saw that He was condemned, repented himself, and brought again the thirty pieces of silver to the chief priests and elders, saying, "I have sinned in that I have betrayed innocent blood." And they said, "What is that to us? See thou to that." And he cast down the pieces of silver in the Temple and departed and went and hanged himself. (TLL, pp. 274-275; *Matt. 27:3-5*)

The stigma of the betrayal is inseparably associated with the name of Judas. Once an honored and respected name, fondly bestowed by parents on their children, it became shunned and disdained because of the man of Kerioth.

After the infamous betrayal of Jesus, Judas never found peace again. It was impossible for him to slip away quietly with the blood-money and to enjoy the ill-gotten gain. He had to stay close to see how things would turn out. Whether Judas remained in the camp of the enemy from Gethsemane to the judgment hall, personally witnessing the proceedings, or whether he observed the procession going to the Praetorium, it was clearly evident to him that Jesus was condemned to die.

WHEN HE SAW THAT HE WAS CONDEMNED

That the betrayer perhaps expected, or even hoped, that Jesus would yet escape from the enemies as He had done before, is nothing more than speculation. When he saw what his betrayal had brought about he "repented himself." His eyes were suddenly opened to the enormity of his sin. How vastly different the sin appeared now that it was done. The scales fell away from his eyes and he saw what a wretched scoundrel he was. Terror gripped his soul. If only he had not made that bargain! If only he had refrained from the evil deed!

JUDAS "REPENTED HIMSELF"

Judas confessed his guilt to his companions in sin, "the chief priests and elders," with a self-condemnation: "I have sinned in that I have betrayed innocent blood." With a cry of despair he acknowledged his treachery and declared the innocency of Jesus. But this innocence of Jesus only magnified his own guilt. Undoubtedly he recalled the awful threat of God's holy law: "Cursed be he that taketh reward to slay an innocent person" (Deut. 27:25). Satan would not miss the opportunity to remind him of it, if he did not remember it, and to torment him with it.

INNOCENT BLOOD

The Law of God convicted Judas, and he regretted the shameful wrong which he had done, but his "repentance" was without faith. He, who knew the private life of Jesus intimately and was competent to judge, credited innocent blood to the Master. But he did not acknowledge that this blood could also make him innocent before God. He did not confess or believe that the Innocent One was *his* Messiah.

WITHOUT FAITH

Desiring to undo what he had done, "he brought again the thirty pieces of silver to the chief priests and elders."

"WHAT IS THAT TO US?" The money, which had seemed so desirable to the avaricious heart of Judas, suddenly became abhorrent to him and seared his soul. The reward of iniquity burned in his hands, and he sought to free himself from the fruit and profit of his sin. Judas carried the blood money back to his partners in crime and offered to return it. He hoped that this would ease the intolerable pressure on his conscience. But the conscience-stricken sinner found no sympathy with these hate-blinded leaders of the Jews. They had no time for Judas, but told him to mind his own business: "What is that to us? See thou to that." Coldly and bluntly they told him that they are not at all concerned about him or his plight. They had no more use for him. They were through with him. They had paid the price for which they bargained, and they concluded that they owed him nothing. They tossed him aside like a broken instrument. The travail of his soul meant nothing to them.

Judas now had no friends, no partners, no savior, no peace — only thirty pieces of silver. The sight of the thirty pieces of silver filled him with utter disgust. "For these he had sold his soul; and these he

ONLY THIRTY PIECES OF SILVER should no more enjoy than Achen enjoyed the gold he buried, or Ahab the garden he had seized" (Farrar). To the One who could have helped him Judas does not go. Instead he yields to utter gloom and despair. No ray of light or hope shines for him anymore.

Judas is possessed with the determination to get rid of the blood money. If the high priest will not take it, he will throw it under his feet where he must step on it. "And he cast down the pieces of silver in the Temple,"

CAST INTO THE TEMPLE not just into one of the courts of the Temple, but as the word 'naos' indicates, into the very Sanctuary, which included the Holy Place and the Holy of Holies. We can picture him, deeply agitated as he was, rushing through the Court of the Gentiles, on through the Court of the Women, up the flight of stairs, into the Court of Israel, up to the low wall which marked off the Court of Priests, or even into the court itself, and then flinging the shekels into the open entrance of the Holy Place. Without stopping to observe the consternation caused by his frenzied action, as silver coins clattered on the marble floor and rolled against the sacred furnishings, he "departed."

Judas was rid of the tainted money, but peace did not come to his troubled soul. He had not gotten rid of his sin, and its guilt gave him no rest. Satan would not relax the pressure of accusation or allow him any comfort

JUDAS HANGED HIMSELF from discarding his gain from the betrayal. So completely had Satan blinded the eyes of his victim that the only way that he could see out of his distress was by means of the rope. The Tempter was already dangling it before his eyes. So he "went and hanged himself." Peter adds the awful detail that the body of the traitor broke free, "and falling headlong, he burst asunder in the midst and all his bowels gushed out" (Acts 1:18). As Ahithophel, the friend and confidant of King David, betrayed his royal master, so

Judas, one of the Twelve, betrayed his Lord and Master. The resemblance also applies to their end. Both went and hanged themselves.

Judas was not lost because he betrayed Jesus, terrible as that sin was, but because he did not believe the Gospel of God's forgiveness in Christ.

The final tragic behavior of Judas was not carried on before the eyes of Jesus; yet He surely was fully aware of it, and by it His sorrow was immeasurably increased.

— D —
The Potter's Field Bought With The Price Of Blood

And the chief priests took the silver pieces, and said, "It is not lawful for to put them into the treasury, because it is the price of blood." And they took counsel and bought with them the potter's field to bury strangers in. Wherefore that field was called the Field of Blood unto this day. Then was fulfilled that which was spoken by Jeremy, the prophet, saying: "And they took the thirty pieces of silver, the price of Him that was valued, whom they of the children of Israel did value, and gave them for the potter's field, as the Lord appointed me." (TLL, p. 275; *Matt. 27:6-10*)

The chief priests now engaged in a remarkable and repulsive piece of hypocrisy. They "said, 'It is not lawful for to put them into the treasury, because it is the price of blood.'" They conceded that its use for the betrayal had made blood money out of the silver. It was tainted with the blood of Christ. For that reason, they argued, it could not be returned to the Temple treasury, from where it had been taken. This position was based on an extension of Deuteronomy 23:18, and possibly of Numbers 35:33,34. These hypocritical leaders had no scruples about participating in the betrayal of innocent blood and plotting "legal" murder; but they were filled with consternation at the thought of violating a law pertaining to the source of money for the Temple treasury. The solution required study, so "they took counsel." The decision with which they sought to salve their consciences was to use it for a needed charitable purpose. "And bought with them the potter's field to bury strangers in." An exhausted clay pit was acquired as a cemetery for strangers who died while they visited the Holy City, such as during the feasts. But even their "charity" betrays the pride of these Jewish leaders. Strangers must be kept at their distance, dead or alive. The wall of partition must be upheld.

A PIECE OF HYPOCRISY

"Wherefore that field was called the Field of Blood unto this day." The keen insight of the common people quickly penetrated the sham of the Jewish leaders and perpetuated the memory of their shameful conduct by branding this burial place as the Field of Blood. Acts 1:19 gives it the Aramaic name, *Aceldema*. The name stuck and was in common use at the time when Matthew wrote his Gospel. Instead of concealing their wickedness, their action established a lasting memorial to it.

ACELDEMA

"Then was fulfilled that which was spoken by Jeremy, the prophet." The action of the chief priests was not a matter of chance. Unwittingly the enemies of Christ were helping to fulfill prophecy and to confirm the ministry of Christ which they were trying so hard to discredit. Matthew makes a free quotation from Zechariah 11:12,13. Ascribing the prophecy to Jeremiah may have resulted from a transcriber's mistake. In Greek, in the abridged form of the names, the change of a single letter would change Zechariah (*Zriou*) to Jeremiah (*Iriou*). Another possible explanation is found in the fact that the entire third part of the Old Testament, commonly known as The Prophets, was sometimes referred to as Jeremy, or Jeremiah, because this book occupied the first position. It is also possible that Jeremiah spoke these words although they are not recorded in his book, and that later Zechariah wrote them in his book.

PROPHECY FULFILLED

As Zechariah, the "shepherd" of Israel in his day, had been valued by his people at thirty pieces of silver, the well known price of a slave; so Jesus, the great Shepherd of Israel, was given the same valuation by the Jewish leaders. This miserable price was meant to be an insult. "As the Lord appointed me" repeats Zechariah 11:13: "And the Lord said unto me." The disposal of the money had to be made according to the Lord's will.

A PRICE OF CONTEMPT

— E —
Pilate Demands The Accusation

But the Jews went not into the judgment hall, lest they should be defiled; but that they might eat the passover. Pilate then went out unto them and said, "What accusation bring ye against this man?" They answered and said unto him, "If he were not a malefactor, we would not have delivered him up unto thee." Then said Pilate unto them, "Take ye him, and judge him according to your law." The Jews therefore said unto him, "It is not lawful for us to put any man to death," that the saying of Jesus might be fulfilled, which He spoke signifying what death He should die. (TLL, p. 275; *John 18:28b-32*)

The whole multitude had brought Jesus to Pontius Pilate, the governor. "But the Jews went not into the judgment hall, lest they should be defiled." The reason their conscience would not permit them to enter the Praetorium was not only that the Gentiles would have leaven in their houses during the season of unleavened bread, but also that coming into personal contact with Gentiles would make them Levitically unclean (cf. Acts 10:28; John 4:9; Mark 7:4). In this they went beyond the Levitical law of defilement. This was an interpretation which the rabbis and scribes had added in the *Mishna*.

FEAR OF DEFILEMENT

"But that they might eat the passover." This does not refer to the Passover meal proper, which had already been eaten the evening before, on the 14th of Nisan, but to the Chagigah, which was observed on the afternoon of the first day of the feast, remembering that their day had already begun at the previous sundown. "Whereas the eating of the lamb on Thursday evening was a sad and solemn celebration, the Chagigah of sacrificial meats on Friday was regarded as a feast of great joy" (Lenski). This the Jewish leaders did not want to miss for fear of defilement. The term "Passover" was commonly used in the wider sense to include the Chagigah and the Feast of Unleavened Bread.

THE CHAGIGAH

"Pilate then went out unto them." Acknowledging that Roman court proceedings were conducted in the open when necessary, Pilate's action unquestionably was a diplomatic concession to the religious scruples of the Jews.

"What accusation bring ye against this man?" Pilate opens the proceedings in the normal Roman manner of hearing the charges or accusations against the prisoner. He begins as a Roman judge should, and he does not allow the impressive delegation to persuade him to endorse their verdict without further ado. Furthermore, Pilate was too familiar with the Jewish leaders to place blind reliance on their court procedure, even when religious matters were involved. Festus said: "It is not the manner of the Romans to deliver any man to die, before he which is accused have the accusers face to face, and have license to answer for himself concerning the crime laid against him" (Acts 25:16).

CHARGES DEMANDED

The Jews retorted: "If he were not a malefactor, we would not have delivered him up unto thee." They acted surprised, as well as hurt in their dignity, that Pilate should hesitate to accept their authority and judgment. They expected him to do their bidding and to waive Jesus' right to a trial under Roman law. When they handed Jesus over to Pilate they did not want him to put Jesus on trial, with the possibility that he might reverse their judgment. They just wanted him to confirm their decision and to execute the punishment.

LOOKING FOR CONFIRMATION

The Sanhedrists put on a great demonstration to give the impression that Jesus was a terrible criminal, yet they avoided making a definite charge, and they only inferred what they wanted Pilate to do. They desired to be the judges. Pilate should be the executioner, and whatever invective the action would produce would conveniently fall on the head of the governor. They expected Pilate to do what their own law did not allow: "Doth our law judge any man before it hear him?" (John 7:51).

NO DEFINITE CHARGE

But Pilate was not deceived by the cunning of the Jews. He replied according to their answer, "Take ye him and judge him according to your law." Pilate could not fail to perceive what the intention of the Sanhedrists was, but his pride in his

"JUDGE HIM ACCORDING TO YOUR LAW"

position as governor and representative of the Roman emperor would not permit him to go along with them. If they did not bring charges against the Accused, he would not accept the case. Therefore he handed it back to the Sanhedrin. But they could only excommunicate, imprison, fine, administer forty stripes less one, etc. They could not inflict the death penalty. This was far short of what they had determined in their meeting. It would not satisfy their thirst for blood.

John adds, "that the saying of Jesus might be fulfilled, which He spoke signifying what death He should die" (John 18:32). Once again our attention is drawn to the hand of God in the course of events. The Father had determined how Jesus was to die. That is why He had to be turned over to the Romans. If it had been in the power of the Jews to execute Jesus, He would have been stoned. This God would not allow. He should not be mutilated and the bones of His body should not be broken. By dying on the cross, the only mutilation of His body would be the nail marks in His hands and feet, and the opening in His side. Furthermore, instead of the execution being quickly carried out in some secluded place, and the body hidden under a pile of stones, Jesus was to be put on public display at one of the great crossroads of the world. Thus His death would receive world-wide publicity.

THE MANNER OF DEATH

— F —
They Begin To Accuse Jesus

Then the chief priests and elders began to accuse Him, saying, "We found this fellow perverting the nation and forbidding to give tribute to Caesar, saying that he himself is Christ, a king." Then Pilate entered into the judgment hall again, and called Jesus; and Jesus stood before the governor; and the governor asked Him, saying, "Art thou the King of the Jews?" Jesus answered him, "Sayest thou this thing of thyself, or did others tell it thee of Me?" Pilate answered, "Am I a Jew? Thine own nation and the chief priests have delivered thee unto me; what hast thou done?" Jesus answered, "My kingdom is not of this world. If My kingdom were of this world, then would My servants fight, that I should not be delivered to the Jews; but now is My kingdom not from hence." Pilate therefore said unto Him, "Art thou a king then?" Jesus answered, "Thou sayest that I am a king. To this end was I born, and for this cause came I into the world, that I should bear witness unto the truth. Every one that is of the truth heareth My voice." Pilate saith unto Him, "What is truth?" And when he had said this, he went out again unto the Jews, and saith unto the chief priests and to the people, "I find no fault at all in this man." (TLL, pp. 275-276)

And Jesus stood before the governor, and the governor asked Him, saying, "Art thou the King of the Jews?" And Jesus said unto him, "Thou sayest." (Matt. 27:11)

And Pilate asked Him, "Art thou the King of the Jews?" And He, answering, said unto him, "Thou sayest it." (Mark 15:2)

And they began to accuse Him, saying, "We found this fellow perverting the nation and forbidding to give tribute to Caesar, saying that he himself is Christ, a king." And Pilate asked Him, saying, "Art thou the King of the Jews?" And He answered him and said, "Thou sayest it." Then said Pilate to the chief priests and to the people, "I find no fault in this man." (Luke 23:2-4)

Then Pilate entered into the judgment hall again and called Jesus and said unto Him, "Art thou the King of the Jews?" Jesus answered him, "Sayest thou this thing of thyself, or did others tell it thee of Me?" Pilate answered, "Am I a Jew? Thine own nation and the chief priests have delivered thee unto me. What hast thou done?" Jesus answered, "My kingdom is not of this world. If My kingdom were of this world, then would My servants fight, that I should not be delivered to the Jews; but now is My kingdom not from hence." Pilate therefore said unto Him, "Art thou a king then?" Jesus answered, "Thou sayest that I am a king. To this end was I born, and for this cause came I into the world, that I should bear witness unto the truth. Every one that is of the truth heareth My voice." Pilate saith unto Him, "What is truth?" And when he had said this, he went out again unto the Jews and saith unto them, "I find in him no fault at all." (John 18:33-38)

Because they saw that Pilate was determined not to condemn Jesus without a trial, the Jewish leaders "began to accuse Him." Having lost the first skirmish with Pilate, the Jews were compelled to formulate definite charges against Jesus. Realizing that the charge of blasphemy, on which the Sanhedrin had condemned Him, would carry no weight with the governor because it was a religious issue, they did not even mention it. Instead they accused Jesus of high treason. The charge against Him was brought from a higher to a lower plane. Originally they maintained that Jesus had sinned against Jehovah; now they said that He had sinned against Caesar, that He was a rebel against the state. "We found" is a legal term. They asserted that they had already given Jesus a full and fair trial on the charges, and that Pilate was being unreasonable in not accepting their verdict. "This fellow" is a highly derogatory designation, particularly in view of the fame which Jesus enjoyed in the land.

ACCUSED OF TREASON

Treason was charged on three counts, not one of which had even been mentioned in their two court trials. First they charged Jesus with agitating the people to disloyalty and insurrection, menacing the peace, and causing tumult. But they were not really concerned that Caesar's influence should suffer (that would have pleased them immensely), but that theirs would. "Our nation" (NIV, NASB) they called it. They used the term for "nation" which describes them merely as a political unit, instead of that which defines them as a spiritual or religious community. They were willing to degrade themselves in order to destroy Jesus. The Jews probably counted on Pilate's having heard of the popular demonstration of the past Sunday when Jesus royally entered Jerusalem, receiving the enthusiastic acclaim and homage of the pilgrims. They hoped to be considered champions of peace and order for their action in bringing Him to justice.

"PERVERTING THE NATION"

The second charge, that Jesus was an obstacle to the collection of taxes, was calculated to receive special attention from Pilate. But the governor might well wonder at

"FORBIDDING TO GIVE TRIBUTE TO CAESAR" — such unexpected zeal for paying tribute to the Romans, quite an about face by a people to whom the Roman taxation had been so galling. They sought to deceive Pilate with a bold and brazen lie, born out of hatred for Jesus. They had surely not forgotten the encounter with Jesus on the right of taxation, when Jesus had declared: "Render therefore unto Caesar the things which are Caesar's and unto God the things which are God's" (Luke 20:25).

This third charge was true, if rightly understood. According to Zechariah 9:9, the Messiah was to be a king: "Behold, thy King cometh unto thee." Since Christ desired only to be a spiritual king, and was rejected as such by Israel, His enemies attributed political aspirations to Him. Thus

"SAYING THAT HE HIMSELF IS CHRIST, A KING"

He, who had shunned the attempts of the people to make Him their earthly king (John 6:15), was accused of being a rival and opponent of Caesar. This was a serious charge, which the governor did not dare to ignore.

Pilate's demand for formal charges had now been met by the Jewish leaders, and so he accepted the Prisoner for trial. "Then Pilate entered into the judgment hall again and called Jesus." By entering the

PILATE ACCEPTS THE PRISONER FOR TRIAL

Praetorium and calling for Jesus, Pilate neatly and officially effected the transfer of the Prisoner from the Jewish authorites to Roman jurisdiction. Only the scruples of the Jews prevented them from also entering the judgment hall. "And Jesus stood before the governor," as a prisoner before his judge. The Son of God submitted to the jurisdiction of civil government.

Standing face to face with the "God-man," Pilate asked, "Art Thou the King of the Jews?" Pilate took up the third charge, that of royal pretension. That charge most directly affected the authority and prestige of the Roman government. But his question seems to reflect incredulity. All appearances denied any pretension to earthly royal power. To have simply answered in the affirmative would have left the impression that the Jews were entirely right in their accusations of treason. Jesus could not create a misunderstanding by permitting a half-truth to stand. In order to have Pilate understand that His kingship depended on what was meant by that term, He asked, "Sayest thou this thing of thyself, or did others tell it thee of Me?" If He were really a rebel, wouldn't Pilate have known this by now? By one deft question Jesus made Pilate consider the source of the charges.

"KING OF THE JEWS?"

Pilate was taken by surprise, and he quickly retorted, "Am I a Jew? Thine own nation and the chief priests have delivered thee unto me." Disdainfully and with Roman pride, Pilate rejected the thought that he was asking this question on his own initiative. No one but a Jew would accuse Jesus of ambition to be a king. It took a Gentile to point out the utter disgracefulness of the chief priests' action: delivering up their own countryman, their own Prophet and King, to the despised alien. A puzzled Pilate

"AM I A JEW?"

asked, "What hast thou done?" It seemed to him that there must be some cause for this violent outburst by His enemies. What had Jesus done?

Jesus Himself answered, "My kingdom is not of this world." He is a king indeed, but not a rival to Tiberius. He has no ambitions for a politically organized realm, or to be any other secularized ruler. His kingdom has no boundaries and cannot be located on a map. His kingship is not dependent on an earthly realm or weapons. It did not originate from this world. It is of an entirely different type. It is not from beneath, but from above, from heaven. Proof that His kingdom is not like other realms is the lack of subjects to fight with earthly weapons to defend Him. "If My kingdom were of this world, then would My servants fight that I should not be delivered to the Jews." Neither Pilate nor His accusers could point to such a force of defenders.

"NOT OF THIS WORLD"

Pilate accepts Christ's statement that He has no claims upon any earthly realm, and he drops the designation "of the Jews," but he does request some further explanation. Jesus affirms that He is indeed a king. "Thou sayest that I am a king." He is not merely striving to become a king. Furthermore, His claim to kingship is legitimate. "To this end was I born." He had not usurped His kingship from another, nor acquired it by conquest. "And for this cause came I into the world," is more than a synonym of being born. It testifies to His existence before coming to this world. His human nativity does not explain His full origin. He had come from another region, from heaven, "that I should bear witness unto the truth." In His declaration concerning the purpose of His coming, Jesus also reveals the nature of His kingdom, and why it is set apart from all of the kingdoms of this world. Although everything which Christ spoke was true, His purpose was not to declare every truth and reality regarding science or the universe, but to bring us that specific truth which we need for our salvation (John 14:6). This salvation truth is summarized in John 3:16. By bearing witness to the truth Jesus was indeed seeking subjects for His kingdom.

"ART THOU A KING THEN?"

And now this unique King, Jesus, offers Caesar's servant, who momentarily happens to be His judge, citizenship in this spiritual realm without renouncing allegiance to his earthly sovereign. He uses the third person, "Everyone that is of the truth heareth My voice." This is both a statement of fact, as to the method in which Christ builds His kingdom, and also a knocking at the door of Pilate's heart — Pilate's hour of divine grace.

AN INVITATION TO CITIZENSHIP

Alas, what a fatal hour it proved to be! The proud Roman's reply is, "What is truth?" He does not inquire about THE truth. He is a skeptic to whom truth is unreal and visionary. To him such a kingdom does not exist. He considers it mere fiction. "And when he had said this, he went out again unto the Jews." Pilate does not wait for an answer. He closes the discussion. He has no interest in this kingdom of Christ. He turns on his heel and leaves, revealing himself as one who is not "of the truth." The humiliation which this attitude of Pilate caused Jesus, Jesus alone knew.

"WHAT IS TRUTH?"

But of one thing Pilate was quickly convinced, that the charges against Jesus were without foundation. Therefore he told His accusers, "I find no fault at all in this man." His findings were the exact opposite of what the Sanhedrin claimed to have found. Jesus had won an acquittal. The next step would properly have been for Pilate to release Jesus and to give Him the protection of the government. This he did not do; neither did he order the dispersal of the crowd which had delivered and accused Jesus.

"NO FAULT AT ALL"

— G —

Jesus Answered Nothing

And the chief priests accused Him of many things; but He answered nothing. And Pilate asked Him again, saying, "Answerest thou nothing? Behold how many things they witness against thee." But Jesus answered him never a word, insomuch that the governor marveled greatly. And they were the more fierce saying, "He stirreth up the people, teaching throughout all Jewry, beginning from Galilee to this place. (TLL, p. 276)

And when He was accused of the chief priests and elders, He answered nothing. Then said Pilate unto Him, "Hearest thou not how many things they witness against thee?" And He answered him to never a word, insomuch that the governor marveled greatly. (Matt. 27:12-14)

And the chief priests accused Him of many things, but He answered nothing. And Pilate asked Him again, saying, "Answerest thou nothing? Behold how many things they witness against Thee." But Jesus yet answered nothing, so that Pilate marveled. (Mark 15:3-5)

And they were the more fierce, saying, "He stirreth up the people, teaching throughout all Jewry, beginning from Galilee to this place." (Luke 23:5)

The acquittal of Jesus from the charges which they had brought against Him only provoked the chief priests to release a flood of accusations. They "accused Him of many things." These were not carefully formulated charges, but an outburst of vicious accusations poured out from all directions, attempting to offer details and particulars to the former charges. Intensely burning hatred for Jesus, combined with the knowledge of Pilate's cowardly weakness, drove them to intensify their demands.

ACCUSED OF MANY THINGS

Against all of these charges Jesus maintained a calm and unruffled silence. All these accusations were not worth an answer. Conscious of His innocence, He gave no heed to what was said against Him. This strange silence impressed Pilate. In astonishment he asked, "Answerest thou nothing? Behold how many things they witness against thee." This was a strange question for a judge to ask a prisoner whom he had just acquitted. Pilate appealed to Jesus to defend Himself.

HE ANSWERED NOTHING

He seemed convinced that Jesus could silence His accusers if He would choose to do so. The appeal exposed Pilate's own cowardice in dealing with the situation that confronted him. "But Jesus answered him to never a word." There was no need to reply. In this case silence was an impressive answer. It was a rebuke to Pilate for even making such a suggestion after he had acquitted Him.

But the silence of Jesus was more than a mere reproof to Pilate and the Jewish leaders. It was also an act of obedience to His heavenly Father. He knew that His

AN ACT OF OBEDIENCE

kingdom could only become effectual through His death on the cross, and the hour for that death had come. Answering the accusations and compelling Pilate to grant Him release, or even only a reprieve, would have conflicted with His Father's will, which He had pledged to do. The prospect of avoiding or postponing the bitter agony of the cross was extremely attractive to the flesh, and was a satanic temptation for Him. But He did not falter in His obedience.

That silence of Jesus struck home. It was more eloquent than speech. "The governor marveled greatly." Strangely enough Pilate was not angered by it. To the Jewish

THE EFFECT OF THE SILENCE

leaders the silence of Jesus was like a direct judgment upon them, "and they were the more fierce." After going through so much effort and coming so close to success, they would not give up so easily. They became more and more persistent. They perceived the weakness of Pilate, and they crowded him relentlessly. He timidly submitted to this indignity. A torrent of new charges were hurled against Jesus: "He stirreth up the people, teaching throughout all Jewry, beginning from Galilee to this place."

— H —
Jesus Before Herod

When Pilate heard of Galilee, he asked whether the Man were a Galilean. And as soon as he knew that He belonged to Herod's jurisdiction, he sent Him to Herod, who himself was at Jerusalem at that time. And when Herod saw Jesus, he was exceeding glad; for he was desirous to see Him for a long season, because he had heard many things of Him; and he hoped to have seen some miracle done by Him. Then he questioned with Him in many words; but He answered him nothing. And the chief priests and scribes stood and vehemently accused Him. And Herod with his men of war set Him at nought and mocked Him, and arrayed Him in a gorgeous robe, and sent Him again to Pilate. And the same day Pilate and Herod were made friends together; for before they were at enmity between themselves. (TLL, p. 277, *Luke 23:6-12*)

To Pilate the mention of Galilee seemed to offer a way out of the unpleasant matter. "As soon as he knew that Jesus belonged to Herod's jurisdiction, he sent Him to

HE SENT HIM TO HEROD Herod." Roman law permitted a man to be tried in any of three courts, the court of his birthplace, of his residence, or of the place where the crime was committed. It was quickly established that Jesus was a resident of Galilee, and thus legally a subject of the tetrarch, Herod Antipas, commonly called a king. Pilate seized the opportunity which the law permitted him and sent Jesus to Herod, in hope that the tetrarch would judge Him as one of his Galilean subjects. By doing so Pilate completely disregarded his own verdict. In fact, he nullifed it, throwing the whole case wide open again. He had buckled under the pressure of the Sanhedrin.

Herod Antipas was a son of Herod the Great and Malthace, a Samaritan. After the death of his father in 4 B.C., Rome placed him over a part of his father's kingdom, the provinces of Galilee and Peraea. He was given the official title of **HEROD** tetrarch, although he seems to have been popularly known as king (Mark 6:14ff). It was his ambition to be king, in fact, that led to his downfall in 39 A.D. When Caligula became emperor, Herod thought the time propitious to go to Rome and to request a crown from him. Instead, the emperor sent him into exile in Lyons for life. This was the Herod who was publicly rebuked by John the Baptist for committing adultery with Herodias, his brother Philip's wife, at whose instigation Herod had the Baptist beheaded. He later feared that Jesus was the Baptist returned from the dead. It was he whom Jesus called "that fox" (Luke 13:32). Like his father, he lavished money on public buildings, and he founded the city of Tiberius on the Sea of Galilee.

To make the transfer of the prisoner to Herod's jurisdiction so quickly was possible because Herod "was at Jerusalem at this time." He had no official duties in Jerusalem. Presumably he was there for the **HEROD WAS AT JERUSALEM** festival, for as a nominal Jew, whose ambition was related to the Jewish land and people, he would naturally strive at least to keep up the appearance of Jewish zeal. The prospect of a holiday in metropolitan Jerusalem, with the palace of his father or the Maccabean palace for a royal residence, must also have been an inviting prospect.

"When Herod saw Jesus, he was exceeding glad; for he was desirous to see Him for a long season, because he had heard many things of Him." Living at Tiberius, on the Sea of Galilee, and ruling the districts **HE WAS EXCEEDING GLAD** where Jesus carried out the greater part of His public ministry, it was inevitable that Herod should hear a great deal about Jesus and His activity. His fear that Jesus was John the Baptist, risen from the dead (Mark 6:14), apparently soon disappeared.

If Herod had been genuinely interested in the mission of Jesus, we suspect that he could have found many an opportunity to hear Jesus prior to this. But his desire was not, like that of Zacchaeus, prompted by the **HOPED TO SEE A MIRACLE** Lord's concern for distressed and troubled sinners. "He hoped to have seen some miracle done by Him." He merely wanted to satisfy his curiosity and to be entertained. He regarded the miracles of Jesus as an exhibition of skill or magic, geared for the enjoyment and amazement of His spectators. There was no sign of interest in His message, as he had once gladly listened to John the Baptist.

"Then he questioned with Him in many words." Herod quickly forgot the purpose for which Pilate had sent Jesus. He made no effort to conduct a trial. He just jabbered away. The "many words" would naturally have to do with the subject that filled Herod's mind at this time, the signs and miracles which Jesus had done. We may be sure that, had they been proper questions of a judicial nature, or a searching after the truth, Jesus would have given him respectful answers. "But He answered him nothing."

MANY WORDS

The Sanhedrin followed Jesus in a group to Herod so that their Prisoner might not be freed for lack of charges. "And the chief priests and scribes stood and vehemently accused Him." As soon as they could, they brought vehement accusations against Jesus. But their efforts were in vain. Herod was not inclined to take over the trial from Pilate, and he turned a deaf ear to the accusations. Besides, what he knew of the actions of Jesus in Galilee branded these accusations as false.

THE SANHEDRIN REPEATS ACCUSATIONS

"And Herod with his men of war set Him at nought and mocked Him." Herod had been offended by Jesus' refusal to answer his questions or to favor him with a miracle, so he and his court amused themselves by heaping scorn and mockery upon the Prisoner. They interpreted His silence and inaction as failure. Therefore they would not take Him seriously, and they treated Him as a man of no consequence. To them He was a joke and worthy only of contempt. The "men of war" were Herod's retinue and bodyguard, not a special military force brought into the domain of the Roman governor.

MOCKED BY HEROD AND HIS MEN

Throwing a gorgeous, or shining, robe over Jesus' shoulders was here an act of mockery, rather than a symbolic declaration of His innocence. It served to inform Pilate that Herod considered Jesus harmless. The word shining (Gr., *lampros*) could mean almost any color, but it was often used in regard to garments of kings and other leaders, as well as of angels, in the sense of being both brilliant and white. It probably has that meaning in this case.

A GORGEOUS ROBE

After Herod had thus taken revenge on Jesus for refusing to cooperate by amusing him and his court, he "sent Him back to Pilate." Herod thereby deepened one of the sorest wounds of the Savior, showing that Jesus was unwanted by those whom He had come to help and to bless. "He came unto His own, and His own received Him not" (John 1:11). The priests would not have Him; the scribes and elders did not want Him; the people cried, "Away with Him!" The governor was eager to get rid of Him and sent Him to Herod, and Herod did not want Him and so returned Him again.

UNWANTED

By sending Jesus to and fro these neighboring rulers exchanged compliments, with the result that an old hostility was turned into friendship. It would have been better by far for both of them if they had become true friends of Jesus!

CHAPTER FIVE
Jesus Condemned To Death

— A —
Pilate Offers To Chastise Jesus And To Release Him

And Pilate, when he had called together the chief priests and the rulers of the people, said unto them, "Ye have brought this man unto me as one that perverteth the people; and, behold, I, having examined Him before you, have found no fault in this man touching those things whereof ye accuse Him; no, nor yet Herod; for I sent you to him. And, lo, nothing worthy of death is done unto Him. I will therefore chastise Him and release Him." (TLL, p. 277; *Luke 23:13-16*)

With the return of the Prisoner, Pilate saw his hope to dispose of the troublesome case by transferring Jesus to the jurisdiction of Herod crumble. As a result he wavered more and more. Then "he called together the chief priests and the rulers of the people" ("and the people" NIV, NASB, RSV) to make an announcement to them. No doubt the anticipated Passover amnesty (see page 108f.) had helped to swell the crowd in front of the Praetorium. In judicial fashion Pilate summed up the case by stating: "Lo, nothing worthy of death is done unto Him." His own examination had turned up no evidence of transgression. Herod, to whom Pilate had sent them, also corroborated his findings (see page 104).

"NOTHING WORTHY OF DEATH"

Two courts had declared Jesus not guilty. We would now expect the governor to follow through with the release of the Prisoner and the dismissal of the case. That would have been consistent with his own verdict and what simple justice required. Instead he offered a most amazing proposition: "I will therefore chastise Him and release Him." Compromise is substituted for justice. Expediency replaces principle. Pilate hoped to satisfy the revengefulness of the Jewish authorities by having Jesus disciplined (Gr., *paideusas*). By letting them gloat over His pain and humiliation, Pilate would spare them the loss of prestige in having made a futile appeal to the governor. At the same time he would soothe his own conscience with the presumption that he had thereby spared Jesus from a worse fate than that which was being demanded by His foes. He was also averting a serious disturbance among the people. At the same time he would be curtailing the popularity of Jesus, teaching Jesus a painful lesson which He would not soon forget.

COMPROMISE PROPOSED

What a fine display of justice! The punishment in this proposal would be inflicted, not for the sake of the Accused, but for the sake of Pilate and the Jews.

— B —
Jesus Or Barabbas

Now at that feast the governor was wont to release unto them one prisoner, whomsoever they desired. And they had then a notable prisoner, called Barabbas, which lay bound with them that had made insurrection with him in the city, who had committed murder in the insurrection. And the multitude, crying aloud, began to desire Pilate to do as he had ever done unto them. For of necessity he must release one unto them at the feast. Therefore when they were gathered together, Pilate said unto them, "Ye have a custom, that I should release unto you one at the Passover. Whom will ye that I release unto you, Barabbas or Jesus, the King of the Jews, which is called Christ?" For he knew that for envy the chief priests had delivered Him. (TLL, pp. 277-278)

Now at that feast the governor was wont to release unto the people a prisoner whom they would. And they had then a notable prisoner, called Barabbas. Therefore when they were gathered together, Pilate said unto them, "Whom will ye that I release unto you? Barabbas or Jesus, which is called Christ?" For he knew that for envy they had delivered Him. (Matt. 27:15-18)

Now at that feast he released unto them one prisoner whomsoever they desired. And there was one named Barabbas, which lay bound with them that had made insurrection with him, who had committed murder in the insurrection. And the multitude, crying aloud, began to desire him to do as he had ever done unto them. But Pilate answered them, saying, "Will ye that I release unto you the King of the Jews?" For he knew that the chief priests had delivered Him for envy. (Mark 15:6-10)

For of necessity he must release one unto them at the feast . . . Barabbas . . . , for a certain sedition made in the city and for murder, was cast into prison. (Luke 23:17-19)

But ye have a custom that I should release unto you one at the Passover. Will ye therefore that I release unto you the King of the Jews? (John 18:39)

Pilate was deeply perplexed. His plan to shift the responsibility had failed. His offer to compromise fared no better; that fell upon deaf ears. The Jewish authorities were unrelenting. They were not minded to yield an inch. How could he extricate himself from this dilemma? Then suddenly he felt he had found the way out. A custom which he thought would save him was called to his attention. He was sure that his new scheme could not go wrong. "Now at the feast the governor was wont to release unto them one prisoner whomsoever they desired." He would use this practice to achieve his goal. The Roman governor went along with an established custom of the Jews whereby a condemned prisoner was set free at the Passover, evidently symbolizing the release of Israel from bondage in Egypt. Normal procedure was apparently followed, nominating two candidates for release and allowing the people to make their choice from them. The stimulus for Pilate to observe this custom came from the people. "And the multitude, crying aloud, began to desire Pilate to do as he had ever done unto them."

A CUSTOM

The people seeking this annual favor from the governor evidently had gathered at the Praetorium and had mingled with the rest of the multitude.

Pilate saw a new way to release Jesus in this request, and so he eagerly seized the opportunity. He proceeded at once to nominate the candidates from whom they might choose. "And they had then a notable prisoner, called Barabbas." He was an especially notorious prisoner and a Jew. He is described as "*episemos*," having a mark placed upon him. He was a seditious person and a murderer. His name, Barabbas, means "Son of Abba." This man Pilate nominated for release, together with Jesus. Pilate personally spoke the proposition: "Whom will ye that I release unto you, Barabbas or Jesus?" This offer was addressed to the people, not just to the Sanhedrists. It was the privilege of the people to make the choice. Treating Jesus as though He were guilty and placing Him on even terms with a public malefactor was another concession to the enemies of truth. With each concession Pilate was only weakening his own position.

BARABBAS

In his offering Pilate identified Jesus as "The King of the Jews, which is called Christ." The way of sin is in itself folly, and those who go that way are bound to add folly on top of folly. It was foolish to try to reason with people as agitated as the Jews were at this time. It was the height of folly for Pilate at this time to fling the title "King of the Jews" into the faces of Christ's accusers while seeking their cooperation. He was not nearly as clever as he imagined himself to be. He was trying to induce the Jews to follow his crooked course, while he was unable to restrain himself from antagonizing them by the manner in which he referred to Jesus.

THE HEIGHT OF FOLLY

The reason for Pilate's disdain of the Jews is stated by the Evangelists: "For he knew that for envy the chief priests had delivered Him." Pilate saw through the pretense of the Sanhedrists. He recognized that the real motive behind their hostility was pure envy. The Sanhedrists feared that Jesus' success among the people would diminish their influence and power, and for that reason they were determined to destroy Him. Pilate saw these Jewish leaders as fanatics who were craving for innocent blood.

FOR ENVY

— C —

Pilate Is Warned By His Wife

When he was set down on the judgment seat, his wife sent to him, saying, "Have thou nothing to do with that just man; for I have suffered many things this day in a dream because of him." (TLL, p. 278; *Matt. 27:19*)

"When Pilate was set down on the judgment seat," on the platform of the Praetorium, where he awaited the choice of the people, a peculiar interruption occurred.

PILATE'S WIFE INTERRUPTS

Pilate's wife chose this critical moment to gain her husband's attention. She had a very serious warning to issue regarding Pilate's judgment of the Nazarene: "Have thou nothing to do with that just man" (literally: "nothing to thee and that Just One"). Her concern was not so much for Jesus, that He should not be harmed, even though she called Him a "Just One"; it was primarily wifely concern for her husband. She feared the consequences for Pilate if he should bring guilt upon himself by condemning Him.

Scripture has left Pilate's wife nameless. Legend has given her the name of Procla, or Claudia Procula, and has portrayed her as a Jewish proselyte who afterward became a Christian. The Greek Church has even canonized her and designated October 27 as the day dedicated to her.

Pilate's wife offered an explanation for her urgent warning: "for I have suffered many things this day in a dream because of Him." Her dream was not an ordinary one. It was vivid enough to disturb her deeply and to cause her great agony. Only a very unusual dream, to be sure, would warrant her action of interrupting the court proceedings to bring word of it to the governor. Legend has transmitted a very elaborate and fanciful account of this dream, but it fails to sound convincing. The dream appears to have been a divine warning for Pilate. Especially in the Old Testament times God often used dreams (even sending them to unbelievers like Pharaoh and Nebuchadnezzar) to convey a specific message to men. Pilate, a typical Roman, reared in a climate of superstition where dreams played an important part, was deeply impressed by the message. This is evident from his feverish efforts to release Jesus. But he lacked courage for his conviction.

A DREAM

— D —
"Release Unto Us Barabbas"

But the chief priests and elders persuaded the multitude that they should ask Barabbas and destroy Jesus. The governor answered and said unto them, "Whether of the twain will ye that I release unto you?" And they cried out all at once, saying, "Away with this man, and release unto us Barabbas!" Now Barabbas was a robber. Pilate therefore, willing to release Jesus, spoke again to them, "What shall I do then with Jesus, which is called Christ, whom ye call King of the Jews?" But they cried, saying, "Crucify him! Crucify him!" And Pilate said unto them the third time, "Why? What evil hath he done? I have found no cause of death in him; I will therefore chastise him, and let him go." And they were instant with loud voices, requiring that He might be crucified, and cried out the more exceedingly, "Let him be crucified!" And the voices of them and of the chief priests prevailed. (TLL, pp. 278,279)

But the chief priests and elders persuaded the multitude that they should ask Barabbas and destroy Jesus. The governor answered and said unto them, "Whether of the twain will ye that I release unto you?" They said, "Barabbas." Pilate saith unto them, "What shall I do then with Jesus, which is called Christ?" They all say unto him, "Let him be crucified!" And the governor said, "Why? What evil hath he done?" But they cried out the more, saying, "Let him be crucified!" (Matt. 27:20-23)

But the chief priests moved the people, that he should rather release Barabbas unto them. And Pilate answered and said again unto them, "What will ye then that I shall do unto him whom ye call the King of the Jews?" And they cried out again, "Crucify him!" Then Pilate said unto them, "Why? What evil hath he done?" And they cried out the more exceedingly, "Crucify him!" (Mark 15:11-14)

And they cried out all at once, saying, "Away with this man, and release unto us Barabbas!" Pilate therefore, willing to release Jesus, spoke again to them. But they cried, saying, "Crucify him! Crucify him!" And he said unto them the third time, "Why? What evil hath he done? I have found no cause of death in him; I will therefore chastise him and let him go." And they were instant with loud voices, requiring that He might be crucified. And the voices of them and of the chief priests prevailed. (Luke 23:18, 20-23)

Then cried they all again, saying, "Not this man, but Barabbas!" Now Barabbas was a robber. (John 18:40)

The brief delay caused by the interruption of Pilate's wife was used to good advantage by the Jewish leaders. They skillfully agitated the crowd to cry out for the destruction of Jesus. "But the chief priests and elders persuaded the multitude that they should ask for Barabbas and destroy Jesus." The high priests took the initiative in asking for the release of Barabbas. The crowd was easily influenced by their authority and readily yielded to their persuasion. Moreover, Pilate had made it too obvious that he was trying to shield Jesus. The fact that Barabbas was a robber and a notorious murderer did not deter them. It has been suggested that the fact that his murder had been committed during an insurrection (see page 109) may even have made him a popular hero in the eyes of many.

THE MULTITUDE PERSUADED

When Pilate put the question, "Whether of the twain will ye that I release unto you?" they were ready with their answer. "Away with this man, and release unto us Barabbas!" They did not just cast a vote for Barabbas, but they prefixed their demand for the rebel and murderer with a repudiation of Jesus. "Away with him" was a demand that He should be put to death. The custom intended to commemorate the deliverance of God's people was used to destroy their Deliverer.

"AWAY WITH HIM"

Pilate had staked everything on the choice of the people and had lost. What had seemed to him a loophole for escape had turned out to be a noose into which he had stuck his head. When he recovered from his shock of disillusionment, he asked in helpless despair, "What shall I do then with Jesus, which is called Christ, whom ye call the King of the Jews?" What a pitiful sight, this Roman governor! His desperate

"WHAT SHALL I DO THEN WITH JESUS?"

attempts to find a formula for releasing Jesus show us that he was well aware of what he should do with Jesus. Only fear and cowardice made him despair of executing the just solution. In his despicable weakness he begged the accusers to offer him the verdict, which he was too fainthearted to pronounce. He even attempted to arouse favorable sentiment among the Jewish people by referring to the Prisoner as "Christ" and "King of the Jews," but the result was the very opposite of what he anticipated.

If Pilate did not know what to do with Jesus, the people had a very definite idea, and they told him. A mighty shout went up, "Crucify him!" So fickle and depraved is the human heart, that the inhabitants of the city which only five days before welcomed Jesus with loud Hosannas now cried for His crucifixion. If the Jews had been permitted to execute Jesus, they would have stoned Him. But lacking this power, they turned Jesus completely over to Pilate so that he should put Him to death for them. Thus they requested a Roman execution. They were unwittingly asking for the very death that Jesus Himself had prophesied (Matt. 20:19).

"CRUCIFY HIM!"

The governor remonstrated, "Why, what evil hath He done?" His vacillation had resulted in a turmoil in which he lost all control of the situation. Forgetting his position as judge and governor, he pleaded with the people to be reasonable. How could they expect to have the Prisoner crucified if they failed to bring proof of any evil on His part? Pilate should have known that it was futile to appeal to reason in such a state of agitation. Once more Pilate testified to the innocence of Jesus: "I have found no cause of death in him." But instead of following through on this pronouncement, he weakly reverted to his former compromise: "I will therefore chastise him and let him go" (see page 107).

JUDGE TURNED SUPPLIANT

The Jews could readily see that Pilate was weakening fast, and they at once exploited his weakness. They ignored his pleas as well as his unprincipled offer of compromise. With increased intensity they yelled, "Let him be crucified!" they were no longer asking a favor. They were "demanding their rights." In the face of this frenzied coercion Pilate retreated. "And the voices of them and the chief priests prevailed." The chief priests not only prodded the rabble on, but they also forgot their position and dignity, and joined in the shouting. Reluctantly Pilate capitulated and permitted the accusers to dictate the verdict.

THE MOB PREVAILED

— E —

Jesus Is Scourged And Mocked

Then Pilate took Jesus and scourged Him. Then the soldiers of the governor took Jesus and led Him away into the common hall, called Praetorium, and gathered unto Him the whole band of soldiers. And they stripped Him and put on Him a scarlet robe. And when they had platted a crown of thorns, they put it upon His head and a reed in His right hand, and began to salute Him, and bowed the knee before Him, and mocked Him, saying, "Hail, King of the Jews!" They smote Him with their hands, and they spit upon Him, and took the reed and smote Him on the head, and bowing their knees, worshiped Him. (TLL, p. 279)

> *Then the soldiers of the governor took Jesus into the common hall and gathered unto Him the whole band of soldiers. And they stripped Him and put on Him a scarlet robe. And when they had platted a crown of thorns, they put it upon His head and a reed in His right hand; and they bowed the knee before Him, and mocked Him, saying, "Hail, King of the Jews!" And they spit upon Him and took the reed and smote Him on the head. (Matt. 27:27-30)*
>
> *And the soldiers led Him away into the hall, called Praetorium, and they call together the whole band. And they clothed Him with purple, and platted a crown of thorns and put it about His head, and began to salute Him, "Hail, King of the Jews!" And they smote Him on the head with a reed, and did spit upon Him, and bowing their knees worshiped Him. (Mark 15:16-19)*
>
> *Then Pilate therefore took Jesus and scourged Him. And the soldiers platted a crown of thorns and put it on His head, and they put on Him a purple robe and said, "Hail, King of the Jews!" and they smote Him with their hands. (John 19:1-3)*

The people had spoken. They wanted Jesus to die, not merely to be chastised. But though rebuffed, Pilate was not ready to give up. Still hoping to save Him, "Pilate took Jesus and scourged Him." He gave orders

PILATE SCOURGED JESUS to administer this terrible and merciless punishment, gruesome even to describe, thinking thereby to satisfy His cruel and cold-hearted foes. Once more he offered them a part for the whole. Pilate's appeal for sympathy (see page 116) does not bear out the contention of some that the order for scourging meant that the governor was thereby sentencing Jesus to death by crucifixion, since the Romans made a practice of scourging a prisoner before nailing him to the cross. They also scourged people who were not sentenced to death.

We cannot say how many blows Jesus received. The Jewish practice of forty stripes less one was not followed by the Romans. At times the victim was literally beaten to death. Since Pilate did not want Jesus to die,

HE SHOULD NOT SUCCUMB he halted the punishment before His condition became critical. Neither would the heavenly Father permit the brutality to be carried so far that His Son would succumb. That would have interfered with Christ's redemptive work, and all the prophecies concerning Him would not have been fulfilled.

To the delight of His foes, and to the added suffering of Jesus, this torture was undoubtedly inflicted before their very eyes in front of the Praetorium. It was after this

A PUBLIC SPECTACLE ordeal that "the soldiers of the governor took Jesus and led Him away into the common hall, called Praetorium." "Praetorium" originally meant the tent of the general in the Roman camp, but it was later also applied to the residence of military and civil magistrates, wherever that might have been. In this case it was probably the Tower of Antonia.

More than the tacit permission of the governor was present in the soldier's mockery of Jesus. There is no evidence that such was customarily connected with scourging; so the soldiers would not have thought to carry out their extremely insulting behavior except with Pilate's consent. It was part of his strategy to satisfy the Jews, without yielding to their demand for the death of a prisoner of whose innocence he was fully convinced. "And gathered unto Him the whole band of soldiers." Upon orders from Pilate the entire cohort, that is, all who were not otherwise on duty, were summoned. A cohort was normally the tenth part of a legion, about 600 men. They were to take part as spectators and participants in the humiliation of Jesus.

WITH PILATE'S CONSENT

The representatives of the church had mocked the prophetic office of Christ (see page 84f.); the state now mocked His kingly office. The form of derision employed by the soldiers was a mock coronation. "And they stripped Him and put on Him a scarlet robe." The manuscripts offer two readings, *ekdusantes* or *endusantes*, "taking off" or "putting on" His clothes. The first reading would mean that Jesus was first stripped for the scourging, then reclothed and stripped once more for the mockery. The second reading would mean that He was led unclothed from the scourging back to the Praetorium, where His clothes were put back on Him, except that in place of His outer garment they put on "a scarlet robe." Wherever the robe came from, it must certainly have been a ludicrous imitation of real royal garb. The more ridiculous they could make Jesus look, the better it suited their coarse sense of humor and their lust for gruesome pleasure.

A CARICATURE OF HIS KINGSHIP

The caricature of the kingship of Jesus continued by equipping Him with a mock crown and scepter. "And when they had platted a crown of thorns, they put it upon His head and a reed in His right hand." A crown would help give the proper "royal" touch, and by making it of thorns, it would be delightfully ridiculous. Somewhere a reed was found for a mock scepter to add the final touch to the caricature of His kingship. This was thrust into His bound right hand. After the "king" was fitted out for His part, they began the mock adoration. "They began to salute Him, and bowed the knee before Him, and mocked Him, saying, 'Hail, King of the Jews!'" A real king is shown respect, doubly so if he is a good king. The feigned homage and sham obeisance by the soldiers made sport of Him and encouraged the spectators to conclude that His kingly claims were mere pretension.

FEIGNED HOMAGE

To the pagan soldiers, accustomed to bloodshed and the bloody sports of the arena, this brand of savage cruelty was but a game. At the same time, it showed what they really thought of Jesus. "They smote Him with their hands, and spat upon Him, and took the reed and smote Him on the head." Vulgar abuse was heaped upon the patient Prisoner as the soldiers filed by to offer their blows, spittle, and feigned obeisance. While

VULGAR ABUSE

earthly kings were accustomed to reach out their scepter to be kissed, the soldiers snatched the mock scepter from Jesus' hand and struck it upon His thorn-crowned head, demonstrating their conviction that His power and authority were ridiculous. By spitting upon the Prisoner, the vilest of insults, the soldiers behaved no better than the churchmen who preceded them (see page 84f.).

With amazing restraint and forebearance, He "gave [His] back to the smiters, and [His] cheeks to them that plucked off the hair; [He] hid not [His] face from shame and spitting" (Isa. 50:6).

HIS ENTIRE BODY HAD TO SUFFER

Not only one of the Lord's members, but His entire body had to suffer the most dreadful pains. His head was wounded by the crown of thorns, by the blows of the fists, and by the reed; His face endured spittle and smitings; His entire body was scourged, stripped, and arrayed in a robe of shame; His hands held the reed; later, His tongue had to taste vinegar and gall. Because sin dwells and is active in all our members, therefore Christ desired to suffer for our sins in all His members.

Chrysostom

— F —
"Behold The Man!"

Pilate therefore went forth again, and saith unto them, "Behold, I bring him forth to you, that ye may know that I find no fault in him." Then came Jesus forth, wearing the crown of thorns and the purple robe. And Pilate saith unto them, "Behold the man!" When the chief priests, therefore, and officers saw Him, they cried out, saying, "Crucify him! Crucify him!" Pilate saith unto them, "Take ye him and crucify him, for I find no fault in him." The Jews answered him, "We have a law, and by our law he ought to die, because he made himself the Son of God." When Pilate therefore heard that saying, he was the more afraid and went again into the judgment hall and saith unto Jesus, "Whence art thou?" But Jesus gave him no answer. Then saith Pilate unto Him, "Speakest thou not unto me? Knowest thou not that I have power to crucify thee and have power to release thee?" Jesus answered, "Thou couldest have no power at all against Me, except it were given thee from above; therefore he that delivered Me unto thee hath the greater sin." And from thenceforth Pilate sought to release Him; but the Jews cried out, saying, "If thou let this man go, thou art not Caesar's friend; whosoever maketh himself king speaketh against Caesar." (TLL, pp. 279-280; *John 19:4-12*)

"Pilate therefore went forth again." He had been in the Praetorium where the mockery was taking place. There is no warrant for trying to excuse Pilate from direct

"I BRING HIM FORTH TO YOU" responsibility for the soldiers' vulgar mockery of Christ. When he thought that Jesus had been abused enough to satisfy the Jews, he halted the cruel sport and brought Jesus out again. He strode out ahead of Jesus and announced, "Behold, I bring him forth to you, that ye may know that I find no fault in him." They should see Jesus as he had seen Him; then they would be content. The manner in which Jesus had borne abuse all the more convinced Pilate of His innocence. Bringing Jesus forth gave Pilate another opportunity to declare His innocence publicly. By thus appealing to the Jews, Pilate passed censure upon his own action. He pronounced himself guilty of a gross miscarriage of justice.

"Then came Jesus forth, wearing a crown of thorns and the purple robe." Pilate was counting on the dramatic effect. The manner in which he played the scene refutes the supposition that the soldiers were mocking and abusing Jesus entirely on their own. Jesus appeared as Pilate wanted Him to appear. He chose to make a display of His misery. When all eyes were fastened upon the wretched figure of Jesus, "Pilate saith unto them, 'Behold the man!'" Pilate has often been pictured as moved to pity at the sight of Jesus. We cannot escape the fact that Pilate himself had deliberately made Jesus an object of pity. Perhaps this was done to excite sympathy or to make Jesus appear so helpless and pathetic that He should be considered never again capable of inspiring a following, and thus rendered harmless. But Jesus did not want to be an object of pity by men. He wanted to be accepted as their Lord and Redeemer. He was ready to be so afflicted in order to remove their affliction.

PLAYING FOR DRAMATIC EFFECT

If Pilate had been a man of any courage at all he would not have appealed to the Jews again for their approval. He had told them: "I will therefore chastise Him and release Him" (see page 107). Consistency would have compelled him to release Jesus now, no matter what the Jews might say. He should have seen in advance what to expect from this last futile attempt to free Jesus.

A LACK OF COURAGE

"When the chief priests, therefore, and officers saw Him, they cried out, saying, 'Crucify him! Crucify him!'" The immediate reaction of the people to the "*Ecce Homo*" ("Behold, the man") is not stated, but it is noteworthy that the suspenseful silence was broken by the chief priests and officers, not by the people. This time the leaders did not prod the people into action, as when they asked for Barabbas, but they themselves sprang forward with frantic yells of "Crucify him!" They either saw that a sympathetic reaction was forming in the crowd, or they feared that it might. They would therefore forestall any weakening by shouting Pilate down and sweeping the people along with the tide.

CRUCIFY HIM!

When the yelling had subsided enough so that he could be heard, "Pilate saith unto them, 'Take ye him and crucify him, for I find no fault in him.'" Pilate struck back with taunting scorn. His reply, to go ahead and crucify Jesus, was no consent, but rather a taunt, reminding them how dependent

PILATE TAUNTS THE JEWS

they were on him to achieve their purpose. For a moment he gave indication of resolute defiance. He declared that, on his part, he could find no justification for such a sentence. Thus for the third time Pilate declared the innocence of Jesus and denied the demand of the Jewish leaders. But they would not give up.

At last the Sanhedrists decided to change their tactics, and truth scored a victory. They were forced to drop their charges of treason and return to His Messianic claims. They were stung by the insinuation that they were demanding "BY OUR LAW" the execution of an innocent person. If Jesus could not be convicted according to Roman law, then they would charge Him according to Jewish law. "We have a law, and by our law he ought to die." The trial was suddenly given a new direction. Jewish law was substituted for Roman law. Not only did the Jews feel bound by this law, but the Romans were also bound to respect it. In accordance with their usual policy of dealing with conquered peoples, national laws were left in force and given the sanction of Roman authority, except for capital punishment.

However, the Jewish leaders did not want Pilate to try Jesus according to their law. They did not consider him competent for that. They were insisting that he should simply accept their verdict and "HE MADE HIMSELF THE SON OF GOD" pronounce sentence upon Jesus. But finally they were ready to become more specific, and they brought their ecclesiastical accusation against Jesus, as Pilate had demanded from the outset (see page 95f.). They charged Jesus with blasphemy: "He made himself the Son of God." The *Torah* (the Old Testament Law) did indeed make blasphemy a capital offense: "He that blasphemeth the name of the Lord, he shall surely be put to death" (Lev. 24:16). But the charge was false because Jesus did not MAKE Himself the Son of God. He IS the Son of God. He had shown and proven Himself to be so in countless ways.

"When Pilate therefore heard that saying he was the more afraid." Instead of persuading Pilate to yield quickly, the revelation of their reason for condemning Jesus made him even more reluctant. Here we learn that THE MORE AFRAID Pilate's strange maneuvering with Jesus had been inspired by fear. There was something about Jesus, His words and behavior, that made Pilate afraid to condemn Him. His wife's dream (see page 109f.) had added to that fear. And now the accusation of the Jews startled Pilate, causing his fear to be still more intensified. His superstitious mind could cause him to expect vengeance for the scourging and mockery which he had ordered.

"He went again into the judgment hall and saith to Jesus, 'Whence art thou?'" Jesus is returned to the Praetorium for another private examination. Pilate does not ask directly: "Art thou the Son of God?" Recalling "WHENCE ART THOU?" the earlier answer of Jesus, "My kingdom is not of this world" (see page 99), he asks with awe and terror, "Whence art thou?" His origin would tell whether there was anything to the charge of His foes.

"But Jesus gave him no answer." For the fourth time in the course of His trial the lips of Jesus remained sealed. He could not deny that He was the Son of God, and yet to affirm it here would have been understood by Pilate in a pagan sense. Besides, Jesus had already given Pilate an adequate answer (John 18:37), which he had scorned by replying, "What is truth?" Further testimony now would serve no purpose.

NO ANSWER

The reaction of Pilate to this silence is the best indication of how fully justified it was. He became angry. Indignantly he demanded, "Speakest thou not unto Me? Knowest thou not that I have power to crucify thee and have power to release thee?" Already greatly irritated by the lack of respect for his authority on the part of the Jewish leaders, Pilate felt his pride deeply hurt when this Prisoner failed to stoop before him. He therefore reprimanded Jesus as though He were disrespectful of authority and ungrateful for the effort which Pilate had made on His behalf. He could not refrain from proudly boasting of his authority as Roman procurator, implying that if Jesus were wise He would take a different attitude and implore his favor. If Pilate had power to release Him, then why did he not use it?

"SPEAKEST THOU NOT UNTO ME?"

Jesus would not be intimidated. He broke His silence to set Pilate straight. "Thou couldest have no power at all against Me, except it were given thee from above." Pilate was merely boasting in vain. He did not at all possess such power as he claimed. And that power which Pilate had came from above, not from Caesar, but from God. These words were also a warning to Pilate that his power was not to be exercised according to his whims, but that he would be accountable for its use to Him who had given it. No human power could of itself determine whether God's Son would live or die.

POWER IS FROM ABOVE

Pilate had already brought guilt upon himself by the abuse of his power in dealing with Jesus. Jesus knew that his guilt would become still greater, and yet his was not the greatest guilt. His was outranked by one even more wicked. "Therefore he that delivered Me unto thee hath the greater sin." Caiaphas and the men associated with him held the chief responsibility for the utter miscarriage of justice in the trial of Jesus because of the unrelenting pressure which they applied to the governor. But Pilate was not thereby absolved. Instead he had to hear his sin placed next to that of the high priest.

"THE GREATER SIN"

"From thenceforth Pilate sought to release Him." The impression left on the conscience of Pilate made him redouble his efforts to release Jesus. He had tried before, but by comparison his former efforts did not count, so strong was his determination now. But whatever form this determined effort of Pilate took, it was met by increased fury from the Jews, coupled with their most dangerous threat: "But the Jews cried out, saying, 'If thou let this man go, thou art not Caesar's friend.' " John is very brief in his account of what occurred here, but to produce such a reaction Pilate must have declared that he would release Jesus. The Jews had tested

"NOT CAESAR'S FRIEND"

the mettle of Pilate before and had found that he could be intimidated. They knew the spot where the governor was most vulnerable — his fear of accusation before Caesar. This they exploited to the full. They employed a tactic that has the stamp of modern subversive propaganda — the insolent flaunting of a discredited falsehood. "Whosoever maketh himself a king speaketh against Caesar." Not only did they brazenly revive the falsehood that Jesus was guilty of insurrection, but with deadly effect they threatened to accuse Pilate before Caesar of being a party to treason if he would dare to release Jesus.

"What a frightful snarl of lies and hypocrisy! Jesus, who bids the Jews to give to Caesar what is Caesar's, is made an enemy of Caesar's by those who know the contrary and is allowed to stand as such an enemy by the judge who also knows the contrary. Pilate, loyal enough to Caesar, is made to face the charge of disloyalty by the Jews who, disloyal to the core, play the role of loyalty; and this while both Pilate and the Jews know that he is loyal and that they are traitorously disloyal. The scene was a devil's masterpiece in lying." (Lenski)

A DEVIL'S MASTERPIECE

— G —
"No King But Caesar"

When Pilate therefore heard that saying, he brought Jesus forth, and sat down in the judgment seat in a place that is called the Pavement, but in the Hebrew, *Gabbatha*. And it was the preparation of the Passover, and about the sixth hour; and he saith unto the Jews, "Behold your King!" But they cried out, "Away with him! Away with him! Crucify him!" Pilate saith unto them, "Shall I crucify your King? The chief priests answered, "We have no king but Caesar." (TLL, p. 280; *John 19:13-15*)

By their threats the Jews utterly crushed Pilate. His courage was broken, and "he brought Jesus forth." Jesus had been kept under protection in the Praetorium. Pilate had gone out to announce his decision to release Him. Bringing Him out again was an acknowledgment of defeat. He "sat down in the judgment seat" for the final, fateful decision. His mind was at last made up. He was now ready to sacrifice Jesus in order to protect himself. In the Greek language the place is identified as *Lithostroton* (the Pavement). The Roman scholar Pliny defines *Lithostroton* as mosaics. The Hebrew, or Aramaic, name *Gabbatha*, was not a translation of the Greek term, but another name for the place. It means "a raised place" or "elevation."

HE BROUGHT JESUS FORTH

"And it was the preparation of the Passover." The word "preparation" was the usual term for the day before the Sabbath, that is, Friday. Combining the term with

THE "PREPARATION" OF THE PASSOVER Passover simply means that it was the Friday of Passover week, and not (as some claim) the day before the Passover. The term was never used in the sense of preparation for a festival. Friday is still called "preparation" in modern Greek.

The designation of time, "about the sixth hour," has also caused some difficulty, since the Synoptists place the crucifixion of Christ at "the third hour." Two time systems were in use. The Jews computed time in twelve-hour periods, beginning at six in the evening, and again at six in the morning. The "third" hour, then, would be 9:00 a.m. The legal, Roman way of reckoning time was from midnight until noon, and from noon until midnight. This was obviously the system which John used, not only here, but also in other passages (1:39; 4:6). It is argued that the time when Pilate mounted the judgment seat could not have been near six o'clock in the morning, since that would not allow sufficient time for the deliberations before Pilate and Herod. But we recall that "it was early" (see page 90) when Jesus was brought to Pilate, and that the Jews pressed for utmost haste to secure the execution of Jesus. We will have to be satisfied with this solution until a better one offers itself.

THE SIXTH HOUR

Pilate is unable to hold back his resentment against the Jews for forcing him to submit. "And he saith unto the Jews, 'Behold your king!'" He lashes out at them in anger while he retreats. Pilate turns the charge regarding Jesus' kingship back upon them and insultingly bids them to look at THEIR King. He probably got some small satisfaction out of seeing that his insult provoked the Jews to yell still more frantically, "Away with him! Away with him! Crucify him!" They loudly repudiate "their" King and again demand His death. When Israel's first king was presented to the people they shouted, "Long live the king!" (1 Sam. 10:24 NASB) When their last King is presented to them they shout, "Crucify him!"

BEHOLD YOUR KING

Pilate exasperates the Jews still more by delaying his decision while he asks in feigned surprise, "Shall I crucify your King?" You have waited long for the coming of your King, and now that He is here you disown Him! What kind of people are you? Stung by the taunt of Pilate, the chief priests answer, "We have no king but Caesar." They not only repudiate Christ, but renounce all claims of hope for national autonomy, acknowledging pagan Caesar as their only king. This declaration was not made by some irresponsible person in the crowd, but the "chief priests" so degraded themselves. It turned out that this statement of the Jewish leadership was an unintentional prophecy. Never again were the Jews to have a king of their own.

NO KING BUT CAESAR

— H —
Pilate Washes His Hands

When Pilate saw that he could prevail nothing, but that rather a tumult was made, he was willing to content the people, and gave sentence that it should be as they required, and took water, and washed his hands before the multitude, saying, "I am innocent of the blood of this just person. See ye to it!" Then answered all the people and said, "His blood be on us and on our children." (TLL, p. 280)

When Pilate saw that he could prevail nothing, but that rather a tumult was made, he took water and washed his hands before the multitude, saying, "I am innocent of the blood of this just person. See ye to it!" Then answered all the people and said, "His blood be on us and on our children." (Matt. 27:24,25)

And so Pilate, willing to content the people . . . (Mark 15:15a)

And Pilate gave sentence that it should be as they required. (Luke 23:24)

At long last "Pilate saw that he could prevail nothing." It was no use. Expediency, compromise, pleading, and taunts had not helped to set Jesus free, nor did they permit Pilate to evade the responsibility of passing judgment on Him. Every move in the direction of what his conscience told him to be right only provoked "a tumult." The mob constantly grew more savage in its demands, and so Pilate finally surrendered. The Sanhedrin had feared that seizure of Christ "on the feast day" would cause "an uproar among the people." It turned out that the uproar, and that on the feast day, was caused by Pilate's effort to save Jesus from death.

A TUMULT

Rather than meet the requirements of justice, Pilate wanted to satisfy the demands of the Jewish leaders and to do what they desired. He "gave sentence that it should be as they required." They were to have their way. They had forced the surrender. Pilate was ready to placate the bloodthirsty mob, but no mention is made of even an alleged crime. The honor of Jesus remained inviolate. However, the name of Pilate would remain forever infamous.

WILLING TO CONTENT THE PEOPLE

Pilate "took water and washed his hands before the multitude." The washing of hands to show innocency was essentially a Jewish rite (Deut. 21:6-9; Ps. 26:6; 73:13), which Pilate imitated with great effect. With this symbolical act Pilate declared his own innocence in the shedding of Jesus' blood, to which he had given unwilling consent. Declaring his innocence, however, did not make it so in fact. Guilt is not washed away so easily. Pilate was guilty of sacrificing innocent blood to the vengefulness of the Jews, and he felt it. It was a guilty conscience that evoked from him his final tribute to Jesus, "that just person." His wife

PILATE WASHED HIS HANDS

had called Jesus that in her message of warning (see page 109f.). That appraisal stuck with him and finally found expression. By its use he only intensified his own guilt.

In the same breath that Pilate exonerates himself he fastens the blame upon the Jewish leaders. "See ye to it," he tells them. They should answer for it before God and the world. The words which they had only last night hurled at despairing Judas (see page 93), now come back to them.

The Jews had far less regard for the holy blood of Jesus than their pagan governor had. While Pilate dreaded to stain his hands with it, the Jews cried, "His blood be on us and on our children." Israel understood the implications of Pilate's act and accepted it.

CHRIST'S BLOOD INVOKED

They were so anxious to gain their end that they were willing, even eager, to take the responsibility away from the governor and to load it upon themselves. They believed that blood unjustly shed would forever cry out in the world for vengeance and would then be upon everyone responsible for shedding it. However, they were not afraid of Jesus' blood. Like Judas, they had been blinded by Satan. They could not see that there was any guilt in shedding this blood. Therefore they did not hesitate to assume accountability for it. Moved by diabolical force, they even included all their future generations in the guilt of trampling on the blood of Christ.

God is not mocked. The curse which they so lightly invoked upon themselves that morning has followed them down through history with fearful consequences. This blood, so lightly dismissed, soon began to haunt Caiaphas and presumably many others. When the Apostles, full of Pentecostal power and zeal, had filled Jerusalem with Christ's doctrine and were hauled before the Sanhedrin, the high priests accused the Apostles of trying to bring the blood of Christ upon them (Acts 5:28). His blood has continued to haunt the Jews ever since. Yet few of them have repented before God and have found peace of conscience.

GOD IS NOT MOCKED

While the shedding of innocent blood called for judgment, the shedding of the sacred blood of Christ was also a sacrifice of highest order to deliver from judgment. By the shedding of this sacred blood God was reconciled with all sinners. It was a ransom by which mankind has been freed from the bondage of sin, hell, and the power of Satan. Thus Jesus' blood can come upon us for salvation as well as for judgment. Those who have faith in Christ's redeeming blood will be truly blessed forever in heaven.

A SACRIFICE TO DELIVER FROM JUDGMENT

— I —
Barabbas Released — Jesus Delivered

Then released he Barabbas unto them, that for sedition and murder was cast into prison, whom they had desired; and when he had scourged Jesus, he delivered Him to their will to be crucified. (TLL, pp. 280-281)

Then released he Barabbas unto them; and when he had scourged Jesus, he delivered Him to be crucified. (Matt. 27:26)

Pilate . . . released Barabbas unto them and delivered Jesus, when he had scourged Him, to be crucified. (Mark 15:15)

And he released unto them him that for sedition and murder was cast into prison, whom they had desired; but he delivered Jesus to their will. (Luke 23:25)

All that remained for Pilate to do was to carry out the sentence which he had rendered. Mentioned first is the release of Barabbas. "Then released he Barabbas unto them." The people had chosen him in preference to Jesus when Pilate used this notorious criminal in a scheme to have Jesus released by popular request (see page 108f.). Though deserving severe punishment, even crucifixion, Barabbas went free because the Jewish leaders were determined that Jesus should be crucified.

BARABBAS RELEASED — JESUS DELIVERED

"When he had scourged Jesus . . ." This had been done in a vain attempt to satisfy Jesus' enemies without requiring Jesus' death (see page 113f.). " . . . He delivered Him to their will to be crucified." This does not mean that Jesus was actually turned over to the Jews. That was not "their will." Their will was that the governor oblige them and order the crucifixion which had to be carried out by the Roman soldiers. Pilate signed the warrant so that it could be done.

— J —
The Via Dolorosa

Then the soldiers of the governor took the purple robe off from Jesus and put His own raiment on Him. And they took Jesus and led Him away to crucify Him. And He, bearing His cross, went forth into a place which is called the Place of the Skull, which is called, in Hebrew, *Golgotha*. And as they came out, they found a man of Cyrene, Simon by name, the father of Alexander and Rufus, who passed by, coming out of the country. They laid hold upon him, and on him they laid the cross and compelled him that he might bear it after Jesus. (TLL, p. 281)

And after that they had mocked Him, they took the robe off from Him, and put His own raiment on Him, and led Him away to crucify Him. And as they came out, they found a man of Cyrene, Simon by name; him they compelled to bear His cross. (Matt. 27:31,32)

And when they had mocked Him, they took off the purple from Him, and put His own clothes on Him, and led Him out to crucify Him. And they compel one Simon, a Cyrenian, who passed by, coming out of the country, the father of Alexander and Rufus, to bear His cross. (Mark 15:20,21)

And as they led Him away, they laid hold upon one Simon, a Cyrenian, coming out of the country, and on him they laid the cross, that he might bear it after Jesus. (Luke 23:26)

And they took Jesus and led Him away. And He, bearing His cross, went forth into a place called the Place of a Skull, which is called, in the Hebrew, Golgotha. (John 19:16b,17)

The trial was over. The warrant had been signed. "Then the soldiers of the governor took the purple robe off from Jesus and put His own raiment on Him." The blood-stained purple robe had disguised Jesus and made Him unrecognizable. Therefore the mantle of mockery is removed from Him, and His own clothes are put on Him again. All who had known Him before should be able to recognize Him. They should know that it was the popular rabbi, Jesus of Nazareth, who by word and deed had proclaimed Himself as the promised Messiah and Savior, who was now being led away to the place of crucifixion.

EXCHANGE OF GARMENTS

By the return of Jesus' own clothes the fulfillment of another prophecy was aided: "They part My garments among them, and cast lots upon My vesture" (Ps. 22:18). Thus while Jesus was on the cross the soldiers were able to cast lots for Jesus' clothes.

Nothing is mentioned about the crown of thorns, but since that was part of His mock-royal attire, we may suppose that it also was removed. Some, such as Origen, hold that Jesus wore it to the cross, and artists, using artistic liberty, have often painted the crucified Savior with the crown of thorns.

Only the soldiers are mentioned in the action, but, of course, they would not act without orders from Pilate.

Other preparations necessary for the execution of the governor's command are implied, for "they took Jesus and led Him away to crucify Him." The haste with which He was led away for execution placed Jesus outside of the law. The humane section of Roman law, stipulating that two to ten days must pass between the death sentence and its execution, either did not extend to the provinces, or did not apply to Jesus "because He had made Himself King." In modern times condemned criminals are not only mercifully given time to prepare themselves for death, but are also given an opportunity to appeal the conviction. Two confessed murderers spent more than six years on death row in the Utah State Prison before their execution in May of 1956. The Jews were anxious to have the greatest possible haste exercised in the execution lest something should go wrong and Jesus should escape. But they were really playing into the hands of God, who wanted the true Paschal Lamb offered at the Feast (see page 4).

THE GREATEST POSSIBLE HASTE

"And He, bearing His cross, went forth." Just as any other condemned man was required to do, so Jesus was compelled to carry His cross. Pressing down upon His

HE BORE HIS CROSS back, lacerated from the scourging, the burden was brutally painful. Being an instrument of death for the vilest of criminals made its bearing cruelly shameful. The shape of the cross was probably the Latin cross, so familiar to us from the symbolism of the Church. It was hardly as tall or as heavy as it is often pictured, since that would have required a couple of men to carry it. If the cross were exceptionally high, it would have put the lips of the Crucified beyond the reach of the sponge on the hyssop reed for quenching His thirst (see page 162). As Isaac had done (Gen. 22:6-9), so Jesus bore the wood for His own sacrifice. HIS cross it is called, but it was also OUR cross. He appropriated it unto Himself, as though it were His own. What a powerful inspiration His cross-bearing should be to us for figuratively bearing out crosses after Him! Can we murmur and complain about the pain and hardship of the crosses which have been placed upon us when we compare it with His cross?

The way that Jesus "went forth" is traditionally known as the Via Dolorosa, the Way of Sorrows. The street that is now pointed out as this way can, at best, only approximate the original way, since Jerusalem has been **VIA DOLOROSA** destroyed and rebuilt several times since Jesus was there. The only sure and certain way to follow Jesus on the Via Dolorosa today is to do so in spirit.

At the end of a way there is always a place, and the Way of Sorrows led "into a place called the Place of a Skull, which is called, in the Hebrew, *Golgotha*." The actual site of Golgotha (in Greek, *Kraniou*; Latinized, "Calvary"; **GOLGOTHA** meaning "Skull") has long been in dispute. All that we can definitely say about the location is that it was located outside the city, as the walls then stood. The law of Moses required that the execution of criminals take place outside of the camp (Lev. 24:14; Num. 15:35,36; Deut. 17:5); therefore also He who was "numbered with the transgressors" must die outside the gate. Likewise the Old Testament scapegoat, bearing the sins of the people, could not remain in the camp (Lev. 16:21). Jesus, the great Sin-bearer, had to carry the sins out of the Holy City. "Wherefore Jesus also, that He might sanctify the people with His own blood, suffered without the gate" (Heb. 13:12). The name, "Skull's Place," evidently refers to the shape of the hill. The suggestion that it might be derived from the skulls that were lying about on the site of execution ignores the fact that the bodies of the executed were buried in pits, and that such exposure of bones would have been unlawful. It is also possible that this name simply arose among the people on account of the use to which the hill was put.

After bearing His cross for some distance, it was necessary to find another man to relieve Jesus of His burden. While the Evangelists do not spell it out in so many words, we will certainly not be wrong in thinking **THE CROSS TRANSFERRED** that the hardship and abuse which Jesus had to endure through the night and morning had left their effect upon Him, making it impossible for Him to stagger on under the heavy burden. This collapse probably occurred just outside the city wall. Unwilling to be delayed, and possibly afraid that Jesus might succumb on the way, the centurion lost no time to get on with the wretched business, being nettled by the jibes of the impatient priests. Acting under the sanction of military law or custom, he requisitioned the services of a man who happened to be passing by.

He was a man of Cyrene, in Lybia, North Africa, either a pilgrim coming to Jerusalem for the festival, or one of those devout men "out of every nation under heaven" (Acts 2:5,10) who had returned to his ancestral home.

A MAN OF CYRENE But since the latter were usually comfortably retired people of advanced years, they were hardly the kind to be pressed into such service. He may well have been recognized as a stranger, thus encouraging the soldiers to take liberties with him. The claim that he was a Moor is nothing more than an interesting possibility, and rather remote at that. This man is identified as "Simon, the father of Alexander and Rufus." The sons were evidently prominent in the Early Church and well known to the reader's of Mark's Gospel. St. Paul also adds a tender reference to the wife of Simon when he writes to the Roman church: "Salute Rufus, chosen in the Lord, and his mother and mine" (Rom. 16:13). The Apostle had been in her home, under her motherly care. It is commonly assumed that Simon's unexpected contact with Jesus on the way of sorrows led to his conversion.

Simon was "laid hold upon." He was caught and forced into a service that he would not have done voluntarily. He was "compelled" to bear the cross after Jesus.

HUMILIATION To be classed with publicly pronounced criminals and to walk side by side with robbers, as though he were on the way to the execution himself, was a humiliation that a man would neither seek nor do cheerfully. Even to touch the cross, an accursed instrument of death, was repulsive to a Jew. It was not until later that this assignment was spoken of in Christendom as an enviable honor. The constraint was put upon Simon by the soldiers. The King of kings is not even consulted, much less left to determine the action. That also was a portion of His deep humiliation.

— K —

The Lamenting Daughters Of Jerusalem

And there followed Him a great company of people and of women, which also bewailed and lamented Him. But Jesus turning unto them said, "Daughters of Jerusalem, weep not for Me, but for yourselves and for your children. For behold, the days are coming, in the which they shall say, 'Blessed are the barren, and the wombs that never bare, and the paps which never gave suck.' Then shall they begin to say to the mountains, 'Fall on us!' and to the hills, 'Cover us!' For if they do these things in a green tree, what shall be done in the dry?" (TLL, p. 281; *Luke 23:27-31*)

As the procession moved on toward Golgotha, the crowd which had demanded the death of Jesus at the Praetorium was augmented by the pilgrims who were coming into the city and by the curious who always gather when something out of the ordinary takes place. News has an astonishingly swift way of traveling from mouth to mouth, especially when it concerns a name which is already on the lips of the people. Crucifixions were often carried on in a carnival spirit, attracting large numbers of spectators.

FOLLOWED BY A GREAT COMPANY

As the crowd swelled, it became less hostile. No doubt there were many there that remembered Bartimaeus, Lazarus, the daughter of Jairus, and the miracles which Jesus had worked for them, as well as the gracious words which He had spoken.

A large part of the crowd was made up of women. They had joined the strange procession and must have gotten rather close to Jesus, for we read that He turned and addressed them. There was much to arouse their sympathy. They saw the bleeding, suffering figure of a man in the prime of life, staggering under the heavy burden of the cross and going forth to an untimely death. No doubt many knew Him, not as a dangerous man, but as a kind and benevolent person, and as a great miracle-worker who had compassion on the poor and needy. While husbands, brothers, and fathers were railing on Jesus, they showed no direct hostility toward Him.

A SHOW OF SYMPATHY

These women made a demonstration by gesture and voice, as was the custom of the professional mourning women of that day. They were raising the Jewish death wail for Him as one who was as good as dead (Luke 8:52; 7:32; Matt. 2:18). By lamenting Jesus they showed that the people were not all hostile toward Him. They also placed themselves open to reproach, for according to Jewish law it was forbidden to show sympathy or compassion to one condemned by the Sanhedrin. It did not matter to them at this time that their conduct greatly annoyed their leaders.

Jesus was not oblivious to the lamentation of the women, and it evoked a warmhearted response from Him. Turning to them, He addressed them. This act of Jesus had implications beyond the importance of the words which He spoke. It was a momentary reassertion of His divine authority. By requisitioning the Upper Room for the Passover meal, and by requisitioning the colt upon which He triumphantly rode into the Holy City, He had asserted His divine authority. It showed that all things are at His disposal. He refused to relinquish this authority; when He acknowledged to Pilate that He was indeed a king, and while His kingship was cruelly mocked by the crown of thorns, the purple robe, and the reed, it still stood. However, on the way to Golgotha this authority to requisition was rudely snatched from Him. Not He, but the soldiers requisitioned the services of Simon of Cyrene to bear the cross. But now He reasserts Himself. He momentarily halts the procession. Until He has had His say, the urgent business of state and church must wait.

AUTHORITY REASSERTED

The objection that Jesus could not have turned around on account of the cross pressing heavily upon His neck ignores the sequence of Luke's record which places this action of Jesus after the transfer of the cross to Simon. What is worse, this objection ignores that the Bible is the inspired and inerrant Word of God.

Once again Jesus assumes His prophetic office to proclaim the will of the heavenly Father. He also reveals His omniscience by foretelling the Judgment to come. He speaks with authority as the Judge before whom all mankind must appear on that great and final Day. Only after He had reasserted Himself could the unholy business proceed. He, who had held His peace before His accusers, makes His last public statement. Never again would He make a public address. His words from the cross were not addressed to the public, and after His resurrection He did not appear to the public, but only to chosen witnesses. What a sober thought — the discourses of Christ to the people to whom He was sent come to an end. The place was not at all inappropriate for Him, who preached more often under the canopy of the sky than in the synagogues and the Temple. His word had wider range here than it could have attained in the palace or the judgment hall.

HIS LAST PUBLIC ADDRESS

How beautifully the completely unselfish nature of Jesus manifests itself once again. There is not a murmur of complaint about His own suffering, or of the terrible ordeal before Him. Instead He shows loving concern for the souls of those who were heading toward a destruction from which they could only escape by faith in Him as their sin offering.

This final public message of Jesus was very short. It was addressed to the "daughters of Jerusalem." Most of these were women who lived in this city, over which Jesus had shed tears because it did not know the time of its visitation (Luke 19:44). What Jesus said to them also applies to all the inhabitants of the doomed city. Some of these women may have been among the multitude which gave royal acclaim to Him on Palm Sunday. They had been swept along by the popular endorsement of the crowd. Their sobbing on the Via Dolorosa was an emotional outburst of womanly sympathy.

DAUGHTERS OF JERUSALEM

Their sentimental outpouring of tears, however, is rejected by Christ. "Weep not for Me," He tells them. They did not understand that He was sacrificing Himself for their sins. Mere sympathy almost certainly implied that Jesus was guilty; it offered an insult rather than homage. It implied rejection rather than an acknowledgment of Him. Jesus does not want to be lamented. He wants to be believed.

> No muted trump, no mourning weeds
> No funeral dirge His body needs.
>
> Anonymous

"Godly sorrow worketh repentance to salvation not to be repented of; but the sorrow of the world worketh death" (2 Cor. 7:10).

When we recognize our own utter sinfulness we do not mourn for what Christ has suffered, but for what He has suffered FOR US. If our Lenten devotions do no more than arouse our sympathy for the suffering Jesus in Gethsemane and the judgment hall; if they do no more than make us weep over the agony

MORE THAN SYMPATHY

caused by the rough, heavy cross pressing upon His lacerated back, or the cruel nails driven through the healing hands of the Friend of sinners; if they do no more than fill us with anger at the self-righteous scribes and Pharisees, or with disgust for a deceitful Judas and a timid Pilate, then they have failed in their purpose.

> Yet, O Lord, not thus alone
> Make me see Thy Passion,
> But its cause to me make known
> And its termination.
> Ah! I also and my sin
> Wrought Thy deep affliction;
> This indeed the cause hath been
> Of Thy crucifixion.
>
> Sigismund V. Birken
> (*The Lutheran Hymnal* 140:3)

But there is indeed a need for their tears. They and their children need them very badly. Jesus Himself had already wept tears over them before (Luke 19:41). He had in mind the terrifying judgment awaiting them. Addressing Himself to the daughters of Jerusalem, He warns them of the impending destruction of their city. As in His teaching on Tuesday, His prophecy of the city's destruction merges with that of the coming of Judgment Day. When the Day of Judgment comes to strike an unrepentant race, it overwhelms men, women, and children alike. Many of the children now playing in the streets of Jerusalem were about to suffer cruel and brutal torture in the siege of the Holy City. They would be starved, killed, or carried away into slavery because they will have heedlessly followed in the footsteps of their elders in rejecting their Redeemer. In those days childlessness, the curse of women in the Old Testament time, would be considered a blessing, and barrenness an advantage. Then an abnormal beatitude would be pronounced upon the childless, who would be spared the sorrow of multiple bereavement. The thought was conversely stated by the Master in a discourse with His disciples: "And woe unto them that are with child, and to them that give suck in those days" (Matt. 24:19). So terrible would be the tribulation in those days, so great the horror, that people who normally count life as a blessing would prefer and beg for a sudden, violent, death. They would call upon the mountains and hills to fall upon them in order to hide them from the righteous wrath of an almighty God. With this, Jesus reissues the prophetic warning of Hosea (10:8), which originally described the destruction of Samaria by the Assyrians.

WEEP FOR YOURSELVES AND FOR YOUR CHILDREN

"For if they do these things in a green tree, what will be done in the dry?" If such a terrible punishment as they are soon to witness is meted out to one who is Himself sinless, but upon whom the Lord laid the iniquity of us all, what will happen to the guilty when they find themselves exposed to the burning fire of the wrath of God? This is stated in the form of a self-answering question (cf. 1 Peter 4:17,18). The green wood is Jesus, the branch out of the root of Jesse (Zech. 6:12; Isa. 11:1). Only green wood is fruitful. Dry wood is unfruitful. Israel could have been a green tree. She was planted by the

A GREEN TREE

rivers of water (Ps. 1:3), but she had become a dead tree, without fruit, fit only to be devoured by fire (Jude 12; Jer. 5:14; Ezek. 20:47). What kind of wood are we? Have we been grafted into the green branch, Christ, or are we a dead branch on a dead tree? When we weep, may our tears be those of repentance, like Peter's, rather than a mere emotional outburst of sympathy!

These words of judgment to come are also words of mercy. They are a warning to repent before it is too late. Now is the day of salvation! The door of mercy is still open and the voice of mercy and love is still calling. If Jerusalem had repented like Ninevah, it could have found grace like Ninevah. Then there would have been no call for its people to gather every Friday for centuries in front of the Wailing Wall (supposed to contain some of the stones from Solomon's Temple) or to lament the loss of their Temple, which has never been rebuilt since its destruction in 70 A.D.

WORDS OF MERCY

CHAPTER SIX
Jesus' Death On The Cross

— A —
The Crucifixion

And there were also two others, malefactors, led with Him to be put to death. And they bring Him unto the place Golgotha, which is, being interpreted, The Place of a Skull. And they gave Him to drink wine mingled with myrrh, or vinegar mingled with gall; and when He had tasted thereof, He would not drink. And it was the third hour, and they crucified Him. And with Him they crucified two malefactors, one on the right hand and the other on the left and Jesus in the midst. And the Scripture was fulfilled which saith, "And He was numbered with the transgressors." Then said Jesus, "Father, forgive them; for they know not what they do." (TLL, pp. 281-282)

And when they were come unto a place called Golgotha, that is to say, a Place of a Skull, they gave Him vinegar to drink mingled with gall; and when He had tasted thereof, He would not drink. Then were there two thieves crucified with Him; one on the right hand and another on the left. (Matt. 27:33,34,38)

And they bring Him unto the place Golgotha, which is, being interpreted, The Place of a Skull. And they gave Him to drink wine mingled with myrrh; but He received it not. And it was the third hour, and they crucified Him. And with Him they crucify two thieves; the one on His right hand and the other on His left. And the Scripture was fulfilled which saith, "And He was numbered with the transgressors." (Mark 15:22,23,25,27,28)

And there were also two others, malefactors, led with Him to be put to death. And when they were come to the place which is called Calvary, there they crucified Him and the malefactors, one on the right hand and the other on the left. Then said Jesus, "Father, forgive them; for they know not what they do." (Luke 23:32-34a)

[There] they crucified Him and two others with Him, on either side one and Jesus in the midst. (John 19:18)

Separated from His own in the Garden of Gethsemane by a stone's cast, and utterly isolated in His civil and ecclesiastical trials, Jesus was at last to have companions. On the Way of Sorrows "there were also two others, malefactors, led with Him to be put to death." Matthew and Mark call them robbers.

GUILT BY ASSOCIATION

Guilt by association was implied, even though this association was not voluntary, but was forced upon Him. He was classified as a criminal among criminals. This was an added indignity for Jesus. It was an even greater insult to be thus grouped with acknowledged thugs and criminals than it was to be hunted with swords and staves (see page 58). The choice of companions in death probably fell on malefactors with some measure of notoriety, whose names, though unrecorded in unimpeachable historical sources, were hardly unfamiliar to the inhabitants of Jerusalem. If it were not for the unsuccessful maneuvering of Pilate (see pages 107-109), Barabbas might have been bound for Calvary rather than celebrating his liberation. Pilate imposed this indignity on Jesus to get some revenge on the Jews for the pressure they had put on him. The shame cast on Jesus was to reflect also on the Jews. By stigmatizing "their king" the governor was casting insult and ridicule into their faces.

The execution date of the malefactors was undoubtedly advanced, if indeed they were scheduled for crucifixion. Respect for the feast and the special requirements placed on the military to maintain security and order would have made such action most unlikely. However, the clamor of the Jews demanded the immediate execution of Jesus; and, ultimately, the Lord had His own timetable for His supreme sacrifice (see page 4).

AN UNLIKELY TIME FOR EXECUTION

The end of the way was "the place called Golgotha" (see page 125). It is frequently spoken of as a hill, e.g., "Calvary's mournful mountain climb." The custom was to choose a prominent place to exhibit the victims publicly. Jesus had to be lifted up, exhibited. A small elevation would aid to make the crucifixion conspicuous. But God is less concerned with places than with events. The Bible simply calls Calvary a *topos* — a place, "The Skull's Place." Its location cannot be definitely determined. In Jerusalem today two sites are pointed out as possible locations of Calvary. But that is of little consequence. The Christian's faith is anchored in the Word, and not in places. An authentic hill of lamentation and mourning, which is what men would be prone to make it, would detract from the resurrection and ascension. To know the place is not important; but to know and to understand what happened there is indescribably important.

A PLACE

The representation of a skull at the foot of the cross refers to an old legend, first mentioned by Origen (A.D. 185-253), that the cross of Jesus rested on Adam's grave.

Unto this Skull's Place "they bring Him." They did not merely lead Him. *Phero*, the Greek verb used here, means to carry, as a burden. Apparently Jesus had become so weak from the strain of all that He had endured during the past couple of days, that He had to be supported on the last part of the way. As the ailing were once borne to Him (Mark 1:32), so He was now borne to Calvary.

After they arrived at Golgotha, preparations for the crucifixion were immediately begun. "And they gave Him to drink wine mingled with myrrh, or vinegar mingled with gall." Jesus was offered sour wine, drugged with myrrh to give it a stupefying effect. Because of its bitter taste St. Matthew calls it gall. Some consider this to have been a merciful custom to deaden the consciousness of the victim, and thus to make the pain more endurable. Others think that it was employed by the executioners to make the victim easier to handle.

A SEDATIVE OFFERED

This sedative was rejected by Jesus. "And when He had tasted thereof, He would not drink." The soldiers tried repeatedly to force Jesus to drink this potion, but He kept refusing. The offer of the stupefying cup was another Satanic temptation for Jesus. His fevered flesh would naturally cry out for the deadening of the senses to the torture that beset it. To have yielded to this temptation would have

HE WOULD NOT DRINK

cost infinitely more than the loss of seven precious sayings from the cross. It would also have disqualified Him as the sin-bearer. It would have nullified His years of perfect obedience and all the arduous work of His lifetime. Fulfilled was the prophecy of David: "They gave Me also gall for My meat; and in My thirst they gave Me vinegar to drink" (Ps. 69:21).

"And it was the third hour" according to the Jewish reckoning of time, or nine o'clock in the morning by our reckoning. It may be conceded that this indicates an approximate time. In an age in which time-measuring devices were rare it was common to give the time of an event to the nearest hour. The language used to record one of the most significant events in history is a marvel of simplicity and restraint. Divine inspiration designed to bring us the fact of the crucifixion rather than the details.

THE THIRD HOUR

Crucifixion was the most cruel form of punishment ever devised by man until the Inquistion came along with its satanic tortures, and modern Communism, which has perpetuated the art of tormenting its victims. This barbaric punishment which the Romans adopted from the Phoenicians was employed against slaves and hardened criminals, but apparently never against Roman citizens. Death by crucifixion was slow, for despite the indescribable pain due to the wounds, the inflammation, and the unnatural strains and tensions, the vital parts of the body — brains, heart and lungs — remained undamaged. Sometimes death was delayed as much as four days. It was a relief for the malefactor to know that he was to die on the very day on which he was crucified.

AND THEY CRUCIFIED HIM

The agonies of Jesus were increased by the wounds on His back, inflicted by the scourging. Added to the physical suffering was the agony of the spirit, caused by the public shame to which He was exposed, and the curse connected with such a death. "For he that is hanged is accursed of God," (Deut. 21:23; cp. Gal. 3:13). By the crucifixion Jesus was being offered as a sacrifice for the sins of the world. This involved violence, as a sacrifice of blood always does. Yet for all the torture of body and soul, Jesus did not in the least falter in His obedience. "He became obedient unto death, even the death on the cross" (Phil. 2:8). He Himself had foretold the manner of death which He was to die (John 3:14,15; Matt. 20:19).

SHAME AND VIOLENCE

Why was the cross chosen by God as the instrument of death? It was the most suitable manner for the slaying of the sacrificial Lamb. Stoning, the Jewish mode of execution, would have broken the bones and mutilated the flesh. To this the heavenly Father would not consent. This He had indicated in the specific command not to break a bone of the Paschal lamb, the prophetic type of the Lamb of God (Exod. 12:46; Num. 9:12). Decapitation had the same objection. Crucifixion, besides fulfilling the requirement of exhibition and the curse, left only the wound marks on His hands, feet, and side, which Jesus showed to Thomas and the other disciples as proof of His resurrection. These wounds had been prophesied in Psalm 22:16. Crucifixion has also left us a more

THE CROSS

comforting picture of the dying Savior. Suspended between heaven and earth He is the intermediary between the two. His outstretched hands signify that He would draw all men unto Himself (John 12:32).

The cross, once an object of shame, through Christ has become a symbol of salvation. It is proudly displayed inside and outside of our churches as a public confession of faith in the Crucified. It is worn as an ornament upon the clothing of Christians. It is a symbol of faith and hope at the graves of the believers. The touch of Christ has hallowed it. The preaching of the cross is the message that brings life and salvation (1 Cor. 1:18,23).

WE SHARE RESPONSIBILITY

"And with Him they crucified the two malefactors." "They," of course, refers in the first instance to the soldiers. Yet they were only the agents who performed the unpleasant task. If we look closely and carefully at "they," we will see in the picture some very familiar faces, faces of the people with whom we work, worship, and play. And there, in the middle of the picture and looking straight at us, we behold our own image. Yes. we too must share responsibility for the crucifixion of the Son of God. Indeed, we were not in that fanatical crowd at Gabbatha crying for His blood; we were not at Golgotha jeering at Jesus; but our sins demanded sacrificial atonement no less than those of the contemporaries of the Lord.

> Ah! I also and my sin
> Wrought Thy deep affliction
> This indeed the cause hath been
> Of Thy crucifixion.
>
> (*The Lutheran Hymnal* 140:3)

NUMBERED WITH THE TRANSGRESSORS

"And with Him they crucified the two malefactors, one on the right hand and the other on the left and Jesus in the midst." It is worthy of note that the two malefactors who shared the Way of Sorrows with Jesus had their crosses placed on each side of Him so that He occupied the prominent position in the middle. It is not known whether Pilate actually ordered this position for the crosses. However, the entire course of events made this arrangement completely logical. It made Jesus stand out among the three as the foremost. In effect, it said that He was the greatest criminal of the three. And indeed He was bearing by far the greatest burden of sin. "The Lord hath laid on Him the iniquity of us all" (Isa. 53:6); (cp. Rom. 4:25; 1 Peter 2:24; Gal. 3:13). Yet this was no personal guilt, it was assumed sin. He was "a lamb without blemish and without spot" (1 Peter 1:19). "And the Scripture was fulfilled which saith, 'And He was numbered with the transgressors.'" The Scripture was Isaiah 53:12. This was not the first time that men had numbered Him with transgressors. During the time of His ministry He was scornfully referred to as "a friend of publicans and sinners" (Matt. 11:19). What was done in scorn has become a badge of honor to Him and a source of comfort to us.

THE FIRST WORD

While the crucifixion was in progress, or shortly thereafter, Jesus cried out. It was not a cry of suffering, complaint, or malediction that came from His lips, but, what was least expected under the circumstances, a plea of pardon springing from divine love. "Then said Jesus, 'Father, forgive them; for they know not what they do.' " Completely forgetful of Himself, and harboring no bitterness, resentment, or lurking desire for vengeance upon His tormentors, the infinite love of Jesus reached out to His persecutors.

"FATHER"

Even though He was delivered into the hands of sinners and was given a very bitter cup to drink, Jesus still addresses God as "Father." Jesus was one with the Father in the eternal Godhead (John 10:30), knowing His Father's heart. Both now, at the beginning of the crucifixion, and at the end Jesus addresses Him as "Father." The plea to the Father is not for Himself; but, in utter self-forgetfulness, His concern is for others.

UTTER SELF-FORGETFULNESS

For whom did He pray? Certainly the soldiers were nearest to Jesus at the moment, and they were causing Him excruciating pain. These same soldiers had participated in the mockery and abuse of Jesus during and after His trial before Pilate. Yet they were here merely executing military orders. Pagans that they undoubtedly were, the soldiers could not comprehend what they were actually doing. But Jesus did not limit His plea to the small number of soldiers who participated in His execution. He prayed for all who brought these torments upon Him. His prayer included the governor who had issued the orders, and especially the guilty Jewish rulers who bore so much of the responsibility for His crucifixion. It reached out into time and space to include all of His adversaries, wherever they might be. Since we, according to the flesh, are all enemies of God, His intercession also included us.

HE MADE INTERCESSION

Why did Jesus appeal to the Father instead of acting on His own authority? Because every sin is an offense against God, which according to divine justice deserves punishment. The Mediator made intercession for His foes and prayed for the forgiveness of this terrible sin which was being done against Him. He implored the Father to withhold the terrible punishment which was due them, to check the flood of His wrath, and to give the sinners another opportunity for repentance. In support of His request Jesus said, "They know not what they do." They could not have been ignorant of the injustice inflicted on Jesus, but they were still ignorant of the fact that it was the long-awaited Messiah whom they were rejecting and slaying (cp. Acts 3:15-17; 13:27). His intercession asks that the divine retribution be withheld until this ignorance had been removed and an opportunity for repentance given. By this intercession Jesus fulfilled the 750-year-old prophecy "He made intercession for the transgressors" (Isa. 53:12).

— B —
The Title On The Cross

And Pilate also wrote a title and set up over His head on the cross the superscription of His accusation. And the writing was: "Jesus of Nazareth, the King of the Jews." And it was written in Hebrew, and Greek, and Latin. This title then read many of the Jews; for the place where Jesus was crucified was nigh to the city. Then said the chief priests of the Jews to Pilate, "Write not, 'The King of the Jews,' but that he said: I am King of the Jews." Pilate answered, "What I have written I have written." (TLL, p. 282)

And set up over His head His accusation, written: "THIS IS JESUS THE KING OF THE JEWS." (Matt. 27:37)

And the superscription of His accusation was written over: "THE KING OF THE JEWS." (Mark 15:26)

And a superscription also was written over Him in letters of Greek, and Latin, and Hebrew: "THIS IS THE KING OF THE JEWS." (Luke 23:38)

And Pilate wrote a title and put it on the cross. And the writing was: "JESUS OF NAZARETH THE KING OF THE JEWS." This title then read many of the Jews, for the place where Jesus was crucified was nigh to the city; and it was written in Hebrew, and Greek, and Latin. Then said the chief priests of the Jews to Pilate, "Write not, 'The King of the Jews,' but that he said: I am King of the Jews." Pilate answered, "What I have written I have written." (John 19:19-22)

"And Pilate also wrote a title, the superscription of His accusation." It was a common practice to place an inscription on the cross, stating why a person was crucified.

THE SUPERSCRIPTION

In the case of Jesus, Pilate was directly responsible for the wording of the superscription. Such superscriptions, written on a board or placard whitened with gypsum, were often carried as a display on the way to the place of execution. It is also claimed that they were sometimes hung from the neck of the victim. No mention of such a placard is made while the procession moved to Calvary. It was probably dispatched there by some other means, since it appears that the high priests did not read the title until it was affixed to the cross.

While the superscription ordinarily contained the accusation or charge on which a person was condemned, John called Jesus' superscription "a title." That was the proper designation for it, for it named no crime whatever. It merely

"A TITLE"

gave Jesus a title by which Pilate desired to insult the Jews and to gain a measure of revenge on them. "And [they] set it up over His head on the cross." Many styles of crosses have found their way into Christian symbolism and art, but the cross on which Jesus hung was a Latin cross, as is clearly shown by the placing of the title. Sentiment has often placed a halo or nimbus above the head of the crucified Christ, where Scripture has placed the superscription.

Presumably the two malefactors also had a superscription over their heads, but no mention is made of it. The sacred record is interested in the malefactors only in so far as their relationship to Jesus is concerned. It does not even mention their names.

The writing on the superscription was: JESUS OF NAZARETH THE KING OF THE JEWS. The variations in the form of the title, as reported by the Evangelists, are due to the threefold language of the title.

The chief question that concerns us here is what the title meant for Jesus. In the first place it was a vindication, in that He was not charged with criminal deeds. The attempts to brand Jesus with wrongdoing had utterly failed.

A VINDICATION   King of the Jews! Should that be a crime? If Jesus had sought to make Himself a political ruler, He would indeed have been an insurrectionist, as His enemies had charged, and His action would have been considered a crime against the state. But Pilate had found Him innocent of this charge, for he perceived that the Jews had delivered Jesus to him out of envy (see page 109). To be the spiritual King of the Jews had no criminal implications, nor were any intended by the governor in that title.

Pilate was shrewd enough to see that he could irritate the Jews by turning the point of their charge against Jesus against them, recalling how he had mockingly asked them whether he should crucify their king. No

INDICTMENT OF THE JEWS   doubt it was the discomfort of the Jews, who squirmed at this jibe, that induced Pilate to incorporate these words into the title. Besides gaining a measure of revenge on his tormentors, by the title Pilate indicted the Jews before the world. He charged them with disloyalty to their King and with rejecting His rule over them. Pilate also subtly served notice to what anyone else could expect if he should dare to make himself a "king of the Jews."

A title of honor? So it is frequently stated. He was indeed a king, but the title was much too restricted. It was limited to one small nation, to one ethnic group. The kingdom which Christ claimed for Himself was

MUCH TOO RESTRICTED   far greater. His kingdom is as broad as the world. It embraces all mankind. If Pilate had called Him "King of Israel," or "King of Zion," we might well look upon it as a title of honor for Jesus. The names Zion and Israel both have a deeper, spiritual, or symbolical, meaning beside their local or national meaning. While the term, "King of the Jews," was indeed used by the Wise Men from the East in their search for the Christ Child (Matt. 2:2), they also betrayed their lack of understanding by searching for the King in the palace of the national monarch. The prophetic voices spoke of the Messiah as the King of Zion (Ps. 2:6; Isa. 40:9; Zech. 9:9; Matt. 21:5). The Jewish leaders themselves used this religious name of honor in mocking Jesus on the cross (cp. Mark 15:32 and page 146).

In the form in which it was placed upon the cross the title was a deep humiliation for the King of kings, adding to the burden of Jesus' suffering. While Pilate was sneering at the Jews for rejecting their King, he was also rejecting his own King by circumscribing His realm. He was a king far greater than Pilate would allow.

There was indeed little of royal appearance present. It is even unlikely that the crown of thorns with which the soldiers had mocked Him was still resting on His brow (see page 124). No kingly dignity was apparent. But He was every inch a king. By His suffering and death He redeemed mankind and established His kingdom of grace. He is the kind of king we need. No other king has the power to deliver us from the bondage of the powers of darkness. May we open our hearts unto Him and let Him rule there!

LITTLE OF ROYAL APPEARANCE

"And it was written in Hebrew, and Greek, and Latin." Pilate seemed intent to give the title the greatest possible publicity. Therefore he had it written in those languages which all the literate people of that time could read. Hebrew (Aramaic) was the mother tongue of Jesus Himself, the language of the Old Testament Scriptures; the language in which God had spoken to Abraham, Isaac, and Jacob of the promised Messiah; the language in which Isaiah and other Prophets had foretold the sacrifice being brought on Calvary's cross; and the language of the Temple and of the Passover Festival, which had drawn the many thousands of Jews to Jerusalem at this time from the four points of the compass. Greek was the world language; the language of culture and commerce; the language most widely known and used in that day, by which people of varying races and nationalities could communicate with one another; and the language in which the New Testament was to be written. Latin was the language of law and Empire, and the official language of the ruling power of the world. Today the story of the crucifixion, with the words of the superscription, may be read in more than a thousand languages and dialects.

HEBREW, GREEK, AND LATIN

Wide publicity was obtained by the trilingual title. Special mention is made of the Jews. Their leaders did not want anyone to read it and to be influenced by it. "This title then read many of the Jews, for the place where Jesus was crucified was nigh to the city." The nearness to the city made it convenient both for the inhabitants of Jerusalem, and for the numerous Passover pilgrims, to read the caption. Bengel suggests that the superscription may have remained longer on the cross than the body of Jesus.

READ BY MANY

"The chief priests of the Jews," as John calls them (to contrast them with "the King of the Jews"), pleaded with Pilate: "Write not 'the King of the Jews,' but that he said: I am the King of the Jews." They were not slow to realize the implication in the title. They felt stung by the insult, which inflamed their minds and poisoned their hour of triumph. Yet they cunningly asked Pilate to make only a small change in the wording. That small change in the wording would have made a great difference in the meaning. Pilate said, "He is king," but the Jews said, "He is not a king, only an imposter who claims to be king."

A CHANGE REQUESTED

This time the Jewish leaders got nowhere with the governor. Exasperated, "Pilate answered, 'What I have written I have written.'" The indignation of the fanatical

PILATE STANDS FIRM Jews must have caused Pilate no little delight after all that he had endured from them. And he had no intention now to relieve their discomfort. He answered with a firmness that had been lacking earlier in the morning. The title will stand! Nothing will be changed! There was nothing that they could do about it. Unfortunately for him, that firmness came too late. It did not undo his cowardly retreat before the onslaught of the Jews, although it probably salved his pride and palliated his conscience a little.

The hand of God is evident, both in the wording of the title and in the firmness which Pilate showed in refusing to change it. Without Pilate himself being aware of it, he was God's instrument to protect the good name of the Savior.

— C —
The Parting Of The Garments

Then the soldiers, when they had crucified Jesus, took and parted His garments, and made four parts, to every soldier a part; casting lots upon them, what every man should take, and also His coat. Now the coat was without seam, woven from the top throughout. They said therefore among themselves, "Let us not rend it, but cast lots for it, whose it shall be"; that the Scripture might be fulfilled, which saith, "They parted My raiment among them, and for My vesture they did cast lots." These things therefore the soldiers did. And sitting down they watched Him there. (TLL, p. 282)

And they crucified Him and parted His garments, casting lots, that it might be fulfilled which was spoken by the Prophet, "They parted My garments among them, and upon My vesture did they cast lots." And sitting down they watched Him there. (Matt. 27:35,36)

And when they had crucified Him, they parted His garments, casting lots upon them, what every man should take. (Mark 15:24)

Then the soldiers, when they had crucified Jesus, took His garments and made four parts, to every soldier a part, and also His coat; now the coat was without seam, woven from the top throughout. They said therefore among themselves, "Let us not rend it, but cast lots for it, whose it shall be"; that the Scripture might be fulfilled, which saith, "They parted My raiment among them, and for My vesture they did cast lots." These things therefore the soldiers did. (John 19:23,-24)

After the crucifixion came the division of the spoils. "The soldiers . . . took and parted His garments." It is generally stated that it was a Roman custom to allow the victim's clothes as a perquisite to the **THEY PARTED HIS GARMENTS** soldiers who had been assigned to the distasteful task of the crucifixion. By taking His clothes from Him another measure of suffering was added to the bitter cup which

Jesus was obliged to drink. Ever since God clothed Adam and Eve in Eden it has been a shame to appear disrobed in public. The shame of nakedness in public constituted severe punishment for Jesus. It was part of the penalty He had to pay. It was also a reflection upon His lordship. Jesus had demonstrated to His disciples that He governed the property of the world. He had His tax money taken out of the mouth of a fish. He requisitioned the boat from which He preached; the colt on which He rode into Jerusalem; the room in which He celebrated the Passover with His disciples — but now He was deprived of the last thing which He owned, as though He were already dead. "Though He was rich, yet for your sakes He became poor" (2 Cor. 8:9). What a complete contrast we have here to what happened on Palm Sunday! On the first day of the week the multitude spread their garments in the way so that the Son of David might ride over them in triumph into the Holy City. On Friday, outside of the city gate, He was robbed of His own garments. He who possesses all things was allowed to retain nothing. He became the poorest of the poor.

In His last will and testament He conveys no earthly treasure. The inheritance He leaves is His body and blood. At the beginning of His earthly life the Orient had sent its gift-bearers, at its close the Occident sends its plunderers.

In a climate such as we find in Jerusalem, clothes are a necessary protection against the burning rays of the sun. To hang disrobed under the sun without any opportunity whatever to obtain relief most certainly added to Jesus' physical agony, which was already more than extreme.

Beneath the Cross we are bound to recall the command of Jesus not to be concerned about raiment, but rather to seek the kingdom of heaven (Matt. 6:25). Instead of costly clothes, which lend themselves to display, and in which pride and vanity often manifest themselves, the garments that we should be most concerned about are Christ's "garments of salvation" and His "robe of righteousness" (Isa. 61:10). Unfading beauty will adorn our robes only when they have been washed and made white in the blood of the Lamb (Rev. 7:14).

CONCERN ABOUT RAIMENT

The parting of the garments was done by "casting lots upon them." This raises the question as to what His clothing consisted of. Only the tunic is mentioned specifically, and for the reason that it was disposed of separately. The usual attire of a Jew consisted of five parts: the headdress, the shoes (or sandals), the chiton, the tunic, and the girdle (or belt). Presumably Jesus wore these five articles of clothing. The articles of comparable value were obviously divided into four parts, since the military detail that crucified Jesus was composed of four soldiers, and, as Mark indicates, were disposed of by lot. All that remained then was the tunic. To give each man an equal part would have required them to tear it, but this would have meant to destroy its value, for it "was without seam, woven from the top throughout." Nothing would seem more natural for soldiers who were accustomed to gambling than to cast lots for the tunic — winner take all. The manner of casting lots varied, and we have no way of knowing how it was done in this particular instance.

LOTS CAST FOR THE CLOTHING

This is as much as the Holy Spirit has willed us to know about the garments of Jesus. Legends about them have sprung up in profusion. Innumerable claims of relics have been made. They are not worthy of discussion. It is infinitely better to have Jesus than a scrap of the garments which He wore. To worship Him who suffered for us on the cross is a most God-pleasing activity, but giving adoration to purported relics of Him is an offense against the Holy One.

What was done with the garments of Jesus was done "that the Scripture might be fulfilled." Hardly anything about the events on Calvary could seem more incidental or more insignificant than the manner in which the clothes of Jesus were disposed of, and yet it was another indisputable proof that this Jesus of Nazareth was indeed the promised Messiah. More than a thousand years before, the inspired David had foretold this detail (Ps. 22:18).

THE SCRIPTURES FULFILLED

The fulfillment of this ancient prophecy was not caused by the followers of Jesus who might be accused of deliberate and planned action, but by hardened, professional soldiers, who were so indifferent to what was happening, that, at the world's most momentous and crucial hour, they gambled for a few garments. All that they were interested in was to perform their assigned task and to get a little, very little, personal gain on the side. While they might have won Paradise, as the malefactor did, their interest and concern rose no higher than perishable rags. They were typical children of the world. They were included in the prayer Jesus made on behalf of those who were ignorant of what they were doing (see page 137).

"THESE THINGS THEREFORE THE SOLDIERS DID"

It was the duty of the soldiers to see that there would be no interference in carrying out the sentence. In addition to the four executioners of Jesus and the two other quaternions who had been assigned to the crucifixion of the malefactors, the guard would normally include a detachment of Roman soldiers, under a centurion, strong enough to cope with any eventuality.

"THEY WATCHED HIM"

— D —

Jesus Mocked On The Cross

And the people stood beholding. And they that passed by reviled Him, railed on Him, wagging their heads, and saying, "Ah, thou that destroyest the Temple, and buildest it in three days, save thyself! If thou be the Son of God, come down from the cross." And the rulers also with them derided Him. Likewise also the chief priests mocked Him, with the scribes and elders, saying, "He saved others. Himself he cannot save. If he be Christ, the King of Israel, the Chosen of God, let him now come down from the cross, that we may see, and we will believe him. He trusted in God; let Him deliver him now, if He will have him; for he said, 'I am the Son of God.' " The thieves also, which were crucified with Him, cast the same in His teeth. And the soldiers also mocked Him, coming to Him, and offering Him vinegar, saying, "If thou be the King of the Jews, save thyself!" (TLL, pp. 282,283)

And they that passed by reviled Him, wagging their heads, and saying, "Thou that destroyest the Temple, and buildest it in three days, save thyself! If thou be the Son of God, come down from the cross." Likewise also the chief priests mocking Him, with the scribes and elders, said, "He saved others. Himself he cannot save. If he be the King of Israel, let him now come down from the cross, and we will believe Him. He trusted in God; let Him deliver him now, if He will have him; for he said, 'I am the Son of God.' " The thieves also, which were crucified with Him, cast the same in His teeth. (Matt. 27:39-44)

And they that passed by railed on Him, wagging their heads, and saying, "Ah, thou that destroyest the Temple, and buildest it in three days, save thyself, and come down from the cross." Likewise also the chief priests, mocking, said among themselves with the scribes, "He saved others. Himself he cannot save. Let Christ, the King of Israel descend now from the cross, that we may see and believe!" And they that were crucified with Him reviled Him. (Mark 15:29-32)

And the people stood beholding. And the rulers also with them derided Him, saying, "He saved others; let him save himself, if he be Christ, the Chosen of God." And the soldiers also mocked Him, coming to Him and offering Him vinegar, and saying, "If thou be the King of the Jews, save thyself!" (Luke 23:35-37)

During these crucial hours on Calvary, "the people stood beholding." A great multitude, including the wailing women, had followed the procession out of the city to Golgotha. Others, coming into the city, certainly stopped to see what was going on, for the place of the crucifixion was prominently public. These stood, looking on with morbid curiosity and grim silence. The spectacle was fascinating to them. They were watching every step. These people had no part in the jeering, but, on the other hand, they also offered no rebuke or reproach to the mockers. In their conduct they showed themselves neither friend nor foe. They were just bystanders. They remind one of the Laodiceans (Rev. 3:15,16), who were neither hot nor cold. If aroused, they could sing "Hosanna!" on Sunday and shout "Crucify!" on Friday. They could wail and lament on the way and stand in spellbound silence at the destination.

THE PEOPLE STOOD BEHOLDING

As we observe them, they seem to be utterly indifferent to the verdict of Jesus, "He that is not with Me is against Me!" (Luke 11:23), and oblivious to the deep suffering that their idle curiosity was causing the Savior. But soon they must smite their breasts and return, either to be touched by the power of Pentecost to confess Christ crucified, or stubbornly to reject the sacrifice made for them, which they had been witnessing.

But while many of the spectators on Golgotha were indifferent to the suffering Savior, "they that passed by reviled Him": the rulers, chief priests, scribes, elders, the thieves, and the soldiers. The mockery on Golgotha served to unite the most diverse human types, the high and the low, the influential and the menial,

OTHERS REVILED HIM

those from the palace and those from the ghettos. Those "that passed by" must have been Jews from the city who had been present at the trial, for we hear them repeating the very thing that was said in the night session of the Sanhedrin by the last two witnesses. This would, of course, not prevent others from coming along the way and parroting the charges that were made against Jesus. More surprising is the part played in the sorry spectacle by the leaders of the Jews. Even here, under public observation, the Sanhedrists discard their dignity and their lofty reputation. They forget who they are and give way to the basest passions. The chief priests are not ashamed to degrade themselves with their taunting cries and their insults upon the silently suffering Christ. While the soldiers had made sport of Jesus in the Praetorium, it is not likely that they would have joined in the mockery if they had not had the evil example of the "noble" Sanhedrists before them. Instigated by all these taunts, even the thieves join in and "cast the same in His teeth." One group takes up the cry from the other. The main guilt, however, rests upon the leaders, who again serve as the instigators, as they had done before outside the judgment hall.

Matthew and Mark call the speaking against Jesus *eblasphemoun,* that is: blaspheming, mocking, speaking against God in anger or derision. The Jews had falsely condemned Jesus as a blasphemer; now they were guilty of blasphemy themselves.

Mocking words were accompanied by mocking gestures and behavior. By "wagging their heads" the people showed what they thought of Jesus and the statements which they attributed to Him, *viz.,* about His destroying the Temple and rebuilding it, and about His being the Son of God. In view of the literal fulfillment of all other prophecies concerning the suffering Savior, it is not assuming too much to find here the literal fulfillment of Psalm 22:7, "All they that see Me laugh Me to scorn; they shoot out the lip; they shake the head." They were mocking Jesus with facial distortions, twisting their features out of shape. It was a vulgar display of bad manners and was intended to demonstrate their contempt for Him. Even if their gestures had been directed against a real criminal, it would have been considered most shameful conduct.

WAGGING THEIR HEADS

The Evangelists proceed to report the substance of their mockery. It was directed against the power and authority of Jesus, and against His faith in His Father. That it was so confined was unwitting testimony to His blameless conduct. Five particulars have been specified in the sacred record:

SUBSTANCE OF THE MOCKERY

1. Christ's prophecy concerning the rebuilding of the Temple was distorted and held up to ridicule. "Ah, thou that destroyest the Temple, and buildest it in three days, save thyself!" This prophecy of Christ was made at the first cleansing of the Temple (John 2:19) in answer to the demand for a sign of His authority. It was misunderstood, but never forgotten. Now they hurled the words back at Him. Let Him begin this miraculous building! The implication is that He had talked big, but was really unable to do anything. If He expected them to believe His tall tales about rebuilding the Temple, then He should

RE: HIS REBUILDING THE TEMPLE

first deliver Himself out of His present predicament. What they failed to see was that even at this time the very prophecy was beginning to be fulfilled. "Come down and build the Temple!" they said, unaware that they were looking at the very Temple of His body, which He was about to rebuild.

2. The second group of jeers was directed against His deity. "If Thou be the Son of God . . ." The IF is a blasphemous challenge expressing their unbelief and contempt.

RE: HIS CLAIMS OF DEITY

It should be nothing for "the Son of God" to come down from the cross — right there before everybody — not harmed in the least. But, of course, they jibe, contending that Jesus cannot do that. All appearances were now definitely against His being the Son of God. Should a few Jewish servants and Roman soldiers really be able to overpower and actually to subdue the Son of God?

3. They continue, "He saved others. Himself he cannot save." The miracles of Jesus are injected into the mockery. These had been performed in city and countryside. They had been witnessed by countless people and

RE: HIS MIRACLES

had been given wide publicity by them. "He saved others," they sneer. Do they really mean to deny that He had saved anybody or rescued anyone from danger or affliction? Can they have been so blinded by their intense hatred as to deny all His miracles? Or were they conceding miracles which were so manifestly clear that even they could not deny them? If it was the latter, then their taunts imply that the conclusive miracle — His saving Himself — is still lacking, and will remain lacking. It was true in a sense that "Himself He could not save," but the reason was not in His own weakness, or in the might of the foe, but precisely BECAUSE He came to offer Himself up to save others. The bonds that held Christ captive on the cross were the bonds of His everlasting love and mercy for the lost human race.

4. The Jewish leaders show a diabolical skill in shooting their cruel barbs deep into the heart of Jesus. They wound Him deeply by ridiculing His Messianic office. "If he be the Christ, the King of Israel, the Chosen of

RE: HIS MESSIANIC OFFICE

God . . ." This sneer is not addressed to Christ directly, but this they "said among themselves." They speak contemptuously of Him in the third person, but what they say is intended for His ears. This makes their scoffing all the more nasty and mean. The Jews are demanding that Jesus save Himself by His Messiahship and prove Himself the true Messiah — if He can. To them the fact of His dying on the cross was plain evidence that God had not elected Him, but rather rejected Him. Instead of using Pilate's wording in the title, "King of the Jews," they mockingly refer to Him as "the King of Israel." This name was the religious name of honor for the people. The term "Jews" indicated nationality alone. But in their manner of speaking of Him they scornfully cast aside His royal qualifications. He — King of Israel? Anything but that!

5. And finally, they jibe, "He trusted in God." With satanic cleverness the enemies seek out the words which will hurt Jesus the most. He had spoken much of His

RE: HIS FILIAL TRUST heavenly Father. He showed a true Son's trust in His Father. Now this very trust is held up to ridicule. His personal faith is scoffed at. They jeer that God will have nothing to do with Him. God has disowned Him. He will not have Him. The proof, they say — God does not intervene. If God wanted Him, He would certainly deliver Him. What makes this mockery cut all the deeper is that the insult is couched in the words of Scripture recorded in Psalm 22:8. The inspiration for such a misapplication of the Scriptures comes from the Tempter, who employed the same tactics in the wilderness. Great David's greater Son is mocked in words reminiscent of the reproach thrown at David: "Where is thy God?" (Ps. 42:10).

The mockers challenge Jesus to demonstrate His divine power — if He has it. The taunts echo what Satan had set before Jesus in the temptation in the wilderness — the challenge to prove His divine power. **"COME DOWN FROM THE CROSS"** Then it was to turn stones into bread; now it is to step down from the cross. Christ withstood both temptations. These mockers only knew and understood power that is used for selfish interests. That Jesus does and will use His power in His own, and far more glorious, way is hidden from them. It is not a Savior who comes down from the cross that we need, but a Savior who ascends the cross; not One who would save Himself, but who desires to save us sinners. Human reason cannot see and understand this. That is a divine mystery.

"That we may see, and we will believe Him," they say. A wicked and adulterous generation frequently asks for a sign, but no sign will be given except the sign of the Prophet Jonah (Matt. 12:39). They want a miracle, **"AND WE WILL BELIEVE"** but one which corresponds to their stipulated conditions. And the condition which they lay down leaves no room for faith. They say that they must have it by sight. It would have been an easy matter for Jesus to come down from the cross. Those four nails would not have held Him, neither would the Roman guard have prevented Him, had He chosen to use His power. But the people still would not have believed. They had seen many miracles performed by Him, but they ascribed them to Beelzebub, the chief of the devils. They doubtless would have done that again if He should actually perform this miracle. Jesus had Himself answered this line of reasoning when He said: "If they hear not Moses and the Prophets, neither will they be persuaded, though one rose from the dead" (Luke 16:31). And that saying was proven to be true on Easter Day, when that same One rose from the dead.

By all this mockery Christ was being provoked to defend Himself. They were goading Him to make a reply. But Jesus held His peace. Suffering the mockery was an act of payment, and therefore He would not reply. He bore **VICIOUS TONGUES** it in our stead. The intensely burning hatred of the enemies of Jesus was revealed in the mockery. They could no longer spit upon Him, so they stabbed Him as deeply as possible with their cowardly and vicious tongues. This mockery represents the "church" at its worst. By it the Sanhedrists were moreover making themselves abominable before God, who says: "He that justifieth the wicked, and condemneth the just, even they both are an abomination to the Lord" (Prov. 17:15).

"The soldiers" put action into their mockery by "coming to Him and offering Him vinegar," or the cheap, sour wine which was provided for them for their refreshment during the long wait. Coming up to the cross, they held out their wine to Him and told Him to come and get it. That was cruel mockery indeed for the Sufferer, who had nothing touch His lips since the night before, was burning with fever, and would have welcomed any refreshment. This mockery took place before the darkness fell. It had no connection with the drink given to Him later by means of a sponge, which took place after the darkness.

MOCKERY IN ACTION

How easily Christ could have put an end to all the mockery! He might have caused fire and brimstone to rain from heaven, etc., but in His divine mercy His enemies were given time for sober reflection and repentance.

Mockery was nothing new for Jesus. Not only had He been reviled and ridiculed during the trial, but even long before it began He repeatedly felt the scorn of those whom He had come to save. At the home of Jairus "they laughed Him to scorn" (Matt. 9:24). He was called "gluttonous and a winebibber" (Matt. 11:19). "The Pharisees derided Him" (Luke 16:14). The Jews said: "Thou ... hast a devil" (John 8:48).

In enduring mockery, too, the disciple is not above his Master. Faithful followers of Jesus should not be surprised if they become the target of ridicule as long as they are living in the same world.

— E —
The Pentitent Malefactor

And one of the malefactors which were hanged railed on Him, saying, "If thou be Christ, save thyself and us!" But the other, answering, rebuked him, saying, "Dost not thou fear God, seeing thou art in the same condemnation? And we indeed justly; for we receive the due reward of our deeds: but this Man hath done nothing amiss." And he said unto Jesus, "Lord, remember me when Thou comest into Thy kindgom." And Jesus said unto him, "Verily, I say unto thee, today shalt thou be with Me in Paradise." (TLL, p. 283; *Luke 23:39-43*)

Even those who were crucified with Jesus joined in the mockery and contempt which was heaped upon Him. Matthew and Mark use the plural when they refer to the malefactors' part in reviling Jesus. (Matt. 27:44; Mark 15:32), while Luke says, "And one of the malefactors . . . railed on Him." Some have sought to explain the difference by ascribing the use of the "categorical plural" to Matthew and Mark, *viz.*, that the scoffers were of every class or category: Sanhe-

EVEN THE MALEFACTORS

drists, people, soldiers, and also the malefactors. A much simpler solution is that Luke is reporting a moment or scene of the great drama on Calvary different from the one the other Evangelists report, and that therefore there is no discrepancy in taking each account literally. Accordingly, both of the malefactors were first swept along by the tide of mockery and ridicule, but, before long, one of them came to repentance. Luke is interested in bringing this fact, particularly because it evoked one of the last words of Jesus from the cross.

Historians have noted the tendency of crucified men to become enraged like trapped animals and to hurl insults and imprecations on the onlookers, and it seems to have made little difference on whom they turned in their excess pain. It appears that at one point both malefactors "railed on Him."

The mockery of the impenitent malefactor follows the pattern set by the Sanhedrists: "If thou be the Christ, save thyself and us." With a bitter taunt he challenges Christ to use His power to prove His claims. If by any chance Jesus could be prodded into action, then He might provide an escape from death for him and his companion. The damnable "if" of the Jewish leaders, which the malefactor repeats, shows that he does not really put any stock in the kingship of his fellow-crucified, neither is there any sign of repentance for his sins. His only desire is to cheat the law of its victim.

THE PATTERN OF THE SANHEDRISTS

We pass by the inference, sometimes made, that the impenitent malefactor was a Jew, while the penitent was a Gentile, as mere speculation.

The penitent malefactor rebuked his companion for his mockery of Jesus, retracting everything that he had previously said in a similar vein. Thus he became the first to protest against the wickedness taking place on Calvary. In fact, his was the only voice raised at Calvary in defense of Jesus. With his rebuke he rejected the popular side, with which he had first cast his lot. Not only were the numbers against him now, but also the appearance of right and the weight of authority. Even Jesus' own disciples had deserted Him.

HE REBUKED HIM

The time and opportunity to confess his faith were very limited for the penitent malefactor, but he made full use of them in rebuking his companion on the other side of Jesus. This was a genuine good work — a kind which many Christians in far more favorable circumstances have shied away from for fear of men.

The tone of the rebuke was in sharp contrast with the mockery. He remonstrated, "Dost not thou fear God?" If common decency would not keep him from heaping scorn upon an innocent person, at least the fear of God should do so. Does he not realize that in a few fours he must stand before his Maker? Does he not know that it is a fearful thing for an enemy of the living God to fall into His hands (Heb. 10:31)? As for the penitent malefactor, the fear of God, which is the "beginning of wisdom," will not allow him to use his tongue against Jesus any more.

"DOST NOT THOU FEAR GOD?"

"Seeing thou art in the same condemnation" — the condemnation was not necessarily for the same crime. Condemnation here means that to which one is condemned, or the judgment pronounced. All three received the same judgment. And yet, what a vast difference there was. In the case of the malefactors the judgment was fully justified. Their own evil deeds were responsible for their shame and suffering. "We receive the due reward of our deeds," the man added. They were only getting what they had coming to them because of their crimes. This was a frank and honest confession of sin, which is evidence of sincere repentance. Contact with Jesus and His Word had led him to repentance. His contrition was coupled with faith. "But this Man hath done nothing amiss." These words were a final, clear testimony to the innocence and purity of Jesus.

"THE SAME CONDEMNATION"

We marvel at such comprehension. How did this evildoer arrive at it? Men have ever been intrigued by the question of this man's background and by the possibility of previous contact with Jesus, or previous knowledge of Him and His Word. As far as we know, he had no contact with Jesus until they started on the Way of Sorrows together. But brief as the time of contact was, the circumstances were most favorable clearly to reveal the true character of Jesus. His enemies even had to confess that "never spoke any man like this Man." It was just as true that never did any man suffer like this Man. His patience and humility under bitter scorn and excruciating pain and His intercessory prayer for His tormentors were so strikingly out of the ordinary, that the malefactor soon recognized that they belonged to an extraordinary person. Likewise, he learned some vital truths about Jesus from the mockery of the Jews, which he listened to for possibly two full hours, and which plainly showed that Jesus did not suffer for any crime, but solely because He claimed to be the promised Messiah and the Son of God.

STRANGELY FAVORABLE

The malefactor's heart had been melted by the Holy Spirit, who led him to bless the One whom the others cursed. He became the last person to testify in favor of Jesus before His death. His rebuke and confession were followed by a plea directed to Jesus: "Lord, remember me when Thou comest into Thy kingdom." He is thus also the first to come to Christ Crucified and to believe on Him as his Lord and Savior. Without doubts or misgivings he addressed Him in prayer. The word "Lord" is missing in some manuscripts. To omit it does not diminish the malefactor's faith in the least, for whether the word was actually used or not, the content of the prayer shows that his heart had submitted to the sovereignty of Jesus. He did not ask for a sign or proof of that sovereignty. His heart needed none.

LAST AND FIRST

With the simplicity of great faith he prays, "Remember me." He believes that Jesus had the full power to grant his request, even though He was about to die upon the cross. How different his plea is from the challenge of his companion, and from what we would expect under the circumstances. He does not ask Jesus to help him down from the cross, nor does he suggest that He might alleviate his physical sufferings.

"REMEMBER ME"

Only to be remembered is his humble request. He wants Jesus to remember his immortal soul. By faith he knows that all that he needs for time and for eternity is to be remembered by Jesus. He does not prescribe or suggest to Him how He should do this. He does not ask for a reserved seat in heaven, either at the right hand or on the left. Standing room will suffice him. He is content to leave the ways and the means entirely to Jesus.

Being remembered is the opposite of being forgotten. To be forgotten by God is to be excluded from His kingdom.

While the Lord's chosen disciples were not yet persuaded of His ultimate triumph, this man confesses that Jesus' impending death will not hinder His kingdom. His eyes remain unclouded by the events on Calvary so that he can see His "kingdom" clearly. He understands what Pilate was unable to comprehend, that Christ's kingdom is not an earthly domain, but a celestial realm. His faith causes him to rise above the Jewish dreams of a political kingdom of earthly power and glory.

"THY KINGDOM"

Jesus often mentioned His "kingdom" in His teachings, and for this reason the plea of the malefactor must have provided Him a moment of great joy in the midst of His suffering.

A variant reading in the manuscripts raises the question of whether the petition should read "into Thy kingdom" or "in Thy kingdom." "Into" His kingdom would mean at the time when He left His earthly life. On the other hand, to come "in" His kingdom would have Him come *in connection with it,* at the end of the world, when the kingdom of God will have its consummation. The answer of Jesus was about to satisfy the malefactor's plea.

In the face of all the taunts and mockery Jesus remained silent, but such a plea as this, even from a contrite criminal, had to be answered without delay. "And Jesus said unto him, 'Verily, I say unto thee, today shalt thou be with Me in Paradise.' "

ANSWERED WITHOUT DELAY

The comforting words which Jesus here addressed to the malefactor were emphasized with a divine oath, "Verily, I say unto thee." The word translated as "verily" is "Amen," a word expressing truth and certainty — a word which Jesus also used as a name for Himself: "These things saith the *Amen*" (Rev. 3:14).

The promise exceeded the petition. The penitent malefactor had spoken to Jesus about the future, and now Jesus spoke to him of "today." To connect "today" with the preceding words, *viz.,* "I say unto thee today," is an arbitrary attempt to bend the meaning of the passage to fit the unscriptural doctrine of purgatory. Of course He was speaking those words on that day. Is it ever possible to say anything at another time than "today"? This word belongs to the promise of Jesus to the malefactor. Death by crucifixion was extremely slow, so that the victim frequently lingered in misery for three or four days. When Jesus promised the malefactor that his suffering would end that same day, it was welcome news to him. The unwitting leaders of the Jews helped to fulfill this promise of

"TODAY"

Jesus by requesting of Pilate that the legs of the malefactors be broken to hasten their death.

But Jesus also promised the penitent a great deal more. He told him that "today," his last day upon earth, would also be his first in heaven. There was to be no waiting, neither was there a purgatory for him to pass through. Implied in the promise is full pardon and absolution for his sins, acceptance into the kingdom of Christ, and an open heaven.

In His promise Jesus does not refer to an earthly habitation, but to heaven, the home of God, of His holy angels, and of the blessed, elsewhere referred to by Him as "Abraham's bosom" (Luke 16:22). Paradise — Jesus called it that

PARADISE — is the ancient Persian word for a pleasant garden or park. It was used by the translators of the Septuagint in Genesis 2:8 for the Garden of Eden, and thus it became associated with dwelling in the presence of God in sinless perfection. Jesus held up to the dying man the vision of Eden restored, a scene of beauty, innocence, and peace, where the stain and defilement of sin was absent and a new and perfect life would begin. Jesus could speak of Paradise as a place native and familiar to Him, because He had come from the Father.

"The devil drove Adam out of Paradise; Christ brings the malefactor into Paradise" (Chrysostom).

To the promise of Paradise Jesus adds, "with Me." Heaven's choicest pleasure is not in the unspeakable loveliness and splendor of the place, but in the fellowship and companionship of Jesus, the beloved Savior. The promise of Jesus

"WITH ME" is completely unrestricted. It is not conditioned upon merit, penance, service or anything else. It is God's mercy and grace, pure and simple, that snatches the malefactor from the brink of the abyss, as a brand from the burning, rescues him from the gates of hell, and escorts him into Paradise. With the admission of the malefactor into heaven, there is no need for us to despair of being admitted.

On the basis of the original word for "he said" (Luke 23:42), in the original Greek: *elegen* (he went on to say), it has been conjectured by some that the malefactor made repeated statements to Jesus before He answered. The word in the original text neither requires nor forbids this interpretation, but it is, finally, of little importance in comparison with *what* was said.

— F —
The Mother Of Jesus At The Cross

Now there stood by the cross of Jesus His mother, and His mother's sister, Mary the wife of Cleophas, and Mary Magdalene. When Jesus therefore saw His mother, and the disciple standing by, whom He loved, He saith unto His mother, "Woman, behold thy son!" Then saith He to the disciple, "Behold thy mother!" And from that hour that disciple took her unto his own house. (TLL, pp. 283,284; *John 19:25-27*)

"Now there stood by the cross of Jesus His mother, and His mother's sister, Mary the wife of Cleophas, and Mary Magdalene." A small group of acquaintances, mostly women, braved the scorn and ridicule and remained on Golgotha. They are described by the Evangelists as standing "afar off" at the time of the death of Jesus. Approximately three hours before the end (according to John) a number of them, including the beloved disciple John and three or four women, managed to approach the cross of Jesus and linger for a while. Mary is mentioned first, though not by name. She is identified simply as the mother of Jesus. The 33-year-old prophecy of Simeon, of the sword passing through Mary's soul (Luke 2:35), was being fulfilled on this day with a surging anguish that left her numb and speechless. Love, pure and deep, as mother love is at its best, would not let her stay away from the gruesome spectacle of the crucifixion of her sinless son. Furthermore, it was necessary for her to be there because Jesus had something to say to her, something that had to be said before many witnesses. He publicly assigned her to her place in the kingdom of God, since in His omniscience He knew of future efforts to exalt her above Himself.

FRIENDS AT THE CROSS

Whether "His mother's sister" refers to Salome, the mother of the disciple John, whom the Evangelist does not wish to mention because of modesty, or to "Mary, the wife of Cleophas," is a question far from settled. From this slender thread of information dangles the question as to whether three or four women stood by the cross. The answer to another question also begs (helplessly) for a resolution from this passage — *viz.*, were James, Judas, and Simon, the sons of Alphaeus (or Cleophas), also cousins of the Lord?

Also present was that devoted worker for Christ, Mary of Magdala, who is often wrongly identified with "the great sinner" in Simon's house (Luke 7:37).

The paintings of artists and the expressions of poets and authors, which place Jesus high above the heads of the little group huddled beneath the cross, unable to touch His body, may be very sentimental, but also very unrealistic. The feet of the crucified were customarily between two and three feet from the ground; and so Mary, or any of the others, could very easily embrace the legs of Jesus or cling to them if they chose to do so and if the soldiers on guard did not object.

UNREALISTIC

Most of the disciples had taken offense at their Master and had gone into hiding. Only John was not afraid of exposing himself to ridicule and danger by being near to Jesus on Golgotha. Thus it was that from His position on the cross "Jesus saw His mother, and the disciple standing by, whom He loved." A very intimate touch in the narrative is here supplied by that same disciple, John. He was the only man in the group, and in Mary's hour of overwhelming grief he stood by her, supported, and comforted her. These two were drawn together in their common sorrow by their love for Jesus. They were the two who stood especially close to Jesus. He saw and understood that they belonged

ONLY JOHN

together. Filled with loving concern for His own, even in this crucial hour of agony, He entrusted His mother to the care of "the disciple . . . whom He loved," as a sacred charge. Nowhere can a nobler, purer example of human love be found than in the love of Jesus for His mother. It even exceeds mother love. He could not be unconcerned about her earthly requirements.

The words which Jesus addresses to Mary, "Woman, behold thy son!" are marvelous in simplicity and brevity, and yet fully adequate for the occasion. They express deep affection and tenderness. In spite of His excruciating agonies of body and soul, He thinks of His mother and her needs and makes provision for them. He speaks with an authority that cannot be disregarded by either John or Mary. By His will and command John is henceforth to occupy the place in Mary's life that He had held hitherto. The command (and it is a command), "Behold thy son!" refers, of course, to the disciple John. It is completely contrary to the spirit of Jesus to want to direct attention to Himself, as some have suggested, to arouse greater sympathy and pity. To interpret the words so as to read, "Behold Me, thy son!" is also completely foreign to the context. Jesus does not want to add to the burden of Mary, but, on the contrary, to lighten it. Corresponding to the words addressed to His mother are those spoken to John, "Behold thy mother!" They do not add anything new. Why then were they added? It was simply good courtesy to address the charge directly to John, as it had been done indirectly in the words spoken to Mary.

HIS WILL AND COMMAND

This was also the last act in Jesus' perfect obedience, that of fulfilling the commandments perfectly — for Mary and for us. Mary understood and was silent in grief. There is no record of any woeful lament, like the one in 2 Samuel 18:33, "O my son, my son!"

The use of the word "woman" has disturbed many people. It seems somewhat disrespectful to them. However, there is nothing disrespectful in the term. It was in common usage in those days. But the term is certainly not as intimate as "mother," and it was not intended to be. It was exactly the right word to convey a very important message from the Lord. Jesus had used the term before in speaking to His mother — at the beginning of His public ministry, just before He performed His first miracle at Cana (John 2:4). Now that His ministry is about to be closed through death, He does so again. In both instances Jesus impresses upon Mary that new relationship to her which began when He entered upon His work of redemption. Though Jesus was still Mary's son, she could no longer command and direct Him as His mother. Her parental position had to yield to a relation far higher and holier. Gently, but firmly, He puts her into her place, and that place is as a member of the Christian Church. There, with all other members of the Church, she must look upon Jesus as her Lord and Savior. The physical relationship of motherhood must give way to the spiritual relationship of discipleship (Mark 3:31-35).

"WOMAN"

John gladly and cheerfully assumed the obligation which Jesus had placed upon him, "and from that hour that disciple took her unto his own house." Luther has

UNTO HIMSELF superbly translated the original Greek, *eis ta idia,* with his German, *der Juenger nahm sie zu sich* (the disciple took her unto himself). It does not necessarily follow that John owned a house at Jerusalem, as some have conjectured. As we would say, John took her into his own family circle. The Greek word for "hour" does not always mean a period of sixty minutes; the text, therefore, does not compel us to assume that John took Mary away from Golgotha at once in order to spare her. On the other hand, the fact that she is not mentioned as being in the group "beholding afar off" (Matt. 27:55,56) a few hours later, strongly indicates that she and John may have left within the hour.

It must be assumed that, as tradition reports, Joseph was no longer living, and that Mary would have been left alone if these provisions for her had not been made.

OTHER CHILDREN OF MARY? While we neither claim, nor try to establish, that Mary lived a "celibate" life with Joseph (Lat., *semper virgo*), we do feel that the words of Jesus, entrusting His mother to the care of His disciple John, do give indirect support to the idea that Mary did not have other children, for then it would have been their filial obligation to look after their mother, and the provision made by Jesus would have been unnecessary. The obligation of the Fourth Commandment would still apply, even if we did assume that such "brethren" still did not believe in Him (John 7:5). The problem of the "brothers" and "sisters" of Jesus has not yet been solved, and it probably will not be solved to our satisfaction on this side of eternity.

Jesus could very easily have provided for His mother without relying upon human help, but His provision is in conformity with the will of God, that His own should care for one another. It was Mary that needed John,

MARY NEEDED JOHN and not John that needed Mary. To picture Mary as the "Mother of the Church," who in the person of John receives all Christians as her children, and bestows blessings upon them, is plainly reversing the facts. The Church has no mother. She has a Father and a King. She has a Bridegroom, and she herself is the bride and is to become a mother (Gal. 4).

We dare not put Mary and her grief in the center of the picture as Mariolatry is constantly doing, often overshadowing the Son. That is doing a grave injustice to

MARY DOES NOT BELONG IN THE CENTER Him. The place belongs to Jesus. He was bearing the burden. He was treading the winepress ALONE, as it had been foretold (Isa. 63:3). He remains our only Mediator with God the Father (1 Tim. 2:5,6). God highly honored Mary by choosing her as the human mother of the divine Son Jesus, and He Himself declared her blessed among women (Luke 1:42). It is nothing short of blasphemy to declare that Mary with her suffering came to the aid of her Son on His cross and helped Him to bear the sins of the world because He could not have borne them alone.

This virtually completes the story of Mary. As far as we know, this may have been the last time that Jesus and Mary saw each other on this earth. The sacred record says

MARY RECEDES INTO THE BACKGROUND

nothing about their meeting after the resurrection. In fact, it has very little to say about her in general. She is mentioned only once after this account in connection with the early Christians in Jerusalem, who were continuing in supplication and prayer (see Acts 1:14), but not as one who was pre-eminent among them. Mary is inconspicuously seated in the background of this account. The Apostles have the place of honor. John, the last of the Apostles to die, in his three Epistles and Revelation never again mentions Mary.

STABAT MATER

Beside the cross in tears
The woeful mother stood,
Bent 'neath the weight of years,
And viewed His flowing blood;
Her mind with grief was torn,
Her strength was ebbing fast,
And through her heart forlorn
The sword of anguish passed.

Medieval Hymn

THE SWORD PIERCED HER SOUL

"But there was worse still — and the sword cut deeper. Had not the angel told her before His birth, 'He shall be great, and shall be called the Son of the Highest, and the Lord God shall give unto Him the throne of His father David; and He shall reign over the house of Jacob forever; and of His kingdom there shall be no end'? This greatness, this throne, this crown, this kingdom — where were they? Once she had believed that she really was what the angel had called her — the most blessed of women — when she saw Him lying in her lap in His beautiful infancy, when the Shepherds and the Magi came to adore Him, and when Simeon and Anna recognized Him as the Messiah . . . And now she stands at the foot of His cross. He is dying; and the greatness, the glory, and the kingdom have never come.

"What could it mean? Had the angel been a deceiver, and God's word a lie, and all the wonders of childhood a dream? We know the explanation now: Jesus was about to climb a far loftier throne than Mary had ever imagined, and the cross was the only road to it. Before many weeks were over Mary was to understand this too; but meantime it must have been dark as Egypt to her, and her heart must have been sorrowful even unto death. The sword had pierced very deep."

James M. Stalker (1894)

— G —
Darkness Prevails — Jesus Forsaken

And it was about the sixth hour, and there was a darkness over all the earth until the ninth hour. And the sun was darkened. And about the ninth hour Jesus cried with a loud voice, saying, *"Eli, Eli, lama sabachthani?"* (That is to say, My God, My God, why hast Thou forsaken Me?) Some of them that stood there, when they heard that, said, "Behold, this man calleth for Elias." (TLL, p. 284)

Now from the sixth hour there was darkness over all the land unto the ninth hour. And about the ninth hour Jesus cried with a loud voice, saying, "Eli, Eli, lama sabachthani?" (That is to say, My God, My God, why hast Thou forsaken Me?) Some of them that stood there, when they heard that, said, "This man calleth for Elias." (Matt. 27:45-47)

And when the sixth hour was come, there was darkness over the whole land until the ninth hour. And at the ninth hour Jesus cried with a loud voice, saying, "Eli, Eli, lama sabachthani?" (Which is, being interpreted, My God, My God, why hast Thou forsaken Me?) And some of them that stood by, when they heard it, said, "Behold, he calleth Elias." (Mark 15:33-37)

And it was about the sixth hour, and there was a darkness over all the earth until the ninth hour. And the sun was darkened. (Luke 23:44,45a)

After Jesus had hung upon the cross for about three hours, at "about the sixth hour," the first remarkable sign in connection with the crucifixion occurred. "There was darkness over all the land." This darkness came at high noon, when the sun was at its zenith and was shining most brightly. Suddenly everything came to a standstill. Labor was halted. Meals were interrupted to find light. The Temple service was disturbed, foreshadowing its imminent cessation. On Golgotha it became very quiet. The tumult ceased. Fear stopped the mouths of the mockers. They dared not continue their sneering jibes. No one cared to speak. Silence prevailed.

"THERE WAS DARKNESS"

Attempts to "explain" the darkness from natural causes leave much to be desired. It could not have been a natural eclipse of the sun, for it took place on the 15th of Nisan, and that was the time of the full moon. An eclipse of the sun is caused by the moon coming between the earth and the sun, and that cannot take place when the moon is full. Attempts to explain the darkness as having been caused by clouds, dust, or vapors do violence to the language of St. Luke, who tells us that the sun itself failed. Only one explanation is possible. The darkness was wholly miraculous. God personally and directly intervened to cause the darkness. He gave a sign from heaven — of the type the Pharisees had so often cried for. Ancient records are of little value to us in this matter. Though some of the Church Fathers, including

WHOLLY MIRACULOUS

Tertullian, Origen, and Rufinus, have boldly appealed to the archives, these have so far failed to produce satisfactory results. But we do not need them. The Scriptures suffice for us.

The extent of the darkness was "over all the earth." The Greek word *ge,* used here by the Evangelists, may mean the "earth" as a whole, or a region or country, hence only part of the earth's surface. This has caused many to limit the extent of the darkness, some more, and some less. But we should not forget that Matthew writes that *pasan* (all) the earth was included, while Mark and Luke write of the *olen* (whole) earth being covered. None of them puts in a word that would restrict it to a given area. The view that the whole earth was blacked out is in agreement with attributing the darkness to the failing of the sun. When the sun fails the darkness is not confined to a limited area, but the entire dayside of the earth is in darkness as well as the other. Once it was dark in Egypt while Goshen had light, but on Good Friday Goshen, too, was plunged into darkness.

"OVER ALL THE EARTH"

This miraculous darkness lasted "until the ninth hour," the very hour in which the lamb for the evening sacrifice was slain. According to our time it was 3:00 P.M.

The darkness hid the climax of the Savior's suffering from human view. No man saw what terrors distorted the face of Jesus in His extreme agonies. In Gethsemane He was removed a stone's throw from His sleeping disciples (see page 48). On Golgotha, where the soldiers and the enemies had taken a position beneath the cross, and the people stood beholding, a veil of darkness concealed His extreme suffering. His followers were spared from witnessing what could have had disastrous results for their faith.

A VEIL

But the darkness was more than just a veil. It was also judgment. Darkness and judgment go together. Jesus was under judgment for the sins of the world. It was during this darkness that the agony of Jesus reached its climax. It was not only an outward darkness. Jesus entered into darkness in His body, soul, and spirit. He endured the judgment for the whole world, and therefore it was fitting that the whole earth should be darkened at this time. This darkness is a reminder of the Judgment to come at the end of the world, when judgment shall strike all those who have not taken refuge in Him who endured the judgment for them on Calvary.

JUDGMENT

How sharply Golgotha stands in contrast with the Mount of Transfiguration! There the brightness of Jesus was so great that His disciples were obliged to hide their faces from the heavenly glory. Here He was shrouded in darkness to hide Him from the gaze of scoffing men.

At the climax of His suffering, just before the darkness lifted at the ninth hour, the stillness was suddenly broken. "Jesus cried with a loud voice" that could be heard for some distance. He had endured the worst that men could do without murmur or complaint, but when God entered into judgment with Him, and poured out His divine wrath upon Him, He could not restrain Himself. He burst forth with an anguished cry from the depths of His terror-stricken soul. The words of the cry were the overture to the Twenty-second Psalm, spoken in Aramaic, "*Eli, Eli,*

THE STILLNESS BROKEN

lama sabachthani?" St. Matthew adds the explanation, "That is to say, My God, My God, why hast Thou forsaken Me?" The Psalm expressed both current experience and prophecy; however, David experienced the abondonment relatively, but Jesus in stark reality.

The terrible gulf which came between Jesus and the heavenly Father during the abandonment is revealed by the language He used. In the agony of Gethsemane, so intense that "His sweat was as it were great drops of blood falling to the ground," His prayer still was, "O My Father" (see page 49). Likewise He addressed Him as "Father" in the first word from the cross as well as in the last. But in this period in which He was forsaken there was no "Father" to whom He could look, but only the righteous and stern "God."

"MY GOD, MY GOD"

We can define the meaning of the language, but to grasp the abysmal depth of the suffering which evoked that cry is a mystery which lies beyond the power of our understanding. The suffering was infinitely more intense than we can ever imagine. Only one who had been actually and completely forsaken by God could explain what that meant, and no human being, still on this side of the grave, has ever been completely forgotten and forsaken by God, nor yet could be. Only in death is impenitent man finally forsaken by God and made to suffer the ultimate curse. But Christ's being forsaken did not occur when He died. When death set in it had already passed over. Only because He was without sin, and perfectly holy within, could He actually be forsaken without being consumed. It is a mystery at which reason falters and which eternity alone will make clear to us.

BEYOND UNDERSTANDING

There is only one cause for which God ever forsakes anyone, and that cause is sin. We see here the full impact of the design of God to make Christ to be sin for us. Only by being truly forsaken by God could the full price of redemption be paid. Indeed we have been dearly bought.

DEARLY BOUGHT

We often complain that we have been forsaken by God when we only begin to suffer. But while we amply deserve to be forsaken by Him, we now know that we need never be forsaken because Christ, our Lord and Savior, was forsaken in our stead.

The cry of Jesus was uttered in the dialect of the people, the Aramaic language. This language of the home and market place was used by God in anticipation of Pentecost, when men should hear in their own tongues the wonderful works of God.

When we speak of Christ's being forsaken by God as being the same as suffering the tortures of the damned in hell (which is frequently done), we must be careful not to identify this with the descent into hell confessed in the Apostolic Creed (based on 1 Peter 3:18-20).

The darkness had lasted so long that the stunning impression which it had first made upon the people gradually began to wear off, and the taunting which had ceased during the darkness was resumed as soon as it had lifted, though not with the same intensity as before. "Some of them that stood there, when they heard that, said, 'Behold, this man calleth for Elias.'" This was horrible mockery. It

THE JEERING RESUMED

must have been first uttered by a Jew, for the jeer was a clear reference to the Jewish expectation of a return of Elijah which was held by the Jewish people. The soldiers could hardly have known about this expectation or applied the words of Jesus to it. Elijah had, in fact, already come (Matt. 11:14), but in a manner which God, and not the Jews, determined. To distort the Scripture and to ridicule its message is a common practice of the unbelieving world.

It should be said that there is, however, another opinion regarding the response to the cry of Jesus. The people uttering the words, it is said, were not really mocking, but were moved to a superstitious fear, resulting from the portents which they had witnessed, and actually believed that Jesus was calling Elijah to His assistance.

— H —
Jesus Dies On The Cross

After this, Jesus knowing that all things were now accomplished, that the Scripture might be fulfilled, saith, "I thirst." Now there was set a vessel full of vinegar, and one ran and filled a sponge full of vinegar, and put it on a reed, and put it to His mouth, and gave Him to drink, saying, "Let alone! Let us see whether Elias will come to take him down." The rest said, "Let be! Let us see whether Elias will come to save him." When Jesus therefore had received the vinegar, He said, "It is finished!" And He cried again with a loud voice and said, "Father, into Thy hands I commend My spirit." And having said thus, He bowed His head and gave up the ghost. (TLL, p. 284)

And straightway one of them ran, and took a sponge, and filled it with vinegar, and put it on a reed, and gave Him to drink. The rest said, "Let be! Let us see whether Elias will come to save him." Jesus, when He had cried again with a loud voice, yielded up the ghost. (Matt. 27:48-50)

And one ran and filled a sponge full of vinegar, and put it on a reed, and gave Him to drink, saying, "Let alone! Let us see whether Elias will come to take him down." And Jesus cried with a loud voice and gave up the ghost. (Mark 15:36,37)

And when Jesus had cried with a loud voice, He said, "Father, into Thy hands I commend My spirit." And having said thus, He gave up the ghost. (Luke 23:46)

After this, Jesus knowing that all things were now accomplished, that the Scripture might be fulfilled, saith, "I thirst." Now there was set a vessel full of vinegar; and they filled a sponge with vinegar, and put it upon hyssop, and put it to His mouth. When Jesus therefore had received the vinegar, He said, "It is finished!" And He bowed His head and gave up the ghost. (John 19:28-30)

The fearful darkness had ended. Light had again returned to Golgotha. Jesus was no longer an outcast from grace. The agony of being forsaken gave way to peace and trust in the heavenly Father.

During the mockery evoked by the Fourth Word, Jesus spoke again. This Fifth Word has given considerable trouble to a large number of expositors. The word itself,

"I THIRST" only four letters in the Greek, is not difficult. Everyone agrees that it means "I thirst," but a great many are not content to let it express purely physical want and desire. Allegories on the word have met with great favor among many expositors and sermonizers and have also infiltrated into our hymnody and liturgy. Support for the allegorical treatment of the word is freely sought in passages which use thirsting in a figurative sense, *e.g.*, which speak of the soul thirsting for God. That Jesus deeply desired the salvation of sinners is beyond dispute, but to claim that this desire was expressed in this word is quite another matter. It is putting something into His mouth for which we have no warrant from the context. Furthermore, there is a grammatical question involved here, as to which of two verbs is modified by the conjunctive *hina* (in order that). If it is connected with *legei* (He saith) it would mean that Jesus spoke the word in order that the Scripture might be fulfilled. This is grammatically possible, and it has set off a search for some statement in the Old Testament to connect with the Fifth Word. However, the effort to find a specific prophecy has fallen short. On the other hand, it is equally correct, grammatically speaking, to connect the *hina* with *panta tetelestai* (all things were accomplished). Then the sense would be: since all things had already been accomplished in order that the Scriptures might be fulfilled, Jesus therefore said, "I thirst." This, I believe, is the correct understanding of the passage.

Jesus knew the Scriptures. He knew what had been prophesied and what was required of Him. He knew that "all" that was necessary for the redemption of mankind, all that which was given Him to do according to the Scriptures, was done. The last act, and the hardest part of the task assigned to Him, took place during the three hours of darkness when He was forsaken by the Father. The last farthing was paid.

ALL THINGS ACCOMPLISHED

Until His great task was accomplished Jesus put aside all physical desires. These could now be attended to. Thirst was one of the most distressing agonies of the crucified. Jesus had gone through more than fifteen hours of enormous strain and torture without a drink, and He must have thirsted long before He came to Golgotha. On His arrival there He rejected the doped wine which was offered Him as a sedative (see page 134). After hanging on the cross for six hours, His naked body exposed to the sun, ridden with fever, emaciated, and by this time dehydrated, the thirst must have become virtually unbearable.

THIRST VIRTUALLY UNBEARABLE

This word was the only expression of physical need to come from the lips of the Savior, but it is evidence of the reality of His human nature and of the reality of His suffering. His was no "phantom body." Yet there also appears to be a purpose beyond the desire for physical relief that caused Jesus to ask for a drink. He was getting ready to surrender His soul into the hands of His heavenly Father. This should be done in a manner that all might know it as an act of His own volition. He could not allow Himself to pass into a coma.

MORE THAN PHYSICAL SUFFERING

The request of Jesus expresses no preference for the kind of drink desired. Anything that will enable Him to make His victorious shout will do. "Now there was set there a vessel full of vinegar" (or sour wine). "*Oxos*" John calls it,

SOUR WINE the cheapest grade of wine which was issued to the Roman soldiers as part of their rations. It was not something unpalatable or undrinkable, but something refreshing.

"And one ran," undoubtedly one of the soldiers on guard, and rendered Jesus this final service. Having filled a sponge with the sour wine, and fastening it upon a hyssop stalk, he "gave Him to drink." The use of the hyssop gives us a good estimate of the height of the cross, since the stem of this plant grows about 18 inches long (see page 153).

While this was going on, the mocking continued. In this the heartless enemies were joined by the soldier who gave Him to drink. Even while he held up the sponge he taunted in words he learned from the Jews, "Let

ELIAS DID NOT COME alone! Let us see whether Elias will come and take Him down." Also this final mockery Jesus endured without reply or rebuke. Elias (Elijah) did not come to the rescue. But this was not the time for a deliverer. The victory was already firmly grasped.

If one were to accept the position that the words, "Behold, this man calleth for Elias," were spoken in superstitious fear, rather than in mockery, one could also hold that the words of the soldier were spoken in the same spirit.

With the drink of sour wine His parched lips were moistened, His burning throat was cooled and cleared, His strength was revived, and He now uttered with His lips the word which was in His heart when He called for a

"IT IS FINISHED" drink. Not with the gasp of a spent life, but with a shout of victory Jesus cries out, "It is finished!" While His foes were gloating over His apparent defeat, the shout of triumph comes from the lips of Jesus.

This word was a report to the Father who had sent Him, but was uttered in a loud voice so that all men should likewise hear. With the greatest single word ever uttered, He announced the consummation of the assignment given Him by the Father. Finished was His redemptive work, the work of reconciliation and atonement. The dominion of the prince of hell had been broken, and Satan had been crushed under His heel. "Paradise lost" had become "Paradise regained."

Satan had tried his utmost to prevent the work of Christ from being finished. He had instigated the murder of the Innocents at Bethlehem and had tempted Jesus in the wilderness. He had entered into Judas and

SATAN'S EFFORTS FOILED had driven him to the act of betrayal. He had inspired the taunts hurled at Jesus to tempt Him to show His power by stepping down from the cross. But all had been to no avail. While most human efforts remain incomplete and unfinished, nothing could prevent the greatest work of God, greater and more glorious than the work of creation itself, from being finished. And proof that all was indeed "finished" was supplied by the return of the light after the three hours of darkness, and especially by Jesus' triumphant resurrection from the dead.

Since Christ has fully redeemed us and has reconciled us unto the Father by His perfect sacrifice, there is nothing left for us to do, there is nothing that we can do, whereby we might merit salvation. It is a waste of time and energy to try to accomplish what He has already finished. But worse than that, when men fancy that they are able to add their own "good works" to those of Christ, they are repudiating His sacrifice and giving the lie to His Word.

Ordinarily the strength of the body diminishes as it gradually becomes weaker. But once more Jesus rallied His strength and "cried with a loud voice." Like the previous triumphant utterance, this one was not meant for the Father only, but it was to be heard and noted by all, His enemies and His friends alike. There was no need to cry aloud for the Father's sake. He could hear the whispered words or even read the thoughts. We note that it was the manner in which Jesus cried out before entering death which made such a deep impression on the Roman centurion.

"WITH A LOUD VOICE"

By divine timing it was the hour of the evening sacrifice when the words rang out over Calvary, "Father, into Thy hands I commend My spirit." The Father was hidden from His consciousness when Jesus had cried out, "My God! My God!" Now He had found Him again as Father. This final word of Jesus is taken from a part of Psalm 31:5, to which He adds the word "Father." It was part of a customary Jewish evening prayer. When Jesus appropriated these words of David He used them in the popular Jewish sense, rather than in the original meaning. In their setting in the Psalm the words constitute a cry of distress, in which the Psalmist is petitioning God to prolong his life by breaking the counsel of his enemies and protecting him. As an evening prayer the thought was that God would stand watch over His child during the hours of darkness and bring him safe and refreshed to the dawn of another day. By this prayer Jesus indicates that He will calmly and peacefully fall asleep, confident of His imminent resurrection.

THE FINAL WORD

The hands of God are in Paradise, the dwelling place of God, of His holy angels, and of the translated saints. "Verily, I say unto thee, today shalt thou be with Me in Paradise" (Luke 23:43). Jesus is going home. Other hands, hostile hands, are eager to lay hold on Him, but He foils the scheming of Satan by depositing Himself for safekeeping into the loving care and keeping of the Father for a little while, for the space of three days.

HOME TO PARADISE

The "Light of the World" was eclipsed, but not extinguished. Through death He was only transferring His existence to another sphere.

The death of Jesus is reported in elegant words: "He bowed His head and gave up the ghost." But the words distinctly report it as a voluntary act on His part. He Himself summons death. He is not conquered by death, but He is its Conqueror. He could have remained alive on the cross for many hours by letting the normal course continue, to say nothing about being able to escape it altogether. He voluntarily laid down His life. Because of the sacrificial nature of His life and suffer-

NOT BY COMPULSION

ing, however, it was necessary that the sundering of Christ's body and soul take place through death, even though He had already suffered the ultimate punishment when He was forsaken. From the foundation of the world it had been determined that the Lamb should be slain (Rev. 13:8).

Jesus died with a prayer upon His lips. His last words have become a pattern and a comfort for countless Christians in their hour of departure out of this life. By His example He has taught us how to die.

— I —
The Veil Of The Temple Rent And The Tombs Opened

And, behold, the veil of the Temple was rent in twain, from the top to the bottom; and the earth did quake, and the rocks rent; and the graves were opened; and many bodies of the saints which slept arose, and came out of the graves after His resurrection, and went into the holy city, and appeared unto many. (TLL, p. 284)

And, behold, the veil of the Temple was rent in twain from the top to the bottom; and the earth did quake, and the rocks rent; and the graves were opened; and many bodies of the saints which slept arose, and came out of the graves after His resurrection, and went into the holy city, and appeared unto many. (Matt. 27:51-53)

And the veil of the Temple was rent in twain from the top to the bottom. (Mark 15:38)

And the veil of the Temple was rent in the midst. (Luke 23:45b)

Past was the hour allotted to the powers of darkness. Jesus had proclaimed its end with a mighty shout. Now it was the Father's turn to speak. Yet He uttered not a single word. When He spoke, it was in

THE FATHER'S TURN TO SPEAK language of His own, one universally known and understood, the language of sign and wonders. With these signs He aligned Himself with Him who expired on the cross. All of these signs occurred simultaneously, at the moment when the lips of Jesus were silenced by death. Human language necessitates their narration in sequence.

First in the narrative we learn that "the veil of the Temple was rent in twain." Although the Herodian Temple had an outer curtain in front of the Holy Place, as well as an inner curtain between the Holy

THE RENDING OF THE VEIL Place and the Holy of Holies, it was unquestionably the inner curtain which was rent. This curtain was never lifted except on the Great Day of Atonement, and it hid the inner sanctuary from every human eye save that of the high priest, and to his eye only on that day. Suddenly, at the time of the evening sacrifice, while priests were presumably ministering in the part of the Temple termed the Holy Place, this heavy and elaborate curtain was torn from the top to the bottom by an unseen hand, exposing the Holy of Holies to the view of eyes which under the old dispensation were not supposed to see it. To attribute the rending to the earthquake, or to a falling timber, is an entirely unsatisfactory explanation in view of the curtain's construction, which was "of the thickness of the palm of the hand." It was miraculous.

The rending of the veil was of great significance, especially to Israel, but finally also to the whole world. It indicated that the ministry of the Jewish high priest and of the typifying sacrifices had come to an end and that the destruction of the entire sanctuary, the pride of the Jewish people, was in the offing. The wall of partition, which allowed the worshiper to come so far and no farther, was swept away. The "Old Dispensation," essentially preparatory, made way for the "New Dispensation," in which all sinners have free access to the presence of God by virtue of the atoning blood of Christ. That the meaning of the rent veil was not lost on all of Israel, particularly on the priests who served in the Temple, appears from the early conversion of a large number of priests (Acts 6:7).

OF GREAT SIGNIFICANCE

At the same time "the earth did quake, and the rocks rent." Only skepticism and unbelief would declare this earthquake to have been accidental. Plainly the Covenant-God was present in His power and greatness at the death of His Son, bringing consternation to the foes of Christ. Rocks were rent by the earthquake, but not the stony hearts of the Jewish leaders.

THE ROCKS WERE RENT

The quake might have been a means of smashing the foe, but instead God mercifully accompanied it with a returning to life. "And the graves were opened: and many bodies of the saints which slept arose." The opening of the graves has often been attributed to the earthquake. That such an effect was possible cannot be denied, but it hardly fits in view of the very select group of tombs which were opened. And certainly the earthquake could have nothing whatsoever to do with the reviving of the dead within those tombs. Only a miracle of God was capable of that. The account leaves out much that our curiosity would desire to know, but was not deemed necessary for our knowledge by the Lord. Much speculation has been done about who these saints were. We cannot settle the question. We can only say that since they were so named by divine reckoning, rather than by human judgment or decree, they were believers who rested their faith in the promised Savior. These departed saints arose. They were made alive again. Death could no longer hold them, but had to yield up its victims again. The resurrection is not merely a future event. It has already begun. These saints are the forerunners of all those who shall be raised on the Last Day.

MANY SAINTS AROSE

According to Matthew, the restoring of life to these saints took place at the time of the sacrificial death of Christ. Where they stayed in the interval between then and the time when, "after His resurrection," they "went into the holy city, and appeared unto many," has perplexed many people,

THEY APPEARED UNTO MANY

but is not answered for us. In my opinion these saints were not raised with the natural bodies in which they once went about, which would have made them subject to death a second time, but they obtained the glorified bodies for which others must wait until the Last Day. With these glorified bodies they could go about unseen, even as Jesus after His resurrection, and could appear briefly to those whose eyes were opened to see them. Who the "many" in Jerusalem were to whom the saints appeared is not reported. The usual assumption is that they were believers like those to whom Jesus appeared after His resurrection. The suggestion that since Jesus did not appear unto His enemies these risen saints may have appeared to them is mere speculation. We simply do not know. The idea that these saints remained upon earth until the ascension of Jesus, when they supposedly accompanied Him to His heavenly abode, is also a pious sentiment without foundation.

The "holy city" was, of course, Jerusalem, still called that in spite of its great wickedness, because the Temple, with its worship of Jehovah, was located there.

— J —
"Truly, This Was The Son Of God!"

And when the centurion, which stood over against Him, and they that were with him watching Jesus, saw that He so cried out and gave up the ghost, and saw the earthquake, and those things that were done, they feared greatly, and glorified God, saying, "Certainly, this was a righteous Man. Truly this Man was the Son of God." And all the people that came together to see that sight, beholding the things which were done, smote their breasts and returned. And all His acquaintance and also many women were there beholding the things afar off, among whom was Mary Magdalene; and Mary the mother of James the less and of Joses; and Salome the mother of Zebedee's children, who also, when He was in Galilee, followed Him and ministered unto Him; and many other women which came up with Him unto Jerusalem. (TLL, pp. 284,285)

Now when the centurion and they that were with him watching Jesus saw the earthquake and those things that were done, they feared greatly, saying, "Truly this was the Son of God." And many women were there beholding afar off, which followed Jesus from Galilee, ministering unto Him, among which was Mary Magdalene, and Mary the mother of James and Joses, and the mother of Zebedee's children. (Matt. 27:54-56)

And when the centurion, which stood over against Him, saw that He so cried out and gave up the ghost, he said, "Truly this Man was the Son of God." There were also women looking on afar off, among whom was Mary Magdalene; and Mary the mother of James the less and of Joses; and Salome, who also, when He was in Galilee, followed Him and ministered unto Him; and many other women which came up with Him unto Jerusalem. (Mark 15:39-41)

Now when the centurion saw what was done, he glorified God, saying, "Certainly this was a righteous Man." And all the people that came together to that sight, beholding the things which were done, smote their breasts and returned. And all His acquaintance and the women that followed Him from Galilee stood afar off, beholding these things. (Luke 23:47-49)

A Roman "centurion," a captain of a hundred, was in charge of the detail on Golgotha. We cannot determine how large the detachment of soldiers was, but it is safe to presume that in the inflammable atmosphere which existed, security considerations would dictate a larger detail than the three quaternians (twelve men) who were the actual executioners. Tradition has invented countless stories to embellish the centurion's person and life. The facts, however, are shrouded in oblivion. We do not know the man, not even his name.

THE CENTURION

His position in command gave the centurion a perfect opportunity to observe and to study all of the events which took place, for he "stood over against Him." All of these things: the long darkness, the loud voice with which Jesus shouted, the earthquake, and the sudden death, had made a deep impression upon the officer. We assume that the centurion was assigned to the duty of safeguarding Jesus when He was turned over to the governor by the ecclesiastical authorities. If so, then he had also witnessed the spiteful maneuvering of the Sanhedrists. He had heard Pilate repeatedly vouch for the innocence of Jesus, and he saw Herod indicate that He was not worthy of death. He had heard Jesus speak of His kingdom, as well as the matchless words from the cross. He was especially impressed by the manner in which Jesus died, that He did not lose His life, but that He surrendered it of His own will.

OPPORTUNITY TO OBSERVE

In sharp contrast to the Jewish mockery and unbelief, the centurion, through sober reflection, came to the conclusion that Jesus was not guilty of the grave charges which His infuriated enemies brought against Him, but that He actually was what He had declared Himself to be. As this conviction forced itself upon him, he disregarded all personal danger and other disastrous consequences of espousing the lost cause of the condemned Prophet, and he came forward with a wonderful confession, "Certainly, this was a righteous Man. Truly this Man was the Son of God." He thus became the first man after Christ's death to confess Him publicly. What the angels had proclaimed at Bethlehem and the Father had testified at the baptism, and again at the transfiguration of Jesus, the centurion confessed before Golgotha's cross.

A WONDERFUL CONFESSION

To explain this confession in the sense of pagan mythology ignores the inspired assertion that the centurion and his underlings "glorified God." That the centurion's knowledge may still have been imperfect is highly probable, but that by no means disproves his faith. A weak faith is still a true faith. The statement has the evident marks of a Christian confession. Spiritual regeneration is wrought in God's own time, place, and manner. This confession was also a sharp indictment of the Jews. An honest and reasonable man had pronounced their passionate condemnation false. They had committed an unpardonable crime. They had not only taken the side of

HE GLORIFIED GOD

unrighteousness and thwarted justice; they had defied the holy and righteous God and had rejected His Son.

Furthermore, it was no less a rebuke of the Roman governor for the sentence which he had passed. And what made it all the more reproachful was that it came from an officer in the Roman army.

Not only was the centurion impressed, but also "they that were with him, watching Jesus," voiced their agreement with the testimony of their superior officer.

OTHER SOLDIERS LIKEWISE Whether all understood what they were saying, or were sincere in their expression, is beyond our ability to determine. We are simply told that those soldiers, some of whom had earlier joined in the mockery, now "feared greatly" after the rocks were rent and other signs had been done, and they seconded the statement of the centurion.

While His own people failed to give Jesus His due respect, the heathen nations sent their representatives to do Him honor. The Magi from the Orient had put to

HONOR FROM THE HEATHEN NATIONS shame the leaders among the Jews when Jesus was born. Now the representatives of the earthly power from the Occident, soldiers from Caesar's army, did the same thing at the time of His death.

Great crowds of people had come to Calvary to see the sight — "a spectacle" St. Luke calls it, which was also the term used for a theatrical show. Their interest in the

THERE TO SEE A SPECTACLE extraordinary events that took place on Calvary was similar to the interest that Herod showed when Jesus was sent to him. He hoped to see something unusual — a miracle. The people had permitted themselves to be blinded and misled by the Jewish leaders. They showed no real sympathy for the popular Teacher, who was the victim of this miscarriage of justice. They were there to see a show, a spectacle. They saw many more spectacular things than they had expected. And when they had seen what occurred they were struck in their hearts. "And all the people . . . smote their breasts."

As they began streaming back into the city the people involuntarily began beating their breasts, indicating the disturbed emotions within. Their equilibrium was gone.

THEY RETURNED IN BEWILDERMENT Dread and bewilderment, mingled with self-accusations and regrets, were indicated by their actions. If only they had not been so hasty! God's signs had had an effect. It had disturbed their minds. Their consciences were aroused. They had come to see a show, but they left with the realization that something terrible had been done when Jesus was crucified. Gone was the haughty mockery. Only the general impression of their reactions is recorded by Luke. Among so many people, feelings and reactions may have varied greatly.

The beating of the breasts does not imply conversion. Men are not converted by witnessing many terrors. If that were the case, then hell would be the ideal place for

NOT CONVERSION conversion. If there had been other converts like the malefactor on the cross and the centurion, it is unlikely that the sacred writers would have failed to make any mention whatsoever of them. But prejudices against the Crucified One may well have been broken down or removed from the minds of many, making them more receptive later to the Gospel message. It is quite plausible that at least some of them may have heard Peter's sermon on Pentecost and were moved to repentance and baptism by his message.

It was all over for the crowd, but not for the followers of Jesus. "And all His acquaintance and also many women were there." The site of the crucifixion grew more and more empty, and soon only a **HIS ACQUAINTANCE LINGERED ON** group of loyal followers of the Lord remained. They did not belong to the multitude, and they did not leave with it. They lingered on. They could not leave. Their love for their dead Master held them. They were concerned about what would become of His body. Their number is not given, but the word "all" suggests that it was not insignificant. They had apparently gathered during the six hours that Jesus hung upon the cross. Many had followed Him from Galilee. Significantly absent were the disciples. They were offended because of Jesus, as He had foretold (see page 45). Only one of them, the beloved John, came there. Peter might have come too except for the bitter experience at the high priest's palace.

The women are mentioned separately as a group because their love and loyalty stood out on Calvary. They were truly "faithful unto death." Some of them already "in Galilee followed Him and ministered unto Him." And while only males were required to come up to Jerusalem for the festival to worship, many women also "came up with Him." The service rendered by loyal women is reported with approval, but only a few of them are mentioned by name.

"Mary Magdalene," or Mary of Magdala, a town on the west side of the Sea of Galilee, had been delivered of seven demons by Jesus (Luke 8:2). For this great favor she gave ardent and unwavering allegiance to Him. As Peter was leader among the Twelve, so she was among the women. This noble woman has been greatly wronged, especially by the Roman Church. To identify her with the woman who anointed the Master's feet at Simon's house is wholly unwarranted. Mary Magdalene is mentioned fourteen times in the New Testament, and not once is there even the slightest suggestion of a moral lapse. The reports are all quite to the contrary.

"Mary the mother of James the less and of Joses" is called the sister of Mary, the mother of Jesus, and the wife of Cleophas (John 19:25; see also page 153).

"Salome, the mother of Zebedee's children" was the mother of James and John.

The silence regarding any presence of Mary, the mother of Jesus, as well as John's silence on this part of the record, leads to the surmise that John may well have led her away from this scene of horrors after Jesus had charged him with her care. Later John was there to witness the piercing of the Savior's side (see page 172).

The "afar off" position of the acquaintances on Golgotha was due to necessity. The soldiers who were stationed there to guard against disturbances occupied the

AFAR OFF area nearest to the crosses. There they could dutifully watch and guard. They apparently kept an area surrounding the crosses clear, where they permitted the mother of Jesus with the other women and John to draw near for a period during a lull in the mockery (see page 153). Nearest to the cross, beyond the soldiers, were the dignitaries — the Sanhedrists, who had come to pour scorn upon the Crucified, and then the curious crowd, who were interested in witnessing a spectacle. That left room for the faithful only in the "area afar off." They may also have been latecomers upon the scene. Their remote position reflected their helplessness. There was nothing that they could do but silently look on, like sheep who have lost their Shepherd and know not what to do or where to go. And they were probably also afraid.

— K —
Jesus' Side Pierced

The Jews therefore, because it was the preparation, that the bodies should not remain upon the cross on the Sabbath day (for that Sabbath day was a high day), besought Pilate that their legs might be broken and that they might be taken away. Then came the soldiers and broke the legs of the first, and of the other which was crucified with Him. But when they came to Jesus, and saw that He was dead already, they broke not His legs; but one of the soldiers with a spear pierced His side, and forthwith came there out blood and water. And he that saw it bore record, and his record is true, and he knoweth that he saith true, that ye might believe. For these things were done, that the Scripture should be fulfilled, "A bone of Him shall not be broken." And again another Scripture saith, "They shall look on Him whom they pierced." (TLL, p. 285; *John 19:31-37)*

As Good Friday is drawing to a close we find our attention once more directed to the Sanhedrists. A delegation of them appear before Pilate with another request.

"THAT THEIR LEGS MIGHT BE BROKEN" "The Jews therefore . . . besought Pilate that their legs might be broken and that they might be taken away." Breaking their legs with a heavy mallet or bar would greatly hasten death. The request of the Sanhedrists, however, was no act of compassion, but they were rather motivated by their law (Deut. 21:23), which they applied to the crucified as well as to such as were hanged. Their bodies were not to remain hanging overnight, lest the land be defiled. The object of the request was to insure the death and burial of the victims before sundown. To obtain the desired action it was necessary to appeal to the governor, for the Roman custom was to let the victims hang until life slowly ebbed away and then to leave the bodies upon the cross until they fell prey to the birds or beasts, or rotted off, unless their bodies had been requested by relatives or others for burial.

An added reason for their grave concern is reported: "because it was the preparation, that the bodies should not remain upon the cross on the Sabbath day (for that Sabbath day was a high day)." The day of Jesus' crucifixion and death is fixed as Friday, the preparation day for the Sabbath.

NOT TO DEFILE THE SABBATH

If the bodies had remained on the cross past sundown, they would then, in their estimation, defile the Sabbath day as well. And no ordinary Sabbath it was, but the Sabbath of the Passover week — doubly sacred for that reason. It was also the day when the wave-sheaf was offered unto the Lord. These hypocritical Jews had greater scruples of conscience about letting a dead body hang upon the cross overnight than about instigating the death of an innocent person.

This zeal for the letter of the law may not have been the only reason for the urgency of the Sanhedrists. The amazing signs which they had witnessed may have filled them with fear. They raised the question whether Christ had really been vanquished or not. They could not rest easily until they had Him securely in the grave. Pilate's assent to the request must have pleased the soldiers as much as it did the Jewish leaders. It would relieve them of an unpleasant and tedious vigil at the site of the execution, since they dared not leave their post until the life of the crucifed was extinct.

THE ONLY REASON FOR THIS ZEAL?

When the orders of the governor had been relayed to Calvary, "then came the soldiers, and broke the legs of the first and of the other which was crucified with Him." The Apostle John beheld how the soldiers carried out their grim orders upon the penitent as well as the impenitent malefactor. He was not spared the earthly punishment for his transgression because he repented. His reward of grace came later (see page 151f.).

THE SOLDIERS BEGAN TO CARRY OUT THEIR ORDERS

The soldiers left Jesus until last. "But when they came to Jesus, and saw that He was dead already, they broke not His legs." At the third cross the soldiers found a situation in conflict with their orders, and they disregarded them. But realizing that they might be called to give an account for acting according to their discretion, rather than strictly adhering to orders, one of the soldiers proceeded to verify the observation, and to make sure that Jesus was really dead. "But one of the soldiers with a spear pierced His side." The wound made by the spearhead was large enough that Thomas might afterward have thrust his hand into it (John 20:27).

ONE PIERCED HIS SIDE

The thrust of the spear quickly produced the needed evidence, "and forthwith came there out blood and water." Much has been said and written about the blood and water. Physiological explanations have been sought. Physicians have been appealed to, but they do not fully agree with what happens or does not happen

BLOOD AND WATER

with corpses. What is usually forgotten is that the sacred body of Jesus was uncorrupted by sin, and what applied to other bodies, where decay normally sets in after death, would not necessarily apply to His body. Imaginations have been given free play, and allegorizations are common on this statement of John. The result has been that the emphasis has frequently been shifted from where the Apostle put it, on the fact of Jesus' death, to the blood and water. Heresies of that day, when John wrote his Gospel, made it necessary firmly to establish and to certify the death of Jesus as a prelude to His resurrection. And that is the chief purpose of this report.

That scene is still so vivid in the mind of John that he testifies, in the third person as he perfers to do, "and he that saw it bore record, and his record is true." Expositors cannot agree on the next phrase, "and he (*ekeinos*) knoweth that he saith true." There is a question as to what is meant by the Greek word *ekeinos* ("he," or more exactly, "that one"). Does it refer to John or to another witness? Those who advocate the idea that another witness is meant, think that John is appealing to Jesus to corroborate his own witness. But putting all speculation aside, John still has only one object in mind by putting these events on record, namely, "that ye might believe."

"THAT YE MIGHT BELIEVE"

Turning from the testimony to the events themselves, John writes, "For these things were done, that the Scripture should be fulfilled." What might appear as mere chance, or the impulse of a Roman soldier, was actually the fulfilling of ancient prophecies. Scripture plainly says that "a bone of Him shall not be broken," in the instructions given concerning the paschal lamb (Exod. 12:46; Num. 9:12), which clearly and unmistakably was a type of the Lamb of God. However, there are also some who have been impressed by the similarity of these words to Psalm 34:20, but the context in the Psalm makes this an unsatisfactory reference. The other Scripture verse, "They shall look on Him they pierced," is found in Zechariah 12:10. John's concern is obviously to present proof of the actual death of Jesus. The evidence was delivered in the spear-thrust into the side of Jesus by the soldier. The more-than-500-year-old prophecy had foretold the precise manner in which the certainty of death should be established. "They shall look upon Him" is generally understood as having their eyes opened to see the enormity of their sin, as the first step toward repentance and the Pentecostal harvest.

THE SCRIPTURE FULFILLED

CHAPTER SEVEN
Jesus' Burial

— A —
The Body Of Jesus Requested

And after this, now when the even was come, because it was the preparation, that is, the day before the Sabbath, behold, there came a man named Joseph, an honorable counselor, a rich man of Arimathaea, a city of the Jews; and he was a good man, and a just, who also himself waited for the kingdom of God, being a disciple of Jesus, but secretly for fear of the Jews. The same had not consented to the counsel and deed of them. He went in boldly unto Pilate, and craved the body of Jesus, and besought Pilate that he might take away the body of Jesus. (TLL, p. 286)

When the even was come, there came a rich man of Arimathaea, named Joseph, who also himself was Jesus' disciple. He went to Pilate and begged the body of Jesus. (Matt. 27:57,58a)

And now when the even was come, because it was the preparation, that is, the day before the Sabbath, Joseph of Arimathaea, an honorable counselor, which also waited for the kingdom of God, came, and went in boldly unto Pilate, and craved the body of Jesus. (Mark 15:42,43)

And, behold, there was a man named Joseph, a counselor, and he was a good man, and a just. (The same had not consented to the counsel and deed of them.) He was of Arimathaea, a city of the Jews — who also himself waited for the kingdom of God. This man went unto Pilate and begged the body of Jesus. (Luke 23:50-52)

And after this, Joseph of Arimathaea, being a disciple of Jesus, but secretly for fear of the Jews, besought Pilate that he might take away the body of Jesus. (John 19:38a)

"And after this," that is, after the death of Jesus and the accompanying signs, "even was come." The day before the Sabbath, or "the preparation" as St. Mark calls it, when everything that was needed for the Sabbath must be prepared, was rapidly drawing to a close. The Sabbath would begin at sundown. The Sanhedrists were concerned only that the bodies should not remain upon the cross, so as not to defile the land (see page 171). What would happen to the body of Jesus after it was taken down was of no concern to them. For all they cared it could be cast into some pit of refuse, or disposed of in the customary manner — thrown with the bodies of the malefactors into a nameless, shallow grave.

THEY SHOULD NOT REMAIN ON THE CROSS

The followers of Jesus, the acquaintances, namely the women and John, the one Apostle who had not failed in his loyalty, were utterly unprepared and helpless in their grief. But God the Father took care of the body of His beloved Son in death. Help appeared suddenly from an entirely unexpected source, help such as would not have been thought possible. Joseph of Arimathaea stepped forward and took full charge of the burial. "Arimathaea" has become Joseph's Biblical surname. It was used to distinguish him from other Josephs, including the one who had been ap-

UNEXPECTED HELP

pointed to provide for Jesus in His infancy. Arimathaea is not otherwise remembered, and there is some doubt as to its actual location. Some think of Ramah in Ephraim, the home of Samuel. The most likely place is Rama in Benjamin, a few miles north of Jerusalem. For a time it belonged to Samaria, but later it was joined to the province of Judah, and hence is called "a city of the Jews."

Joseph did not now live in Arimathaea, for he had a new tomb made for himself in Jerusalem, since he was a member of the Sanhedrin, "an honorable counselor." But since it was from the Sanhedrin that the most determined opposition to Jesus had come, the Evangelists supply the explanation that "the same had not consented to the counsel and deed of them." Joseph was not of the mind and spirit of the body to which he belonged, as far as its attitude toward Jesus was concerned. The "counsel" referred to was that taken at the first meeting of the Sanhedrin on Tuesday evening at the palace of the high priest, where it was decided to take Jesus by subtilty and kill Him (see page 5). The manner in which he showed his opposition, whether by speaking against their plans, by casting a negative vote on their resolution, or in some other way, is not known. His absence from the later meetings on Thursday evening and Friday morning seems certain, for here we are told that all who were present condemned Jesus to death.

AN HONORABLE COUNSELOR

Not only was Joseph a man of high character and position, but he was also "a rich man." This is mentioned to show that the burial of the Lord was in fulfillment of Isaiah 53:9: "And He made His grave with the wicked, and with the rich in His death." As long as He was still making payment for the souls of transgressors, Jesus was numbered with the transgressors. But once the ransom had been paid, His shame and disgrace were turned into honor, and He was buried as an aristocrat.

"A RICH MAN"

Joseph belonged to that small, spiritually-minded company in Israel who had set their hopes on the Messiah — those "who waited for the kingdom of God," to which group also Simeon, Anna, Zacharias and others had once belonged. He had become convinced that Jesus was that Messiah and had become His disciple. But until now Joseph had failed to profess his faith in Jesus, and the reason, frankly stated, was that fear of the Jews had sealed his lips ("being a disciple of Jesus, but secretly for fear of the Jews"). That fear was felt, not by Joseph alone, for there were others who were likewise intimidated by it (John 7:13). If we wish to appreciate his difficulty, we must consider that such profession would have meant expulsion from the synagogue and becoming an outcast among his people (John 9:22). It was the honorable position which Joseph had in the community which made the step of avowal so difficult.

FEAR KEPT HIM A SECRET DISCIPLE

Now, under circumstances which had become especially unfavorable, Joseph did an astonishing thing. He cast all fear and cowardice aside and boldly "came" forward. He must have been standing among the spectators on Golgotha, but now he step-

LOVE FOR JESUS PRODUCED BOLDNESS

ped forward and spoke to the centurion who was responsible for the body of Jesus, telling him of his intention to ask Pilate for it. This would keep the body from hastily being taken down and cast into the common grave with the malefactors. Then he hastened on into the city. Time was getting short. Impelled by love for Jesus, Joseph's former timidity turned into fervor, and "he went in boldly unto Pilate and craved the body of Jesus." Once the decision had been made he acted with courage and forthrightness. What his fellow members of the Sanhedrin refused to do in the morning for fear of ceremonial pollution, because they wanted to eat the Chagigah (see page 96), he did not hesitate to do. He went in boldly unto the judgment hall to speak to Pilate. It did not matter to him now that he should become ceremonially unclean, since he intended to bury Jesus, and according to the law he would become unclean anyway from handling a dead body. His only concern now was to bestow upon the dead body of Jesus whatever honor he could. Nor was he deterred by the judgment of the ceremonial law which declared a man accursed who died upon the tree.

— B —
The Body Taken Down From The Cross

And Pilate marveled if He were already dead; and calling unto him the centurion, he asked him whether He had been any while dead. And when he knew it of the centurion, Pilate gave him leave and gave the body to Joseph. And he bought fine linen. He came therefore and took the body of Jesus down. And when Joseph had taken the body, he wrapped it in the clean linen cloth.

And there came also Nicodemus (which at the first came to Jesus by night), and brought a mixture of myrrh and aloes, about a hundred pound weight. Then took they the body of Jesus and wound it in linen clothes with spices, as the manner of the Jews is to bury. (TLL, p. 286)

Then Pilate commanded the body to be delivered. And when Joseph had taken the body, he wrapped it in a clean linen cloth. (Matt. 27:58b,59)

And Pilate marveled if He were already dead; and calling unto him the centurion, he asked him whether He had been any while dead. And when he knew it of the centurion, he gave the body to Joseph. And he bought fine linen, and took Him down, and wrapped Him in the linen. (Mark 15:44-46a)

And he took it down, and wrapped it in linen. (Luke 23:53a)

And Pilate gave him leave. He came therefore, and took the body of Jesus. And there came also Nicodemus (which at the first came to Jesus by night), and brought a mixture of myrrh and aloes, about a hundred pound weight. Then took they the body of Jesus and wound it in linen clothes with the spices, as the manner of the Jews is to bury. (John 19:38b-40)

There were probably two things that made Pilate marvel, though only one of them is mentioned. In the first place, he must have marveled at who it was that made the

PILATE MARVELED request for the body. He belonged to the very assembly of judges who had so urgently insisted upon the death of Jesus. Then, he "marveled if He were already dead." Death by crucifixion was extremely slow, as we have stated, sometimes dragging out for as many as four days. Even with the breaking of the legs, as Pilate supposed had been done, it seemed hardly possible.

Pilate decided to move with caution, for he was dealing with a Jew, and a Sanhedrist at that. So he called the centurion who was in charge on Golgotha and **HE GAVE THE BODY TO JOSEPH** "he asked him whether He had been any while dead." When the centurion assured the governor that Jesus had indeed died, Pilate "gave the body to Joseph." Thus Jesus, who had been spurned by the Jews and turned over to the Gentiles, was now returned to "His own" for burial. This was not an unusual favor. It was a regular procedure of the Romans to grant the bodies of the crucified to friends or relatives who requested them. There is also nothing to show that Pilate granted this privilege for money, as was sometimes done. Neither is there any indication, as has been suggested, that this request was granted to spite the leaders of the Jews.

At this opportune time Joseph received help from another like-minded leader of the Jews — a man by the name of Nicodemus. He had first come to Jesus in the early part of His ministry, about three **AND THERE CAME ALSO NICODEMUS** years earlier. But John reminds us that he had come by night (John 3:2), implying that he then lacked the courage to come to Him openly. At the Feast of the Tabernacles, about six months before the crucifixion, Nicodemus had challenged his fellow Sanhedrists who were plotting against Christ: "Doth our law judge any man before it hear him and know what he doeth?" (John 7:51). But this was as much a defense of the law as a defense of Jesus, and when he was shouted down with the angry retort, "Art thou also of Galilee?" he held his peace. But now his attitude was different. Like Joseph, Nicodemus was made bold by the death of Jesus, and when all seemed lost forever, he surprisingly showed his true colors. Jesus had predicted that when He would be lifted up He would draw all men to Himself (John 12:32). He was already doing so. First His companion on the cross, then the centurion who "glorified God," and now these two Jewish aristocrats openly confessed Him as their Lord.

Time was growing short, and the shopkeepers would soon close up for the Sabbath; so Joseph and Nicodemus hurried to make the purchases needed to give Jesus an honorable burial. Joseph "bought fine linen" for **SHARED ASSIGNMENT** burial clothes while Nicodemus bought the spices — and in a most generous amount, which revealed not only an ardent love on his part, but also his ample means. The pound (*litra* or *libra*) was about 11 oz. Hence the purchase amounted to about 70 pounds in our weight. Imagine what Judas would have said if he had been there to estimate the price! That the purchases were thus divided indicates that these two prominent men were working together, and that each had knowledge of what the other was doing.

Myrrh was used in both liquid and powder form. Mary used the liquid (John 12:3). Nicodemus brought the powder. It was made from the aromatic gum resin of the "Balsamodendron myrrha" and was also used by the Egyptians for burial purposes. Aloes, a powdered wood, was mixed with the myrrh. It was highly prized for the odor it released as the wood decayed. The choicest variety of aloes was grown in India.

MYRRH AND ALOES

"Then took they the body of Jesus and wound it in linen clothes with the spices." It was Joseph who took down the body of Jesus, helped of course by others. He took charge of the burial, and the others readily followed his lead. In the short time and under the conditions prevailing on Golgotha, it was not possible to wash and to anoint the body of Jesus as desired, though the blood from the wounds was undoubtedly rinsed away. But at Bethany Mary had already anointed Jesus beforehand for His burial (Mark 14:8). Because of the circumstances the body was quickly wrapped in the linen with generous amounts of spices scattered between the layers. For the Gentile readers John adds the remark: "as the manner of the Jews is to bury." He wants them to know that the body was not mutilated. Unlike the Eyptians, the Jews did not disembowel the bodies when they "embalmed" them, but they wrapped the spices in the folds of the burial clothes.

AFTER THE MANNER OF THE JEWS

— C —

Jesus Laid In The Tomb

Now in the place where He was crucified there was a garden; and in the garden a new sepulcher, that was hewn in stone, wherein never man before was laid. Therein they laid Jesus therefore because of the Jews' preparation day; for the sepulcher was nigh at hand, and the Sabbath drew on. And they rolled a great stone to the door of the sepulcher and departed. (TLL, pp. 286-287)

And laid it in his own new tomb, which he had hewn out in the rock: and he rolled a great stone to the door of the sepulcher and departed. (Matt. 27:60)

And laid Him in a sepulcher which was hewn out of a rock, and rolled a stone unto the door of the sepulcher. (Mark 15:46b)

And laid it in a sepulcher that was hewn in stone, wherein never man before was laid. And that day was the preparation, and the Sabbath drew on. (Luke 23:53b,54)

Now in the place where He was crucified there was a garden; and in the garden a new sepulcher, wherein was never man yet laid. There laid they Jesus therefore because of the Jews' preparation day; for the sepulcher was nigh at hand. (John 19:41,42)

The body was ready for burial, but Jesus, who had no place to lay His head during His life, also had no tomb of His own. Mortal man has been accustomed to provide a tomb for himself, but Jesus, the Son of God, was not intended for death. It was only for our sakes that He needed a grave — and then, only for three days. That Jesus might be with the rich in His death (see page 175f.), the place of the crucifixion had been providently located near a place where a suitable grave was available.

NO TOMB OF HIS OWN

"Now in the place where He was crucified there was a garden." A garden was the scene of man's first sin, whence death came into the world, and a garden was to be the scene of Christ's final triumph over death. It was in a garden that His last agonies began, and it was in a garden that He was placed when they were over.

"And in the garden a new sepulcher that was hewn in stone." Matthew tells us that it belonged to Joseph. He had it cut out of the side of the cliff, probably at no little expense, and intended it for his own use. It was "a new sepulcher . . . wherein never man before was laid," therefore fresh and clean. No odor of death or decay clung to it. Its very newness made it a fitting place for the sacred body of Jesus, which, according to Psalm 16:10, should see no corruption or decay. New things were customarily used for sacred purposes. The colt on which Jesus rode into Jerusalem on Palm Sunday was one "whereon never man sat" (Mark 11:2). The Ark of the Covenant was brought to Jerusalem on "a new cart" (2 Sam. 6:3). "A red heifer upon which never came yoke" was specified for the sacrifice. (Num. 19:2). "A new sepulcher . . . wherein never man before was laid" became the resting place for the Lord's body.

A NEW SEPULCHER

"Therein they laid Jesus therefore because of the Jew's preparation day." To Joseph the sacrifice was not too great. Where there is great love for Jesus, the cost of serving Him is not counted. Because of the Sabbath it was necessary that the burial must be completed by sundown. And there could be no thought of finding a burial place any distance away from Golgotha, as "the Sabbath drew on" (literally, was dawning). He, the Lord of all things, who borrowed a boat to preach from, a colt to ride upon, and a room to celebrate in, now rested in a borrowed tomb. He allowed Himself to be laid in the grave, that He might hallow our graves. A portion of the rich supply of spices was undoubtedly scattered around the body in the tomb, for this appears to have been the custom when special honor was to be shown (2 Chron. 16:14). In all this Joseph and Nicodemus performed a God-pleasing and good work. The poor they could always help, but Jesus they could only bury once.

BY CONSTRAINT OF THE SABBATH

There was no ceremony at the burial of Jesus. No funeral oration was spoken. No trace of earthly pomp was present. The body was simply laid away and the grave closed. "And they rolled a great stone to the door of the sepulcher." This was not an irregular boulder, which could only have blocked the entrance. Rather a stone for this pur-

NO CEREMONY

pose was cut in the shape of a large flat wheel, like a huge grindstone. It was then fitted into a groove in front of the tomb, and thus held in position. This done, they "departed." The followers of Jesus made no attempt on their part to guard the grave. The thought of its necessity never entered their mind.

— D —
The Women At The Tomb

And the women also, which came with Him from Galilee, followed after and beheld the sepulcher and how His body was laid. And there was Mary Magdalene, and the other Mary the mother of Joses, sitting over against the sepulcher, and beheld where He was laid. And they returned, and prepared spices and ointments, and rested the Sabbath day according to the commandment. (TLL, p. 287)

And there was Mary Magdalene, and the other Mary, sitting over against the sepulcher. (Matt. 27:61)

And Mary Magdalene and Mary the mother of Joses beheld where He was laid. (Mark 15:47)

And the women also, which came with Him from Galilee, followed after and beheld the sepulcher and how His body was laid. And they returned, and prepared spices and ointments, and rested the Sabbath day according to the commandment. (Luke 23:55,56)

A very simple funeral procession made its way from Golgotha to the garden. The men carried the body "and the women also, which came with Him from Galilee, followed after." The procession included two women previously mentioned: Mary Magdalene and Mary the mother of Joses (see page 169). The love and loyalty which had caused them to follow Jesus from Galilee held them now, even though their Master had died.

A VERY SIMPLE FUNERAL PROCESSION

The women did not lend a hand in the preparation of the body, neither could it be expected of them since two distinguished Sanhedrists had taken charge. While the last rites were performed "they beheld where He was laid." They just looked on and gave careful attention as to where and how the body was laid. They also noted that in the great haste required, the body had not yet, in their estimation at least, been properly and completely embalmed. It was here that the decision was made to return on Sunday morning to complete the task in a manner not now possible.

THEY BEHELD WHERE HE WAS LAID

Leaving the tomb, the women "returned and prepared spices and ointments." This preparation does not mean that the women mixed or compounded them, but

THE WOMEN PREPARED SPICES AND OINTMENTS rather that they bought the materials and arranged them in readiness for an early start to the tomb on Sunday morning. The *aromata* were costly spices in powder form and the *myra* were perfume liquids or extracts. The sequence in Matthew gives the impression that the two Marys lingered on at the tomb after it had been closed and the others departed. This would help to explain Mark 16:1, that they bought sweet spices "when the Sabbath was past," *viz.*, on Saturday evening after six. Because they lingered, either the shops were already closed on Friday evening when they got there to buy, or they closed before the women were able to complete their purchases. The need for preparing materials for the trip to the tomb early on Sunday morning did not keep the women from strict obedience to the Jewish Sabbath law prescribing complete rest. They "rested the Sabbath day according to the commandment." This was the last Sabbath of the Old Covenant.

The divine timing involved was very beneficial to the Church, even in its less obvious details. Because the sacrifice of the Lamb of God occurred in a year in which the Passover proper fell on the day of preparation (between sundown Thursday and sundown Friday), Jesus was not only given the new tomb near Golgotha, but the Sabbath rest kept the women from going out to the grave on the morning after the burial of Jesus, to be rebuffed by the Roman guard, and thereby to lose the incentive for appearing there on the glorious resurrection morn.

GOD'S TIME WAS PERFECT

— E —
The Guard At The Sepulcher

Now the next day, that followed the day of preparation, the chief priests and Pharisees came together unto Pilate, saying, "Sir, we remember that that deceiver said, while he was yet alive, 'After three days I will rise again.' Command therefore that the sepulcher be made sure until the third day, lest his disciples come by night and steal him away, and say unto the people, he is risen from the dead; so the last error shall be worse than the first." Pilate said unto them, "Ye have a watch. Go your way; make it as sure as you can." So they went and made the sepulcher sure, sealing the stone, and setting a watch. (TLL, p. 287; *Matt. 27:62-66*)

While the women carefully observed the Sabbath rest, the Sanhedrists were prevented from doing so by their own uneasy consciences. The dead Jesus seemed to have caused them even more concern than the living Jesus had done. They remembered

NO SABBATH REST FOR THE SANHEDRIN

that He had prophesied His resurrection on the third day (Matt. 12:38-40), and they were greatly troubled. Among the happenings of that eventful day, they were probably most deeply moved by the confession of Jesus which two distinguished members of their own body had made. The result was a hasty policy meeting on "the next day that followed the day of preparation." That was the Passover Sabbath, which was especially sacred to the Jews, and its desecration was viewed most gravely. According to Jewish reckoning, it began at sundown, and unquestionably the events recorded took place that very evening, before darkness had fully settled over Jerusalem. To imagine that they waited until morning before they acted does not make sense. The likelihood of the disciples stealing their Master away was just as great on the first night as on the second. After reaching agreement on the action they would take, "the chief priests and Pharisees came together unto Pilate." We are not to suppose that they marched over to the governor's residence in a body. That would have been too conspicuous, even in the gathering dusk. But the language indicates that at least a sizable part of the Sanhedrin was present.

A striking example of the hypocrisy of the Pharisees, which Jesus had denounced (cf. Matt. 23:27ff.), manifests itself in their conduct here. On Friday morning, when they had a Jewish crowd around them, they refused to enter the Praetorium for fear of ceremonial pollution (see page 95f.). Now, even on this high feast day, they had no scruples about entering the residence of the Roman governor. These same people, who had so often decried Jesus as one defiling the Sabbath when He had done only good and had healed people on it — those people, who had this same day asked Pilate to remove the bodies so that the great Sabbath day might not be desecrated, now contemptuously trod their Sabbath law under foot. They were willing to ignore their own strict regulations when it served their selfish interests. The people smote their breasts when they returned from Calvary (see page 168f.), but the hearts of their leaders remained unchanged.

NO SCRUPLES NOW

They swallowed their pride and in flattery addressed Pilate as "Sir" (literally, Lord), to gain a favorable hearing. To explain their third request pertaining to Jesus since He had been nailed to the cross, they told Pilate, "We remember that that deceiver said, while he was yet alive, 'After three days I will rise again.' " It was indeed remarkable that the enemies of Jesus remembered this particular word so well, while His own disciples had never grasped its meaning, and now, stunned by grief, had completely forgotten it. It was only after Jesus had risen from the dead, and after they had been reminded of the prophecy, that they too remembered.

"WE REMEMBER"

The utter contempt in which these leaders of the Jews held Jesus is seen in this, that even now when He was dead they would not refer to Him by name. With venomous lips they called Him "that deceiver." By this epithet they were referring to the Messianic claims of Jesus, which they regarded as a lie. Isaiah had prophesied concerning Christ, "Nor was there any deceit in His mouth" (53:9, NASB). And St. Peter testifies: "Who did no sin, neither was guile [or, deceit] found in His mouth" (1 Pet. 2:22). Yet the holy and sinless Christ, who spoke only words of truth and life,

"THAT DECEIVER"

was branded a deceiver by unscrupulous plotters and schemers, to whom deception was nothing strange or foreign.

After this explanation of their presence before Pilate, the Sanhedrists requested, "Command therefore that the sepulcher be made sure until the third day." They did not believe it possible that Jesus would really rise from the dead, and hence did not want the burial place made sure against the resurrection. What they claimed to be concerned about was a disturbance from without, "lest his disciples come by night and steal him away." They easily suspected others of being as evil and deceitful as they themselves were. So they pictured the disciples before Pilate as being potential grave robbers, willing to do anything to supply a fictitious fulfillment of their Master's predictions. The Jews did not tell Pilate how the grave should be secured, but the obvious way was to assign a military guard to watch it.

"THAT THE SEPULCHER BE MADE SURE"

The Jewish leaders expressed grave concern over the consequences if the disciples should succeed in a scheme to convince the people that Jesus was risen. "So the last error shall be worse than the first," they argued. The "first error" (literally, first deception) was what Jesus had done during His lifetime, causing many of the people to free themselves from the power and influence of the Jewish religious leaders. The "last error" (literally, last deception) would take place after His death. If any great number of the people should believe the reports of a resurrection, it would very likely undermine the authority of the leaders even more. This proved to be a shrewd observation by the Sanhedrin, in the light of the impact which the reports of the resurrection really did make later on.

THEY FEARED THE EFFECT

Pleased that the proud Jewish leaders thus acknowledged his authority, Pilate readily yielded to the request and gave them a guard of his soldiers, with the words, "Ye have a watch." He too may have felt some uneasiness because of the strange course of events. During the trial he had publicly washed his hands (see page 121f.), with the hope of removing his personal guilt, but the still small voice within is not so easily put aside. Now the responsibility of making the grave secure was also masterfully placed upon the Sanhedrists when Pilate told them, "Go your way; make it as sure as you can." He did not want them to come back and to blame him again if things should not turn out according to their wishes. He was, in effect, washing his hands again.

REQUEST GRANTED

Successful in their mission to Pilate, the Sanhedrists then engaged in a most unsabbatical activity. They "made the sepulcher sure, sealing the stone, and setting a watch." All possible precautions were taken to prevent theft or robbery at the grave. As a special precaution, the stone was sealed. The purpose of sealing was not to fasten the slab to the front of the grave, or to close all the crevices, but merely to provide evidence that the stone closing the grave had not been tampered with. A method which may have

"THEY MADE THE SEPULCHER SURE"

been used was to stretch a string across the stone and to seal it to the rock at both ends, stamping it with an official seal. The fact that Pilate left it up to the Jews to secure the grave as best they could, makes it seem more likely that the great seal of the Sanhedrin was used rather than the seal of the Roman governor. Still all that really matters is that by their careful precautions the enemies of Christ helped to establish the certainty of the resurrection of Jesus. Against their will and intentions, the enemies of Christ did the Christians a real service. By having the tomb securely guarded they made certain that there was no deception. Thus the Holy Spirit forced them to provide a proof of the resurrection and to help confirm our faith in it.

CPSIA information can be obtained at www.ICGtesting.com
Printed in the USA
LVOW07s0406071215
465699LV00005B/6/P